IMAGES
of America

ESSEX ON LAKE CHAMPLAIN

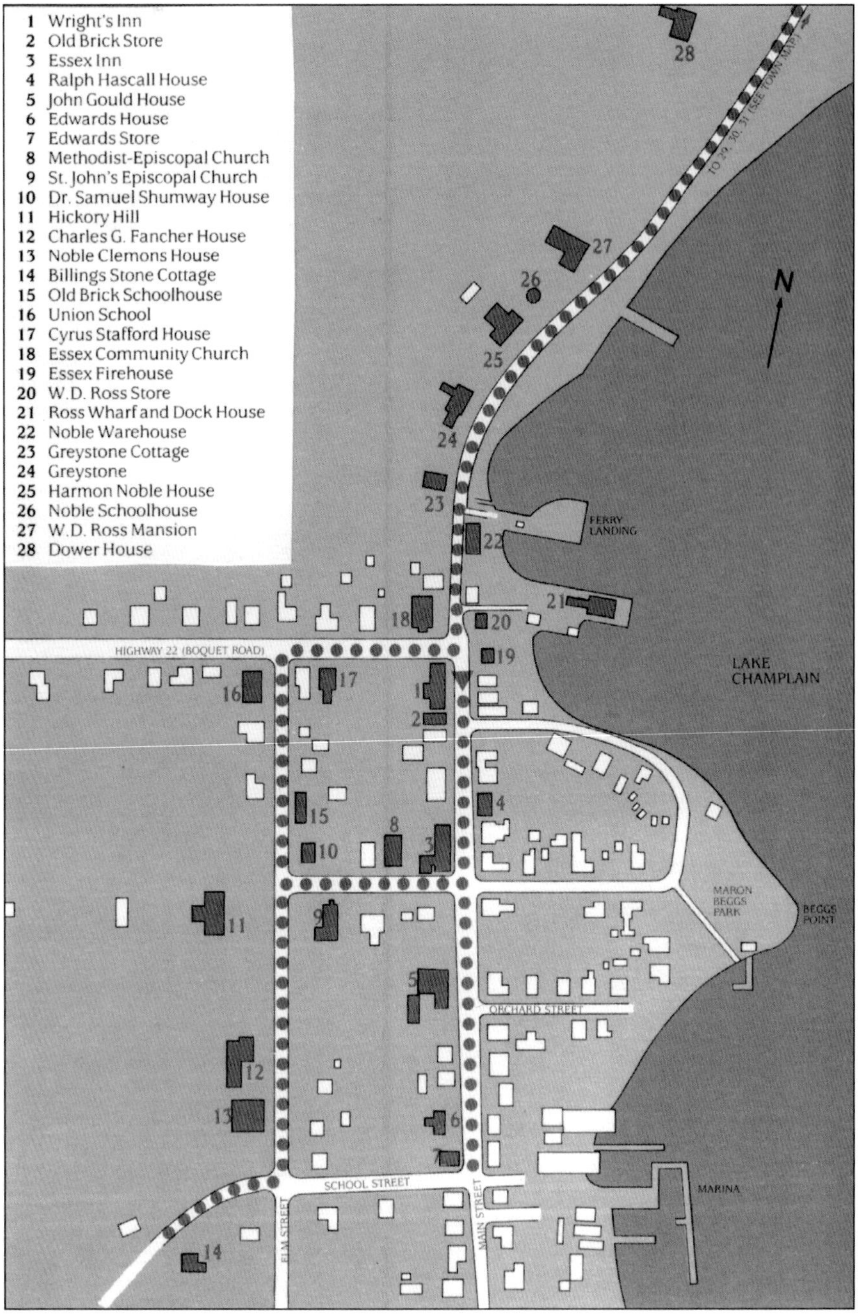

ESSEX HISTORIC DISTRICT MAP. A plan of the Essex hamlet streets and houses that were placed on the National Register of Historic Places historic district of 1975 is seen here. (Courtesy of Essex Community Heritage Organization.)

On the cover: **ESSEX HARBOR FROM LAKE CHAMPLAIN.** The historic district of Essex resulted from maritime commerce. Multiple wharves and piers extend into the north harbor and are reminders of the heyday of Essex, 1820–1860. By the 1920s, as here, heritage tourism and recreational boating prevailed. (Courtesy of Essex Community Heritage Organization.)

IMAGES
of America

ESSEX ON LAKE CHAMPLAIN

David C. Hislop Jr.

ARCADIA
PUBLISHING

ISBN 978-0-7385-6369-5

Published by Arcadia Publishing
Charleston SC, Chicago IL, Portsmouth NH, San Francisco CA

Printed in the United States of America

Library of Congress Control Number: 2008936854

For all general information contact Arcadia Publishing at:
Telephone 843-853-2070
Fax 843-853-0044
E-mail sales@arcadiapublishing.com
For customer service and orders:
Toll-Free 1-888-313-2665

Visit us on the Internet at www.arcadiapublishing.com

Dedicated to the establishment of the Essex Heritage Center in 2009 by the Essex Community Heritage Organization that will for the first time provide a permanent location for the collections of photographs, articles, manuscripts, and artifacts about the remarkable town of historic Essex

Contents

Acknowledgments		6
Introduction		7
1.	The Natural Environment	11
2.	Maritime Merchants	27
3.	Village Views	41
4.	Business and Industry	55
5.	Civic Life in Public Buildings	67
6.	Village Life and Country Life	93
7.	Merchant Row Mansions	107
Bibliography		127

ACKNOWLEDGMENTS

I am especially grateful to Historic Essex/Essex Community Heritage Organization board members for their permission to digitalize and use many selections from the extensive photographic, document, and artifact collection of the Essex Heritage Center library. Historic Essex/Essex Community Heritage Organization is the 40-year-old local historic preservation organization founded in 1969 to protect and preserve the unique heritage of Essex.

Also thanks go to Tilly Close for permission to use many images from the Ross family photographic collection. The following were also generous with their input, professional advice, and encouragement: Stephen Maselli, Sally Johnson, Lauren Murphy, Steven Kellogg, Todd Goff, St. John's Church, and the Greystone Archives. Research from my master's thesis, "One of the Most Architecturally and Culturally Significant Greek Revival Villages in America: Essex, New York," advised by John Mesick, AIA, Antoinette Lee, Ph.D., and Hugh Miller, FAIA, was used extensively throughout. Images and research by George McNulty, Margaret Scheinin, Howard Hayes, and others on file all contributed to the documentation. Unless otherwise indicated, all images are courtesy of the Essex Community Heritage Organization.

Finally I would like to thank my editor at Arcadia Publishing, Rebekah Collinsworth, for her guidance and enthusiasm throughout the project.

With the publication of *Essex on Lake Champlain*, 10 years of research and writing have come to fruition on a truly historic and special place.

INTRODUCTION

The historic hamlet of Essex, located on the western shore of Lake Champlain, is remarkably preserved yet today is located within a half day's drive of 75 million people in the northeastern United States.

Essex is especially known for its picturesque Greek Revival architecture enhanced by its location along a scenic lakeshore set among rolling farmlands all within sight of the Adirondack Mountains. This combination of architectural integrity and environmental purity makes it one of the most intact early-19th-century villages in America still existing today.

The history of the hamlet of Essex begins just before the American Revolution and extends forward in time to today's era of successful historic preservation. The time period of architectural significance for Essex on a national level is during the great era of maritime commerce on Lake Champlain in the early to mid-19th century, that is, the years between 1820 and 1860. Essex developed as a remarkably successful commercial enterprise under the guidance of two patron families and hundreds of merchants and workers. The physical record of this period is essentially intact, with the merchant mansions, worker houses, shops, inns, wharves, shipyards, churches, schools, and surrounding rural and agricultural countryside still very recognizable and well preserved today.

The geographical town of Essex is located in Essex County, forming the county's eastern boundary along the 121-mile divide Lake Champlain forms with the border of Vermont. For over two centuries, this relatively remote region has been accessed first by roadways then by steamboat routes, railroads, and finally highways. Despite such inroads, Essex County remains largely Adirondack Park wilderness and is one of the least-populated counties in New York State.

The hamlet of Essex is an unincorporated part of the town of Essex, often currently and historically called Essex Village, a term that includes the entire named Essex Village Historic District listed on the National Register of Historic Places in 1975.

In 1764, the New York adventurer and former Irish soldier William Gilliland was granted land patents that included vast portions on the west shore of Lake Champlain. The following year, he established a settlement near the mouth of the Boquet River, and the area was soon named after him as Willsborough. The American Revolution destroyed most of the settlement, but the pioneers rebuilt, and in 1805, Essex was separated from Willsborough and became its own town. When the fortunes of war again came to the Champlain Valley during the War of 1812, Essex was developed enough to participate as a supplier and indeed profit from the demand for goods and war materials. The shipyards produced several hundred bateaux, small, agile boats that were vital in stalking and monitoring the actions of larger enemy vessels. The Essex shipyards built the sloops *Growler* and *Eagle* that saw action surrounding the decisive battle at Plattsburgh in Cumberland Bay under Commodore Thomas Macdonough. When the final treaties were signed, Essex had fully developed its shipyard and had built several wharves on the lake. The prosperity following the War of 1812 lasted long enough to continue development in Essex until the great New York State era of canal building began in the early 1820s.

The socioeconomic development of Essex began just before 1800 with the establishment of two great family dynasties: the Daniel Ross family and the Ransom Noble family. Daniel Ross had the good fortune of marrying William Gilliland's daughter Elizabeth. He thus was heir to his father-in-law's land claims. The Ross children eventually came to own most of the original patents covering Essex Village. The Noble family followed the popular immigration path of the late 1800s, migrating from New Milford, Connecticut, up to the northern portion of Vermont. Then, according to the family Bible records, they crossed Lake Champlain in January 1800 and settled in Essex.

Even though Noble and Ross founded the family dynasties that dominated the social and economic life of Essex for the duration of the 19th century, they still lived in close proximity to their businesses and their workers. This new social pattern of the owners, workers, and businesses living and working in close proximity was established in the early years of the Industrial Revolution. The still-intact street plan of Essex has a combination of merchants' mansions and workers' housing all within walking distance of one another in this quintessential Greek Revival town. The grid pattern of the village solidified as a central core of shops and commercial enterprises surrounded by residences.

The idea of adding to the natural waterways of America evolved from the successes of canal systems throughout Europe. The connection of Lake Champlain to the Hudson River waterway system was proposed at the extreme southern tip of the lake at the town of Whitehall. The canal then was dug to reach the Hudson River south of Lake George. The success of the Champlain Canal began a boom, and merchants and shippers now used the southerly route, as opposed to shipping north in the direction that Lake Champlain flows. The opening of the Champlain Canal in November 1822 richly rewarded the Essex community and proved the key to its ultimate financial success. Now, for the first time, shippers could easily move their products south to the burgeoning East Coast markets of the New York state capitol at Albany, the industries at Troy, and farther south to New York City and Philadelphia. When the new Erie Canal was completed in 1825, they could connect with it near Albany and ship to all the markets of the Midwest. The wharves on the north side of the two Essex harbors served the shipping trade. This allowed merchants to ship Adirondack timber, potash, tanned hides, agricultural products, and later iron ore south to New York City and to the new western markets as well. Brought back from points south beyond the Hudson River were furnishings for Adirondack buildings, coal for heating purposes, and finished wood products.

The shipyards in the south bay area continued to construct vessels throughout the mid-19th century. Many were used on the Champlain Canal as Essex built over 50 documented vessels between 1814 and 1870. Many were the sloops and schooner-rigged canal boats that sailed the lake until the dawn of the 20th century. The Hoskins, Ross and Company shipyards in Essex constructed the canal boats and sailing sloops in such numbers that they were among the largest shipyards on the lake.

As with most waterways in America, Lake Champlain is best remembered for the palatial and elegant steamboats of the late 19th century. While these stately ships capture the imagination best, they were in fact far outnumbered by the sailing vessels plying the lake. Indeed, the workhorse of the early 19th century was the sloop, a single-mast boat that could be sailed by two men. It was used for both lake commerce and ferry service, often landing at various points on the other side depending on the winds.

The Champlain Canal led to the need for specially designed boats that were small enough to transverse the narrowest locks of canals yet capable of sailing on the broad lake. A boat was designed with a sloop mast added to the canal boat that could be lowered to go through locks.

Many of these canal sloops were constructed at the shipyards in Essex. Some were made in the double-mast schooner form. Upon entering the Champlain Canal, the masts were lowered and the boats converted from wind power to locomotion provided by towpath mules.

As prosperity for the Noble and Ross families increased, more people were needed as workers and to manage related services such as stores, inns, and legal and medical care. This furthered the economic multiplier effect. The town of Essex population peaked in the early 1850s near 2,500 people and gently declined in the later part of the 19th century. The population of the town of Essex in the year 2000 was 713. The decline after about 1860 is attributed to the vast shift in natural resources to the new opportunities of the American West. The Champlain Valley and the Adirondacks had been mined and the timber cut. Natural resources were available cheaper elsewhere and the new national system of railroads could transport goods far faster than the old canal system. Essex went into a long but gentle decline. Many of the major families relocated but importantly still maintained their Essex homesteads and often stayed in Essex during the long summer months when the cool summers were highly desirable in an era before air-conditioning. The same features of sparkling summers and beautiful countryside began to attract others, and the region developed a summer tourist economy. Construction of summer cottages specifically aimed at vacationers such as the Crater Club in Essex helped keep the village intact and picturesque.

Then in the late 1960s, the first stirrings of the historic preservation movement began, and the remarkable survival of a whole town of antique structures was first noticed. Pioneer preservationists banned together and formed the Essex Community Heritage Organization in 1969. They inventoried all the historic structures in the village and submitted a completed nomination that was listed as the Essex Village Historic District in 1975.

Since then, preservationists have continued to study the buildings of the historic hamlet, and the survival of a small town with such an intact Greek Revival building stock has become more and more unique in 21st-century America. An analysis completed in 2002 shed new light on the construction, design, and type of historic buildings in Essex. The hamlet buildings are 68 percent wood frame with clapboard siding, reflecting the location of Essex near the Adirondack forest. Despite being located on a limestone ledge, only 8 percent of the buildings are constructed of stone, reflecting its greater labor cost. Most of the buildings in Essex maintain their original use at 87 percent, and the majority, over 90 percent, are located on their original sites.

Indeed, a full 50 percent of structures are in the Greek Revival design. A further 20 percent are in the earlier but closely related Federal style. Combined, nearly 70 percent of all buildings in the historic area reflect neoclassical design. A village with 80 percent of its buildings constructed before 1900 with nearly half in the same historic Greek Revival style argues for national significance in architecture. With 70 percent of buildings constructed before the Civil War, Essex maintains the feel and ambience of a mid-19th-century village.

Essex residents seem to have always lived in a setting that represents perhaps the most modern of times while retaining the best of the past. A sense of history, possibly instilled by the Yorker and Yankee ancestors and also a sense of thrift pervaded Essex over the decades and indeed the centuries. Today thrift is finally being viewed as a form of conservation, an environmentally friendly philosophy. Retaining and maintaining older homes conserves the embodied energies used to construct them in the past. That is, the excavation of the raw materials in 1820 or so and the manual labor used to build the houses are all embodied in the structures as they exist today. The 150 structures of Essex have been used and lived in by generations of the original owners then by successive waves of other devoted owners. In this way, the embodied energy is conserved, and new energy, such as that required to construct new houses, is avoided, and the carbon footprint of new construction is eliminated. Once again, the persistence of old houses speaks to modern times.

Of course, Maud Noble, during her long life living at Greystone, knew nothing of embodied energy, but she did know that her father's homestead was a sound and superbly constructed residence that she had no intention of abandoning, even when life dictated she reside half of the year in Washington, D.C. She took great care in planning for the future of the house after her own death, suggesting that it be used as a convalescent home for children if her estate could afford it or otherwise it be left to a beloved relative who would care for it properly. This early and unnamed form of preservation was repeated by example throughout Essex and helped maintain it in good stead until the mid-20th century.

Dr. Bates Lowry was the director of the Museum of Modern Art in New York when he arrived in Essex in the 1960s. At that time, the past was banished by modernism, and many historic buildings across the country were being neglected, pulled down, or bulldozed for urban renewal. One of the few strands of the past that was acceptable was folk art, with its simple forms and naive design that seemed to many to be proto-modernist. To Lowry, the simple forms of Greek Revival architecture related to American weather vanes, duck decoys, quilts, and carousel figures and thus deserved attention. He painted many Essex buildings, such as the immense 1867 schoolhouse, in Nantucket blue or yellow and even added a cod weather vane or rooster. Slowly, others did notice, and by the late 1960s, several new homeowners banded with concerned local citizens to form the Essex Community Heritage Organization, soon known by its acronym, ECHO.

One of the first projects ECHO undertook was a comprehensive scholarly survey of the town. Since then, several generations of restoration have occurred, beginning with rescue in the 1980s of such structures as the Noble Clemons house and the original Hascall house. By the 1990s, a more detailed and thorough restoration began in many structures, as the newer owners chose to restore every possible detail and undue abuses of the past, such as inappropriate siding. The Dr. John Stafford residence on Main Street is an excellent example as is the Henry Gould house nearby. Finally, in the first decade of the 21st century, with time and financial resources at their peak, elaborate structural and environmental restorations, such as at Rosslyn and the Mesick residences, insured that Essex would survive and even prosper architecturally for at least another century.

The survival of the approximately 150 restored village buildings in their original location was even more remarkable and rare in America by the first decade of the 21st century. The hamlet was studied again and documented as Essex celebrated the Hudson-Fulton-Champlain quadricentennial in 2009.

One

The Natural Environment

Two distinctive geographical regions, the high peaks of the Adirondack Mountains to the west and the Green Mountains of Vermont to the east, frame Lake Champlain and form the Champlain Valley. The altitudes of the earth's surface in the valley region vary extremely from 5,344 feet in height on the top of Mount Marcy in the Adirondack High Peaks to 400 feet below sea level in Lake Champlain off Whallons Bay in Essex.

As an 1824 description from *A Gazetteer of the State of New York* by Horatio Gates Spafford states,

> The County of Essex comprises a large portion of the . . . region of this State, the land being rough, broken into hills and mountains, but affording a tolerable proportion of arable lands of a pretty good quality. It is situated about midway between the cities of New York and Quebec, having the navigation of the lake and rivers each way, made continuous to each by the Champlain Canal.

At first, in the middle of the 18th century, pioneer settler William Gilliland referred to the region as "a howling wilderness, more than one hundred miles removed from any Christian settlement." The land patents granted to him in the 18th century by the king of England covered what is now the east coast of the state of New York near the Adirondack Mountains. The region was settled after the American Revolution, and shipping began north on Lake Champlain. The War of 1812 provided the natural harbors of Essex with the opportunity to engage in shipbuilding for the cause, and the region prospered. Essex gained its maximum population ever, about 2,500 people, by 1850.

Essex County was formed from Clinton County to the north in 1799, making it, even today, one of the largest counties in New York State. Similarly, the town of Essex was separated from its neighbor to the north, the present town of Willsboro, in 1805. The town of Essex, including the historic hamlet of Essex, is about 23,798 acres of gently rolling Champlain Valley land, crossed by the Boquet River.

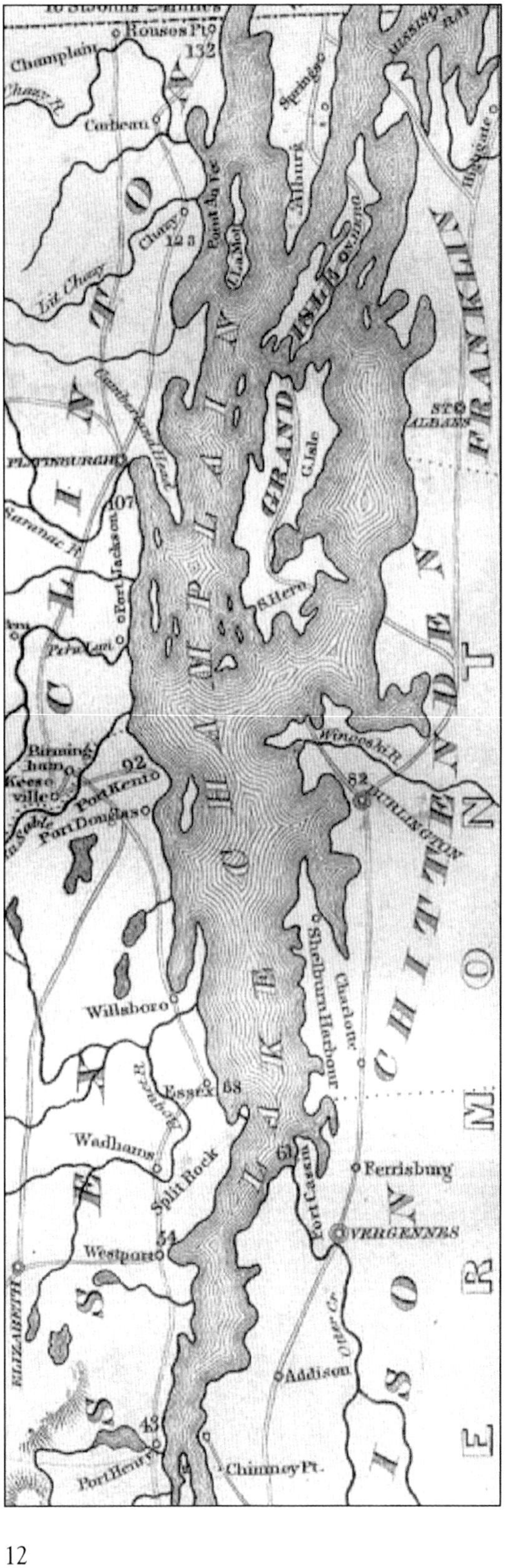

HISTORIC MAP OF 1844. Maps of Lake Champlain changed dramatically from the 17th century to the present day. After its exploration by Samuel de Champlain in 1609, the lake that took his name was one of the most prominent waterways in early maps of North America. Lake Champlain had a strategic location that featured it in military struggles from the Seven Years' War through the War of 1812. Thus the lake appears on the earliest cartography as a significant body of water in North America. This is particularly true during the 17th century when rival European forces involved Native Americans in political conflicts. As America formed in the next century, important Revolutionary War battles made the defense of Lake Champlain still a serious concern. Only in the 20th century did Lake Champlain fade from military or political importance and also faded from prominence on most maps. Hence today, even though it is the sixth-largest body of freshwater in North America, Lake Champlain is barely visible on many national maps.

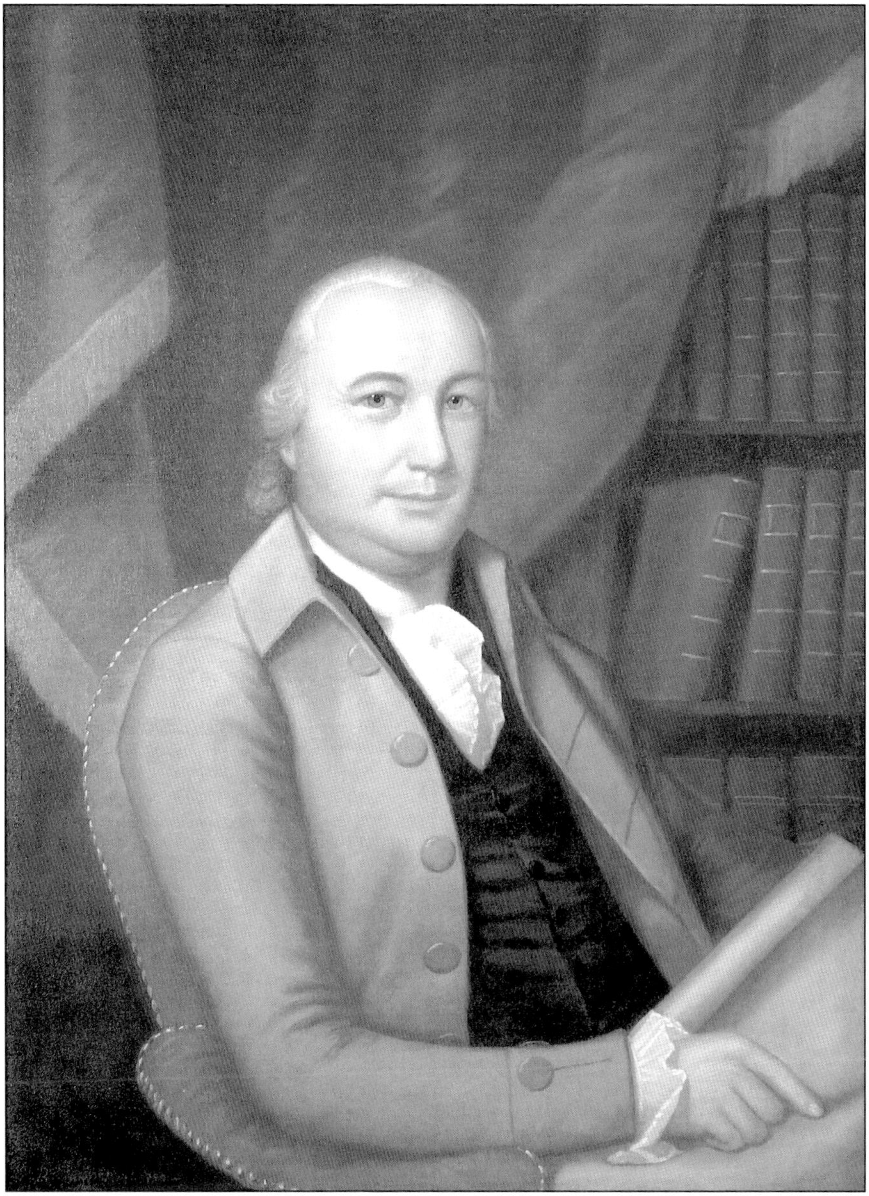

PORTRAIT OF WILLIAM GILLILAND. Published here for the first time is a recently discovered portrait of William Gilliland as painted by Ralph Earl in 1789. Gilliland met Earl while both were in a debtors' prison in New York, thus illustrating the extremes of fortune in 18th-century American life. In 1764, New York adventurer and former Irish soldier Gilliland was granted land patents that included vast portions of the west shore of Lake Champlain. The next year, in 1765, Gilliland and friends moved north from New York and made plans to settle the region. They arrived near the Boquet River from Skeenesboro near Fort Ticonderoga. Fort Ticonderoga was an eminently important fortification long established by the French and then captured and used by the English to guard the militarily strategic region between Lake George to the south and Lake Champlain to the north. Gilliland established a settlement near the mouth of the Boquet River, and the area soon became known as Willsborough. Gilliland maintained a journal, the *Willsborough Town Book*, detailing the settlement. (Courtesy of Fort Ticonderoga Museum.)

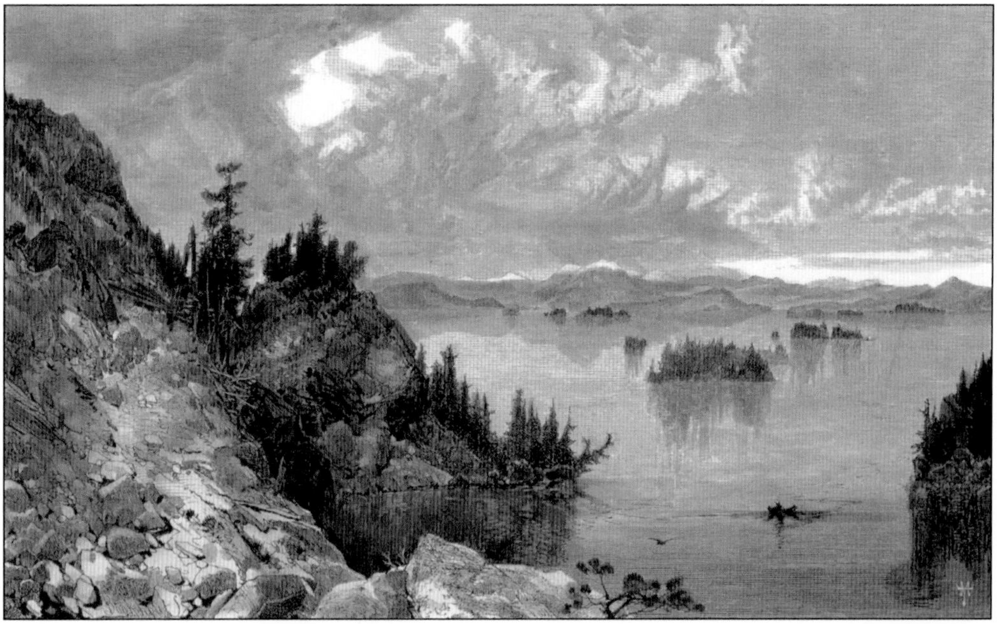

LAKE CHAMPLAIN, 1850. John M. Duncan, a Scotsman who toured the area in 1818 and 1819, described the lake in an 1823 book on his travels: "Lake Champlain . . . is about ninety-five miles long. . . . The body of the lake is exceedingly irregular in shape; flowing round a good many islands, some of which are of considerable size. . . . The banks are in general flat, and covered with wood to the water's edge."

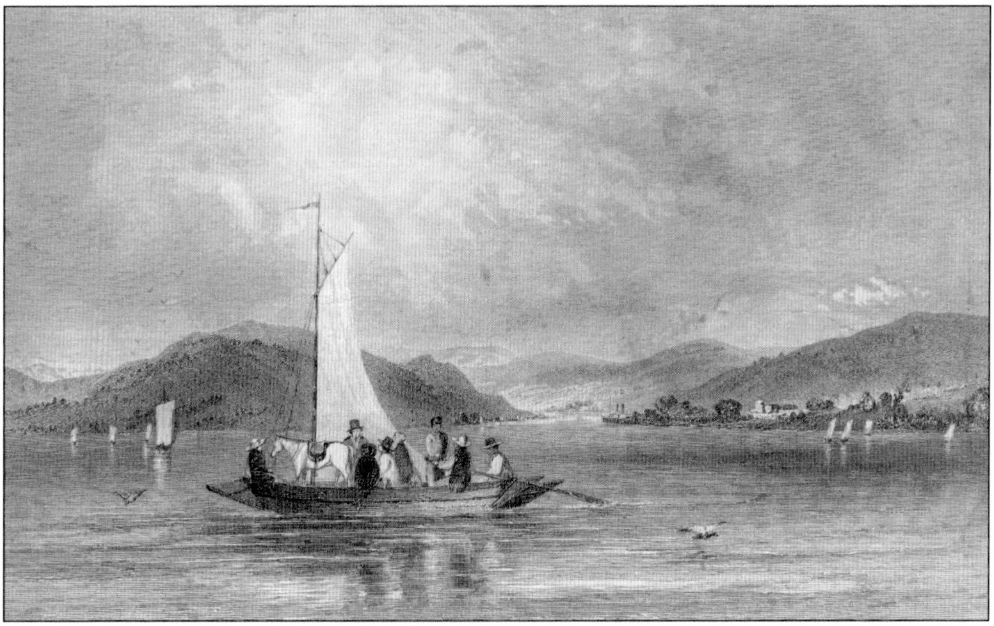

SCENE ON LAKE CHAMPLAIN. As in all of 19th-century America, the earliest views of a region that were reproducible for the general public were wood and then later steel line engravings that could be reproduced as lithographs. The steel engraving of *Scene on Lake Champlain* dramatically illustrates the local geography, picturing the abrupt transition from majestic mountains to deep lake. The ruins of Fort Ticonderoga are in the distance.

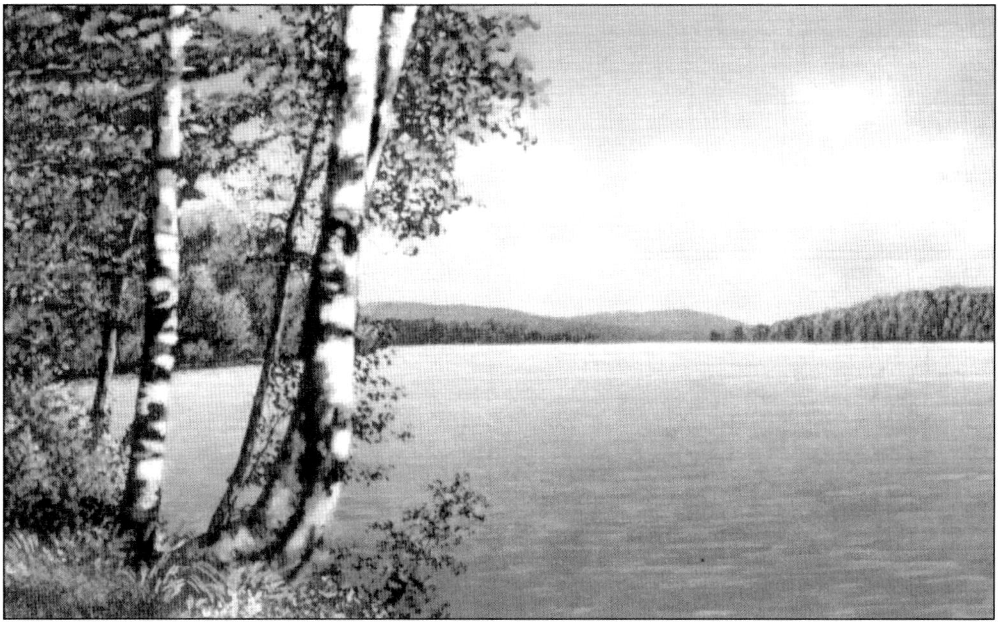

LAKE CHAMPLAIN VIEW. Some 300 years after the first exploration, this view of Lake Champlain has changed emphasis from a wilderness being tamed by commerce to a peaceful scene with the lake appearing as placid as an Adirondack pond. Birch trees do flourish but far more typical along the shoreline are the eastern white cedars. The scene seems to relate Lake Champlain to the Adirondacks in an early effort to promote cooperative vacation marketing.

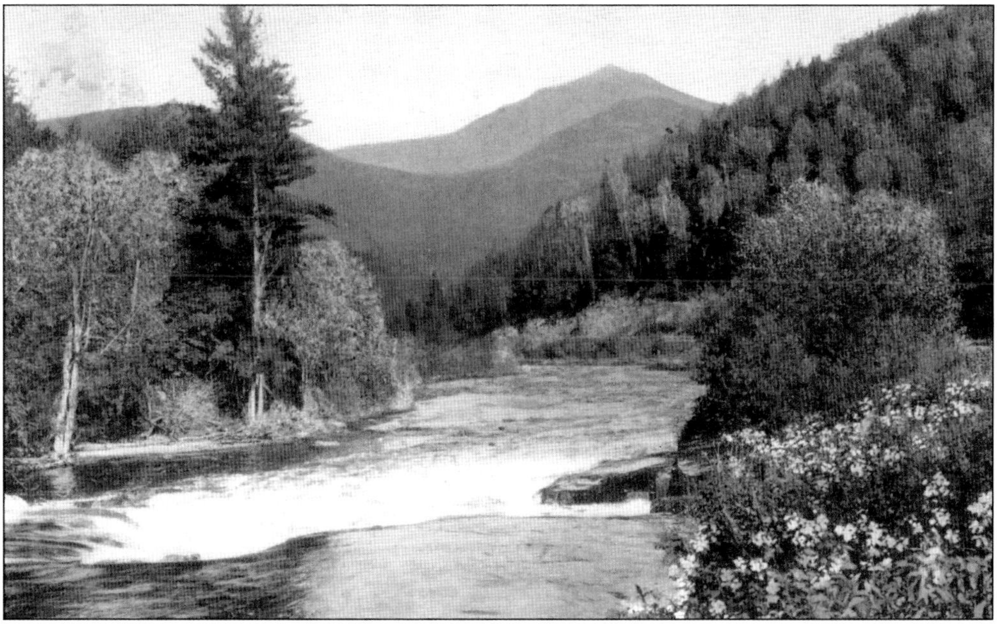

ADIRONDACK MOUNTAINS. Late in the 19th century, concerned citizens in New York State began lobbying to preserve the special wilderness aspects of the Adirondack Mountains, some of the oldest mountains in the world. Such prescient environmental concern led to the formation of the Adirondack Park under legislation enacted in 1892. This set aside nearly three million acres of land in Upstate New York and designated them as a forest preserve.

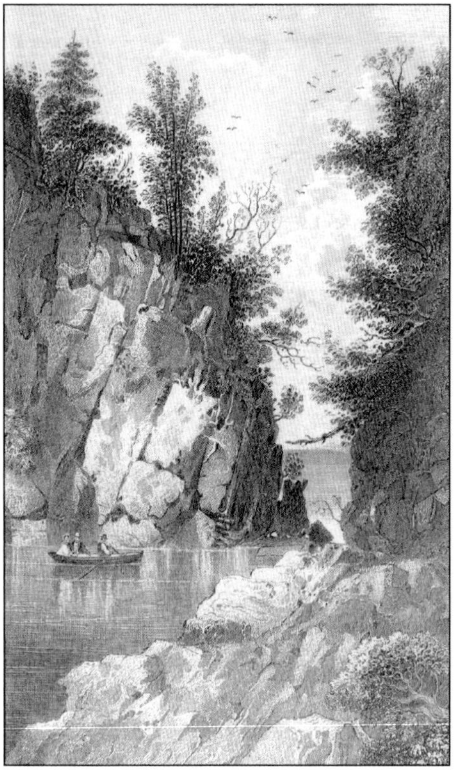

Split Rock Engraving. Split Rock is a prominent natural feature of Lake Champlain. Its cliffs are about 400 feet above the surface water level. First known as Roche Regio by Native Americans, it was the boundary between the Mohawk and Algonquin tribes. On the earliest maps, it was called Cloven Rock by 17th-century French explorers. The rock was first used for navigation purposes, but by the late 19th century, it was popular with tourists and explorers.

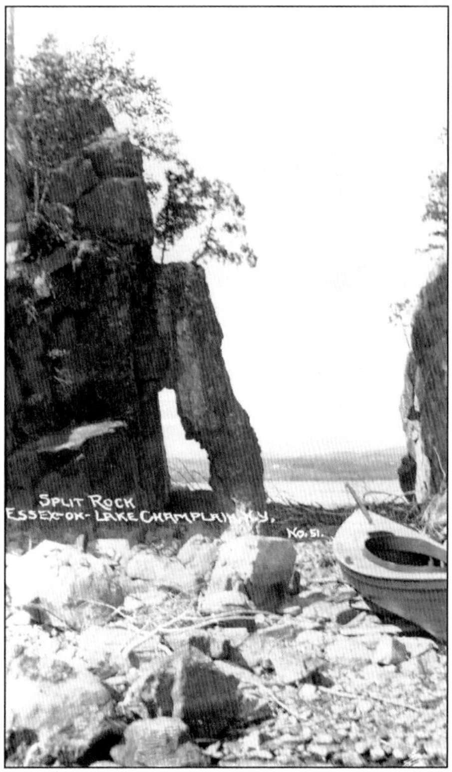

Guide Boat. The serenity of an Adirondack guide boat belies the real threats to Lake Champlain that came in the mid-20th century, when powerful government forces planned to route the St. Lawrence Seaway down it. Had this occurred, the endless freighter and tanker international shipping traffic would have polluted extensively. However, local activists managed to stop the project. The same coalition of forces was later able to defeat the construction of a nuclear power plant in Charlotte across the lake from Essex.

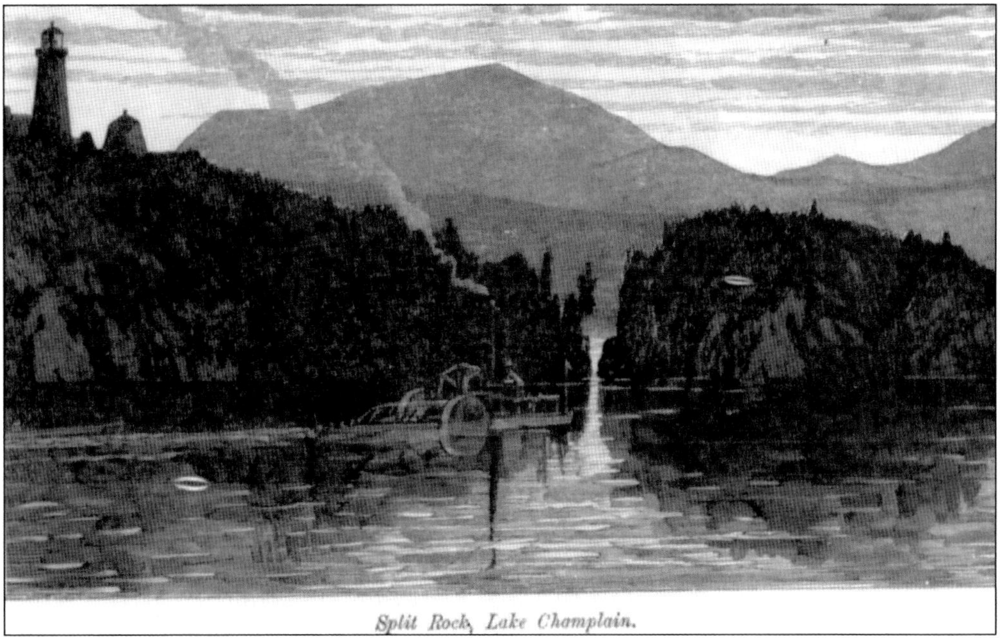

EARLY LINE ENGRAVING. The magic of Split Rock with a passing steamboat is visible in this chromolithograph. Lake Champlain was spared the environmental consequences that still plague other American bodies of water, such as the Hudson River and the Great Lakes. As a result, the significant and pristine environment of Lake Champlain has been declared a UNESCO world biosphere reserve. As a port village, Essex rests on a lake that is a unique environmental survivor.

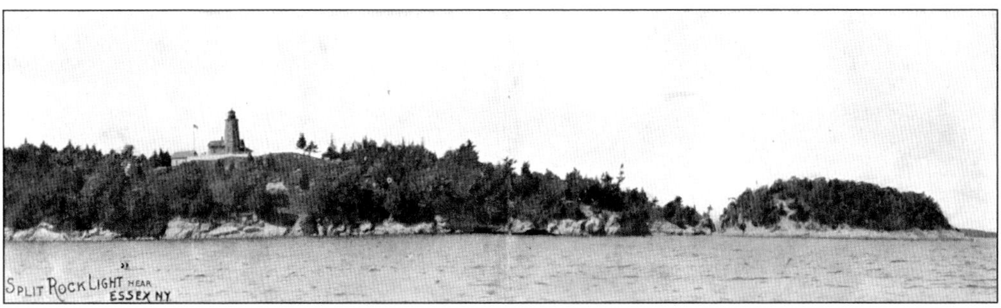

IMAGE OF SPLIT ROCK. The present octagonal limestone block lighthouse was constructed in 1867 on a site where a station was established in 1838. Now privately owned, the light was recently relit and today operates again. By the late 1970s, the boundaries of the Adirondack Park had been extended to include all of the Champlain Valley and all of the waters of Lake Champlain that were contained within New York State borders.

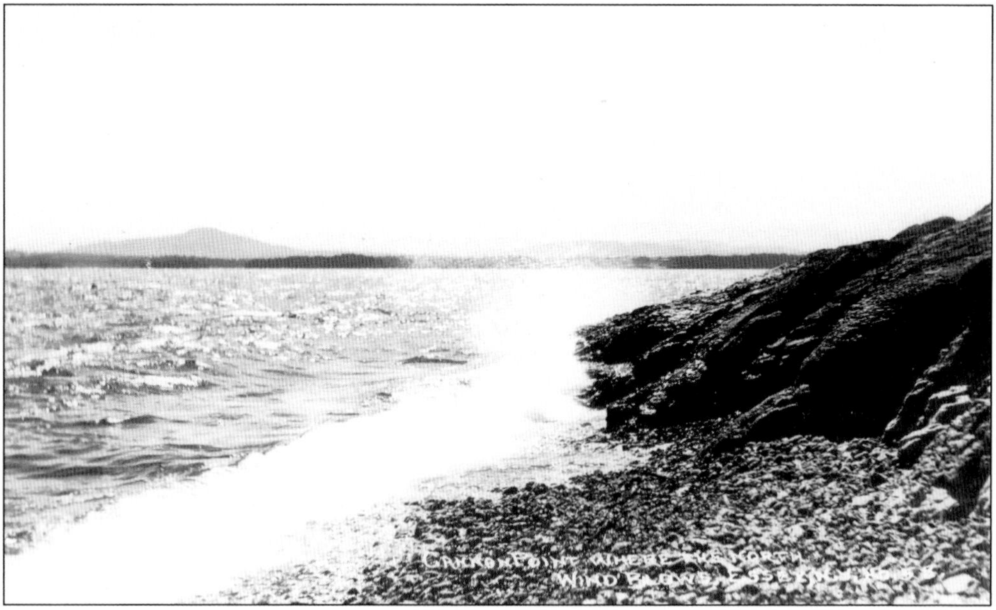

"CANNON POINT, WHERE THE NORTH WIND BLOWS." The types of land use in Essex include those of shipping, shipbuilding, and commerce at the waterfront. Also important is the early-19th-century history of clear-cut timbering, done both for its own commercial sake and to open up the land for agriculture. The land was then used for farming—first wheat and domestic foods then hay and oats for animal feed.

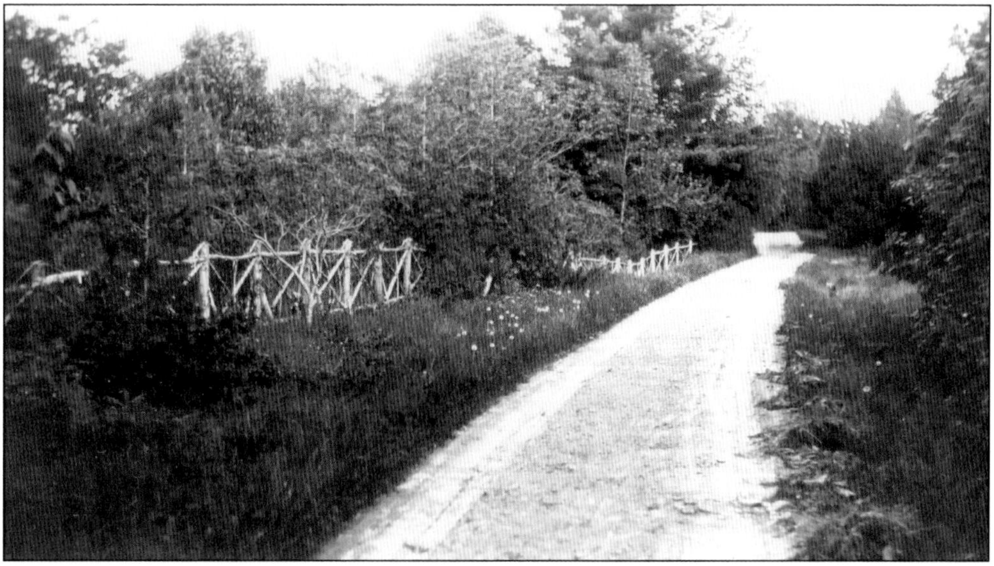

THE SOUTH ROAD. Presenting an Adirondack rustic association is a log white birch fence along part of the lakeshore. Once called the South Road, this rural pathway was long unpaved and rutted from wagon wheels, as shown here about 1911. The sender of this postcard wrote, "This is a way down the road from our Camp. . . . Everybody is just grand to me and the lake is four miles and a half rite here and the widest part is twelve."

THE ROAD SOUTH. The south end of Lake Shore Road leads eventually to the next town of Westport. The road is particularly scenic; the appeal was due to the narrow tree-lined road meandering over gentle hills with occasional breaks in the birch and aspen trees affording spectacular views of Lake Champlain. Again, this wooded area still exists immediately up to the first house in the Essex hamlet, locally known as Champ Watch.

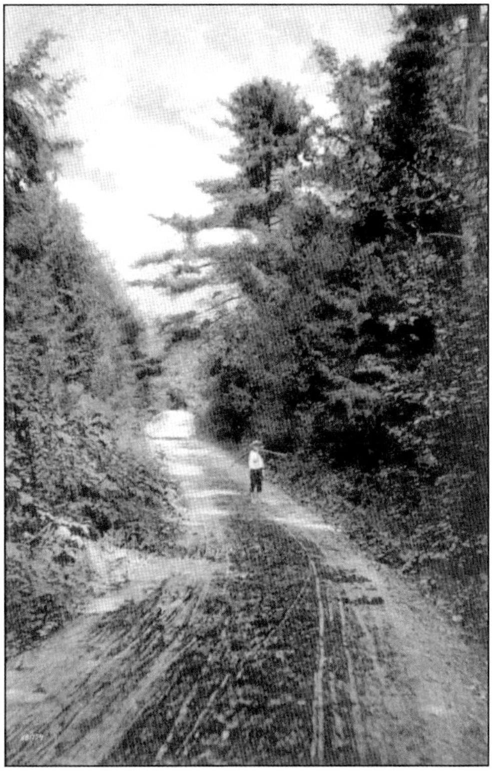

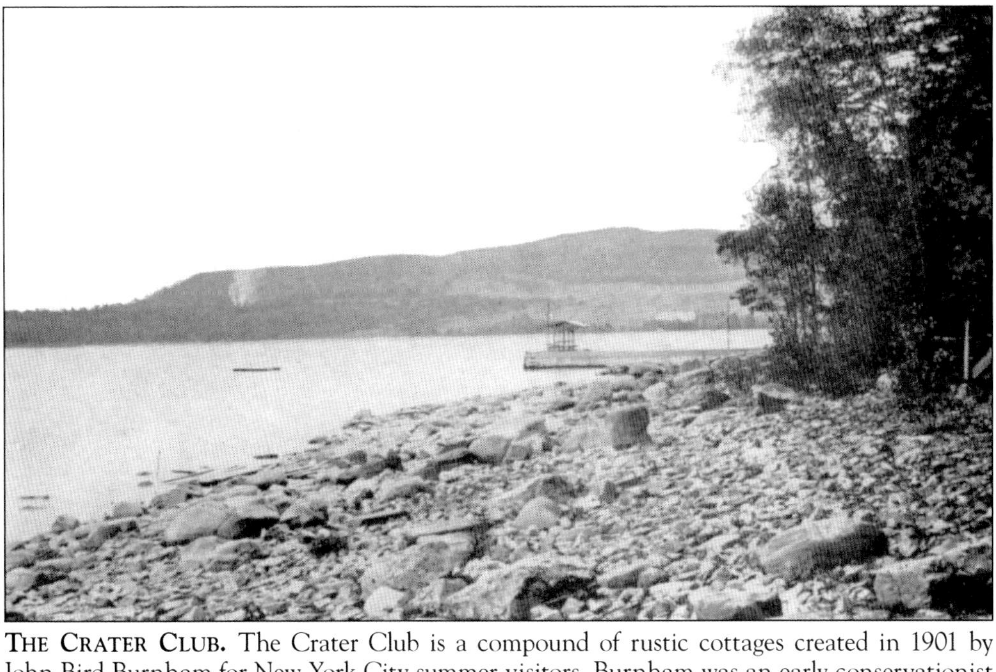

THE CRATER CLUB. The Crater Club is a compound of rustic cottages created in 1901 by John Bird Burnham for New York City summer visitors. Burnham was an early conservationist and believed that the natural environment was owned by all, and the public had a right to an opinion in the use and protection of natural resources. The Crater Club was named for what was once believed to be an ancient extinct volcanic crater.

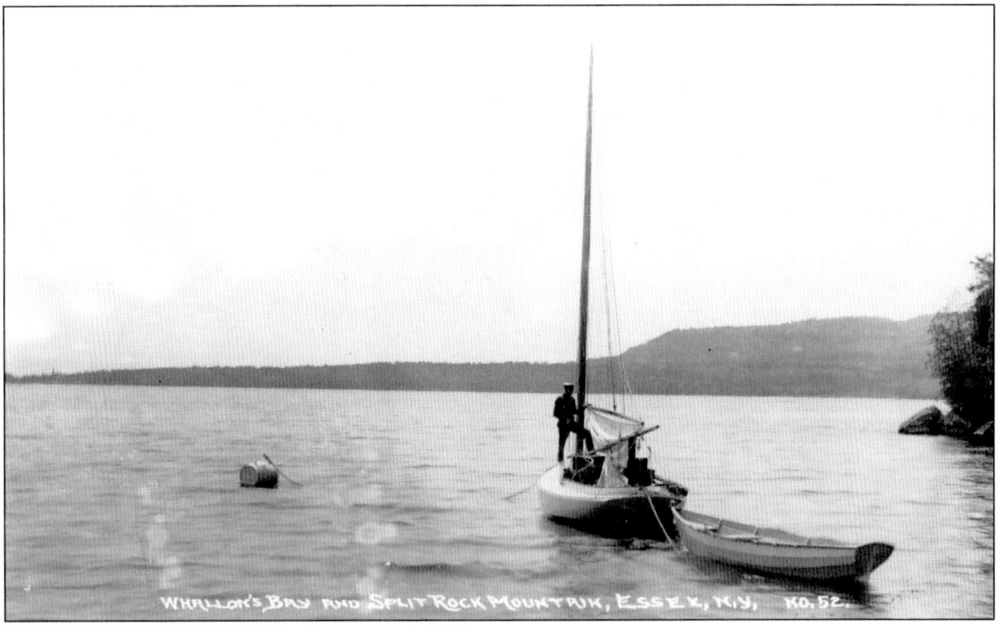

WHALLONS BAY. Named after early pioneer Judge Reuben S. Whallon, the bay that bears his name extends east toward Split Rock. Whallon was the first documented supervisor of the Town of Essex, and he was elected to the House of Representatives in the Pres. Andrew Jackson–era Congress. Whallon owned all the land to the west of his bay and formed the hamlet of Whallonsburg, which still exists to this day.

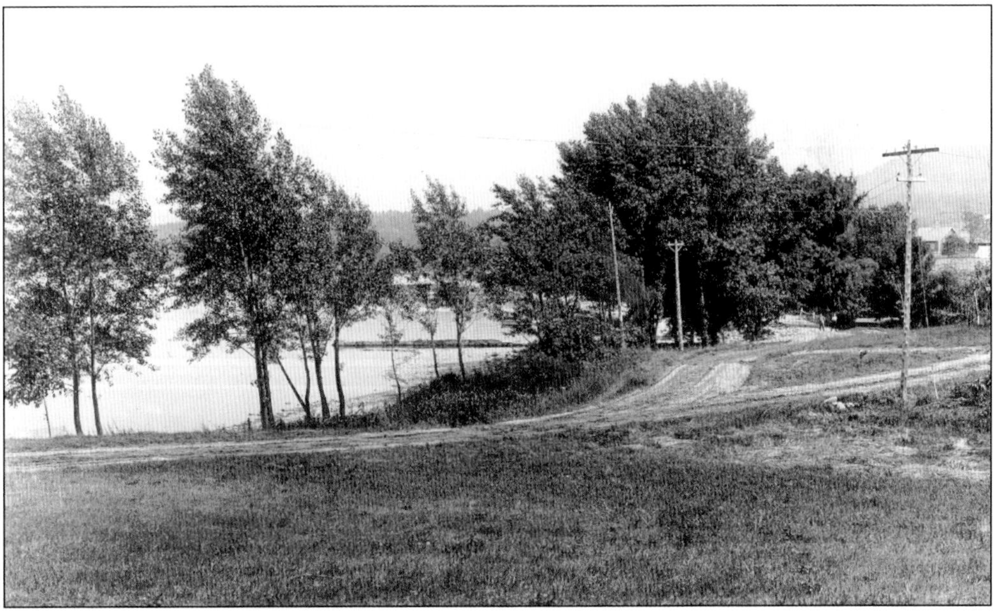

ROAD AT WHALLONS BAY. The roadway today forms the same traffic triangle at Whallons Bay, with only the addition of a stop sign or two. Fewer trees line the lakeshore than when this postcard was sent in 1915. Despite repeated citizen interest in burying them, telephone or telegraph poles and wires have existed for over 100 years along area rural roadways.

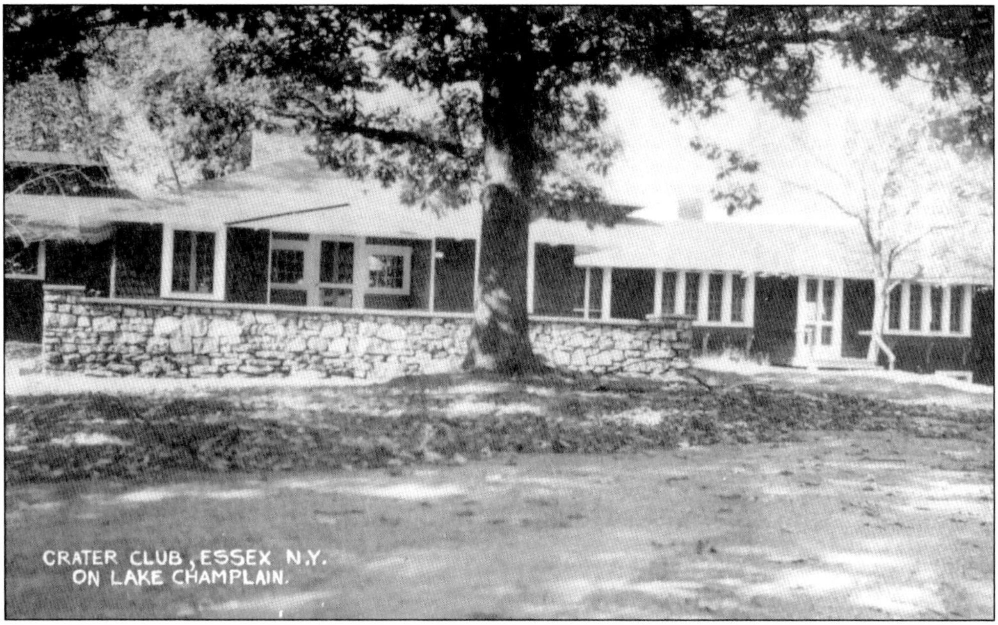

CLUBHOUSE. The main clubhouse of the Crater Club continues to serve the function of central meeting area and recreational pavilion today just as it did 100 years ago. It is designed in a simple rustic style with few Great Camp pretensions. Now most of the cottages are privately owned, and the club no longer rents individual units exclusively.

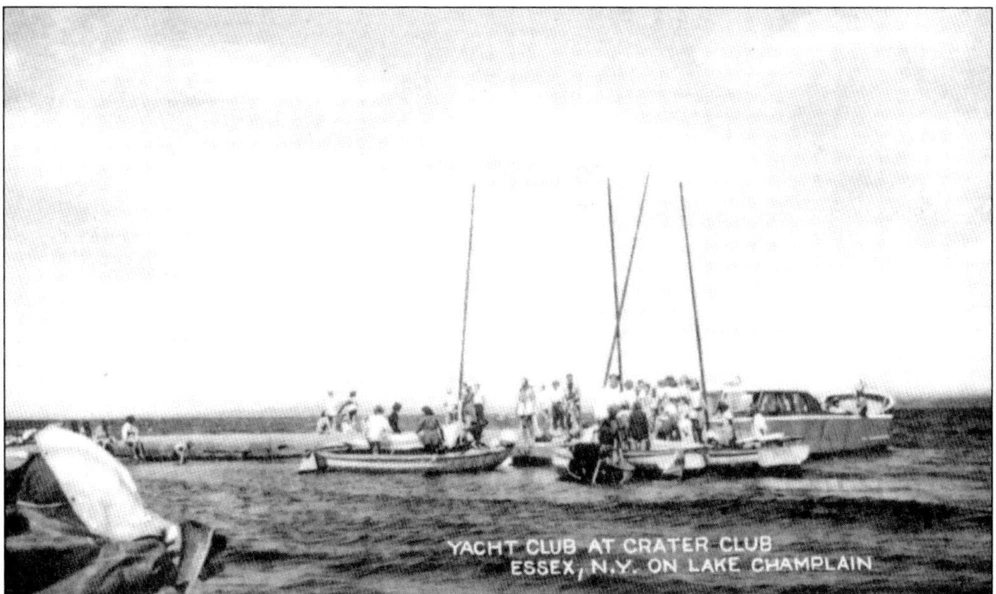

MARINA AT THE CRATER CLUB. The 1920s prosperity in America is reflected in the appearance of numerous pleasure yachts on Lake Champlain. The marina at the Crater Club formed its own regatta and owned its own pier

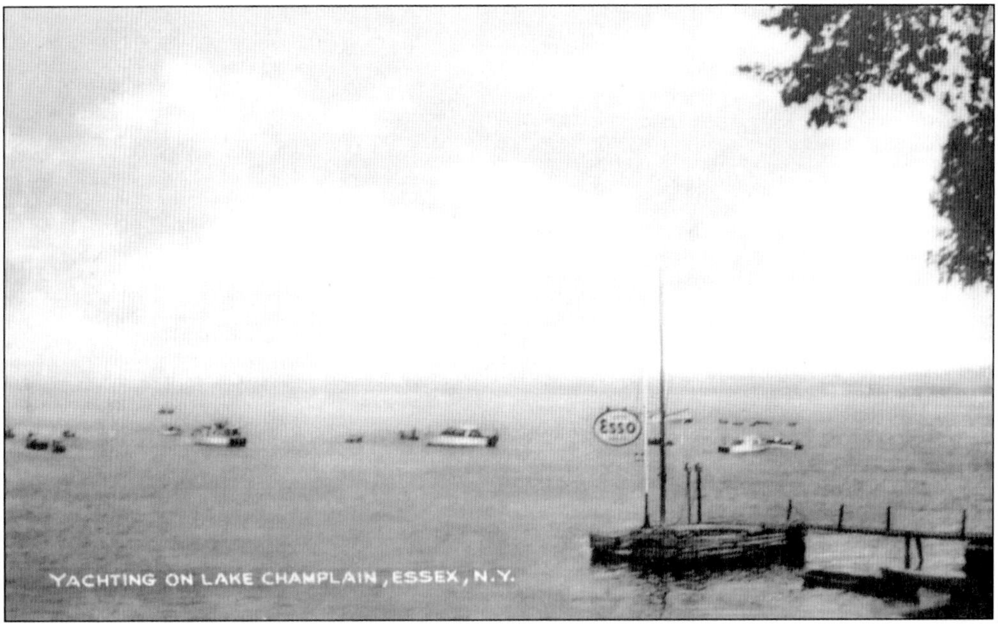

MURPHY'S MARINA. As tourism became the dominant local business, many historic structures were adapted to service the automobile. Motor touring on the newly paved roadways became a pastime of the 1920s, and motorboating became an attraction on the waterways. Both required a ready supply of petroleum products, such as those supplied by Murphy's Garage, an annex to an 1830s house.

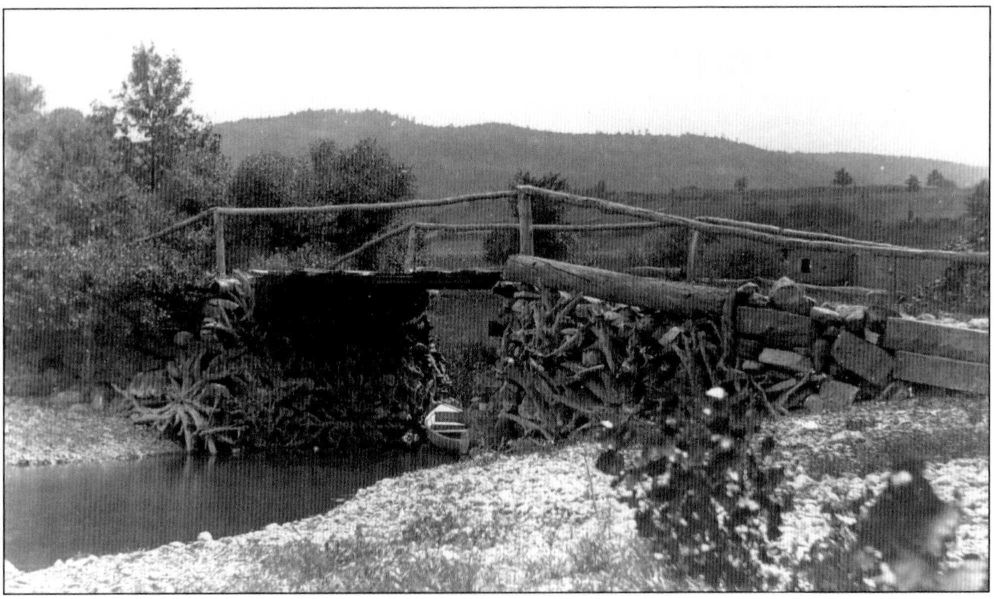

RUSTIC STUMP BRIDGE. The wonderful old stump bridge just south of Essex at Whallons Bay added rustic charm to the area around 1920. The elaborate cedar-root bridge would today be associated with the fashionable Adirondack style. Boundary demarcations are prominent along Lake Shore Road. A five-mile-long stone pile fence still exists, lining this roadway to the north. Early photographs show poles stuck at intervals in the stones and wires between them, increasing the height of the fence.

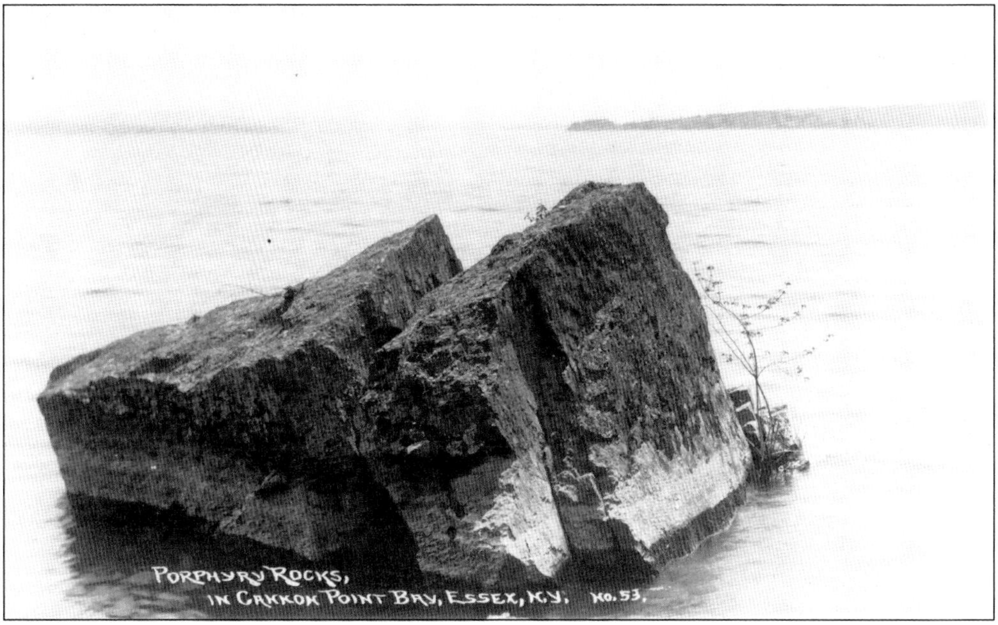

PORPHYRY ROCKS. Another oddity along the shoreline of Lake Champlain is the presence of the Porphyry Rocks. These ancient stone outcroppings represent a stone type uncharacteristic of the Chazy limestone beneath the hamlet of Essex. To the west is a street where there is an area that has been quarried for limestone for at least a century.

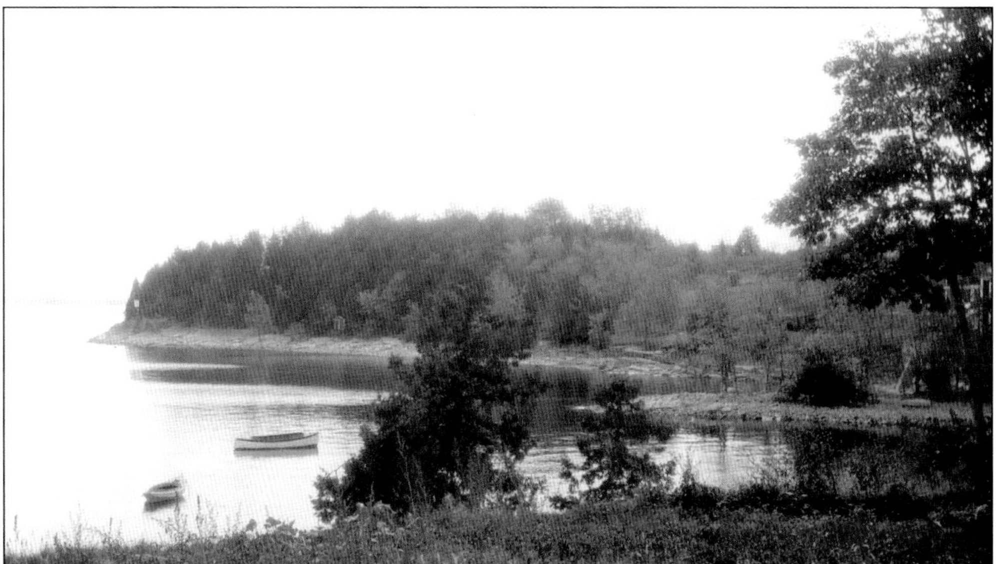

BLUFF POINT BAY IN SUMMER REPOSE. After the Essex Horse Nail Company factory burned in 1918, the land on the point was converted into a park. The idea of local park creation was still rather new in the 1920s, although the Adirondack Park, not yet including Essex, was formed in 1892. Bluff Point in the distance remains unchanged and undeveloped to this date, and easements exist to insure the compatibility of any future development.

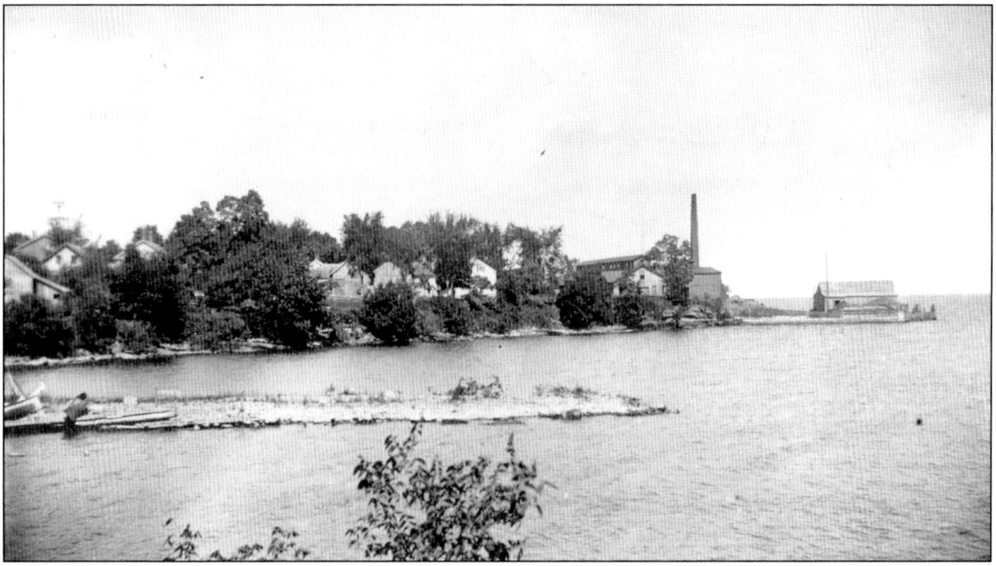

SHIPYARD. Remains of the shipyard wharf in the foreground highlight the industrial shift from shipbuilding to the distant factory of the blind and sash manufacturing company by the late 19th century. Lake steamers heading southward down toward Westport docked at the point on the far right.

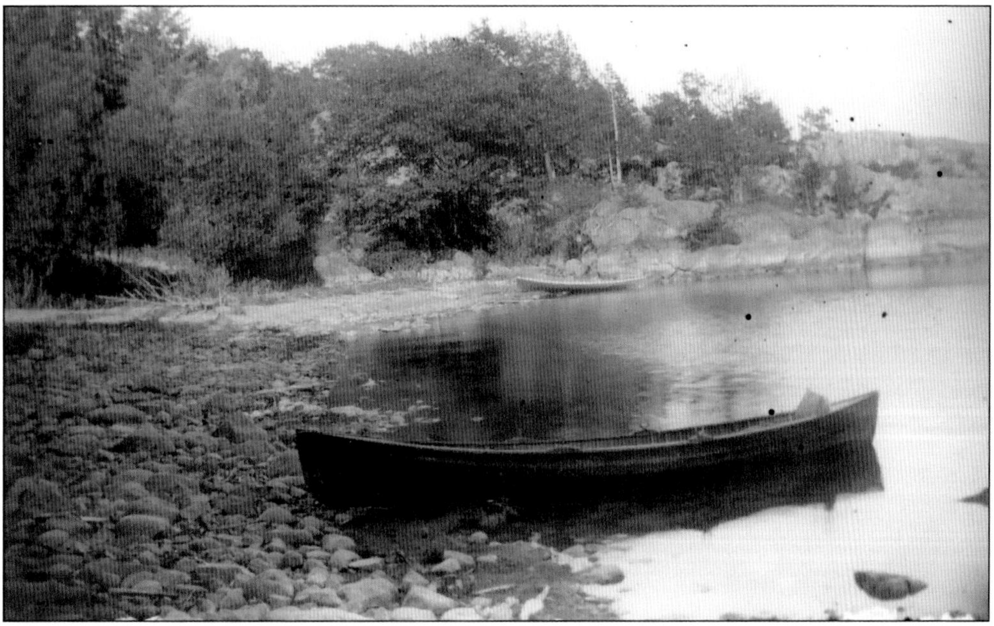

ADIRONDACK GUIDE BOAT. The simple summer pleasure of rowing the indigenous Adirondack guide boat was enjoyed on Lake Champlain. Guide boats could be carried by one man, referred to as a guide, over his back like a shell when portaging between bodies of water. They were constructed of lightweight woods like northern cedar with spruce ribbing. Guide boats could be pulled up easily on shore while the owners left to explore on land, as here near Essex.

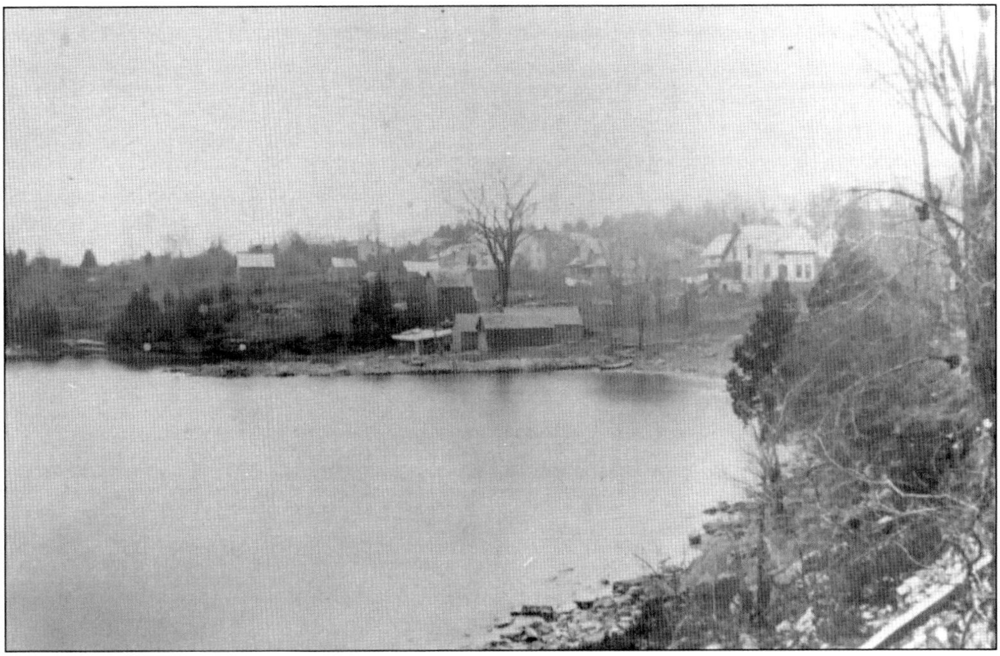

SOUTH BAY. The south end of the marina, where today a waterfront restaurant and series of docks are sited, reveals only a few sheds in this view from about 1910. The large Greek Revival house from about 1850 at the right has impressive presence and belies the beginning of the row of smaller cottages extending southward up the hill known as Bull Run.

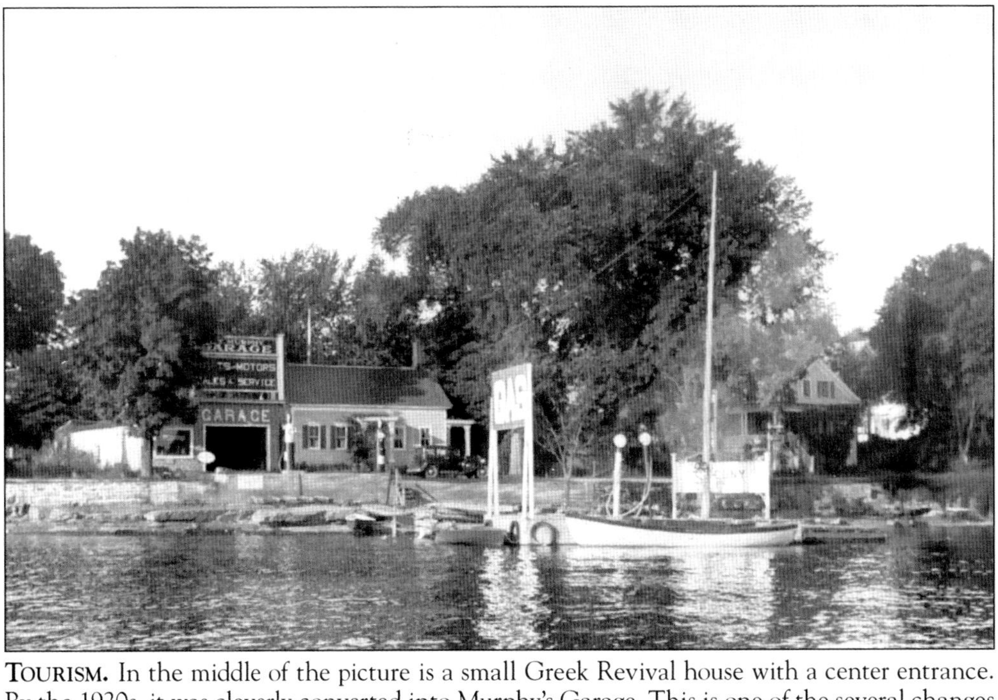

TOURISM. In the middle of the picture is a small Greek Revival house with a center entrance. By the 1920s, it was cleverly converted into Murphy's Garage. This is one of the several changes in use of a building that the tourism era spurred. Today most of these automobile changes have been reversed and the structures often returned to exclusively residential use.

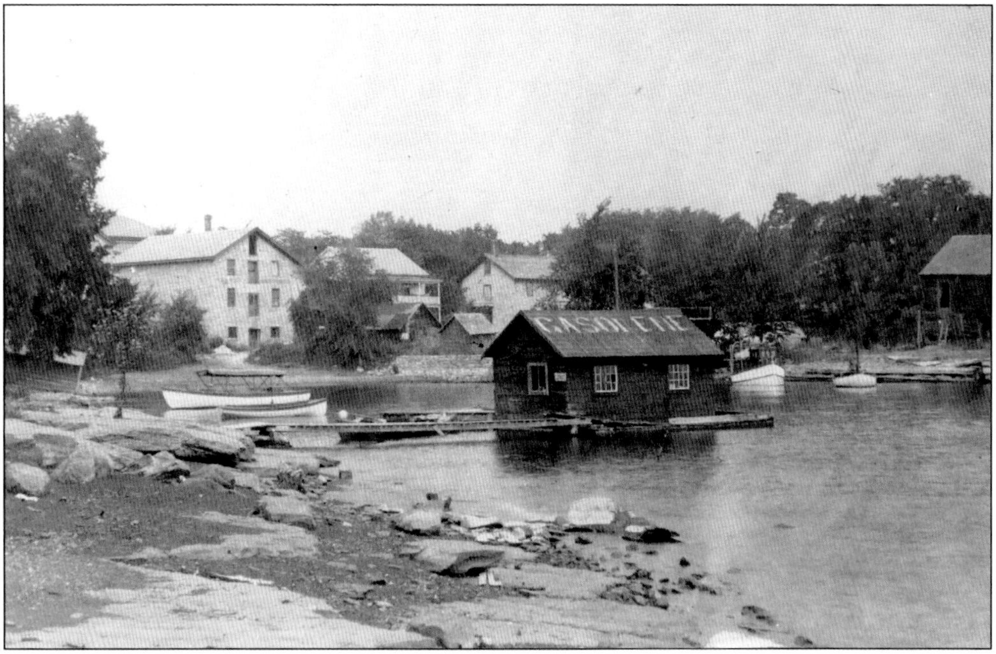

Maritime Murphy's. This view looks from the vicinity of Murphy's Garage over toward its shed that served the watercraft. The building of the old dock house on the far right, a relic from the earlier canal schooner days, sits neglected and awaiting a future use. The white hulls of boats, like white shoes on men, were popular in the era.

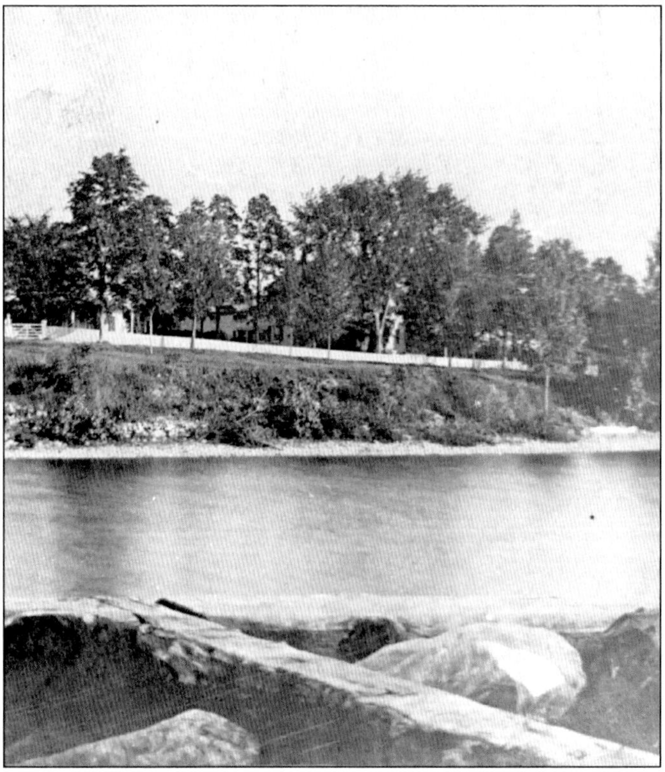

North Coast Houses. The four great houses on the north shore are united in both their Georgian architectural style and in the continuous wooden fence that runs between them. In the foreground is the stonework cribbage of the Noble family wharf. The octagonal Noble schoolhouse/office on the left and the William D. Ross home, called Rosslyn, are visible through the foliage. This view documents the wood spindle fence that appears to enclose the front of both in the 1880s.

Two

MARITIME MERCHANTS

The evolution of maritime commerce on Lake Champlain is important nationally because it represents how hundreds of small American communities developed. From the skills of a few entrepreneurs with the support of dozens of merchants and workers, vast fortunes were created in a manner that played out across the national scene. Maritime commerce helped Lake Champlain become one of the gateways to early industrial America. Surprisingly, despite several towns existing on both sides of Lake Champlain, only Essex seemed in a position to truly prosper from the construction of the Champlain Canal in the 1820s. Essex was located on the broadest, deepest part of the lake and possessed two fine natural harbors. The roadways to the west from Essex headed directly to the regions that held the largest concentrations of natural resources then available in the Adirondacks. Thus Essex became the largest and most successful port on Lake Champlain in the early 19th century.

The first vessels of Lake Champlain were undoubtedly Native American canoes, such as the ones Samuel de Champlain and his explorers used on their first voyage in 1609. By the early 19th century, sailing ships had been fully developed for two centuries. Fully rigged sailing ships under the command of Thomas Macdonough won the day for the Americans at the battle of Plattsburgh victory during the War of 1812. Several ships for that conflict were constructed at the shipyards in Essex, such as the *Eagle* and the *Growler*. Government contracts during the conflict enabled Essex to develop its shipyards and prosper as a community.

The first sloop on the lake, the *Euretta*, was built in Essex about 1810 by Richard Eggleston. He went on to construct about 10 150-ton vessels, over 100 freight vessels, and 250 row galleys or bateaux. Sloops transported livestock and travelers to both sides of the lake. The commerce on the Champlain Canal fed into commerce on the Erie Canal, strengthening the new cities in western New York State, such as Syracuse, Rochester, and Buffalo. Ultimately this led to a participation in the great westward expansion to the broad plains and future cities of the middle and western United States.

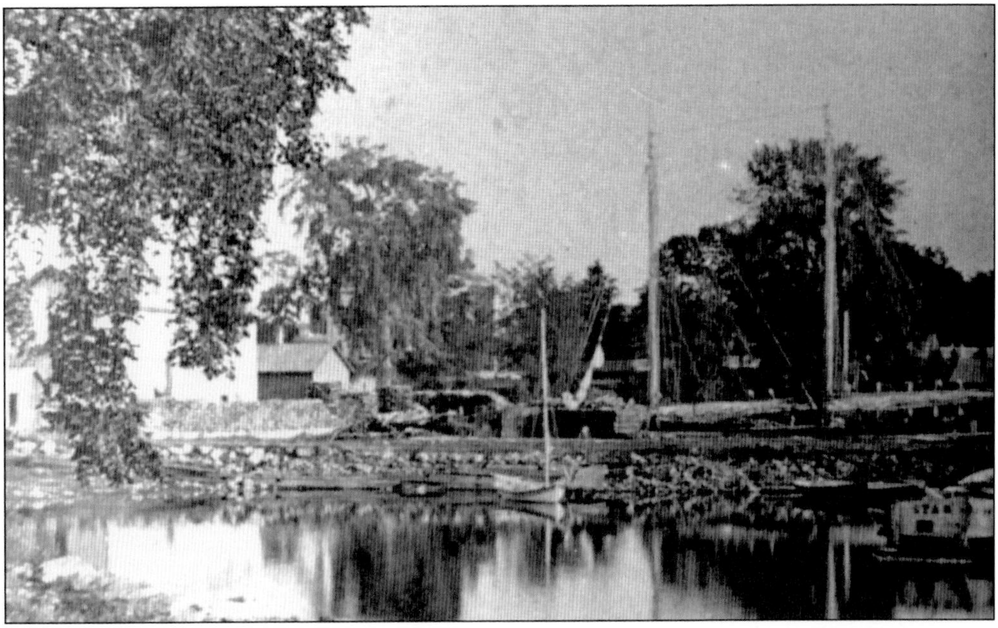

OLD SAILING BOATS, C. 1890. Lake Champlain flows to the north, eventually emptying into the St. Lawrence River. Thus when early settlers used the waterway for trading, they tended to ship goods north toward the Canadian region. Trade was not particularly lucrative, so wise investors such as the Noble family of Essex promoted the construction of the Champlain Canal connecting the southern end of Lake Champlain to the waters of the Hudson River.

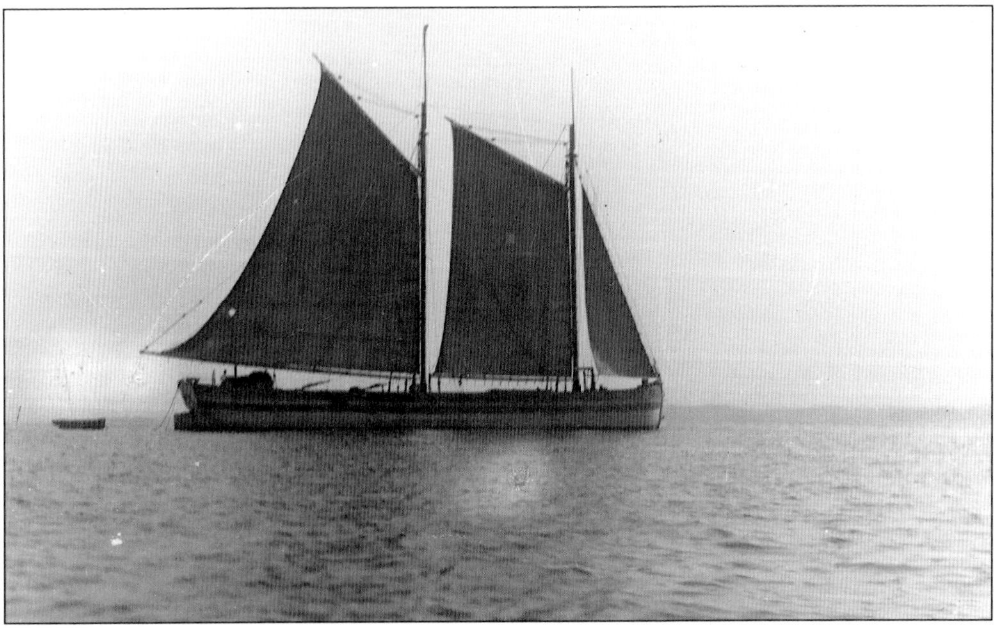

CANAL SCHOONER. An economic boom soon followed, but one problem remained, as the full rigging of sailing ships could not navigate through the low bridges of the canal. So inventive souls developed the canal schooner, a vessel that had collapsible masts. The masts could be stored flat during canal journeys and when the boat was towed by mules. When open waters of the lake were reached, the masts could be installed upright and the sails employed.

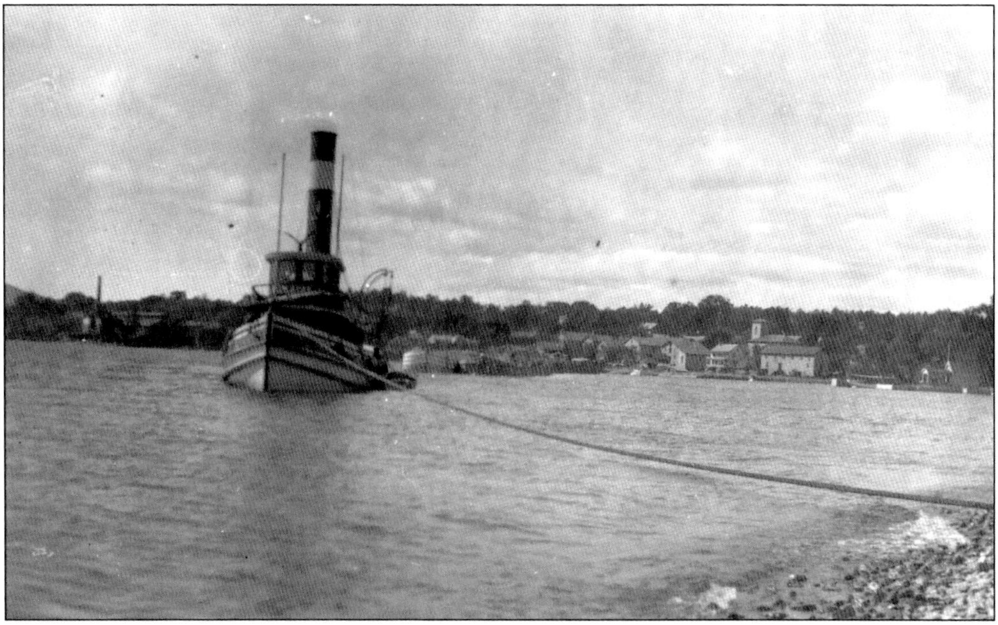

IN TOW ON LAKE CHAMPLAIN. Once steam power became widely available, the canal boats could be towed like barges and grouped together for more efficient transport. Eventually the sails became redundant, and all lake transport occurred by towing. The last barges, filled with fuel oil destined for the Plattsburgh Air Force Base, were towed on the lake into the 1990s. With the closure of the base, the final chapter of lake commerce ended.

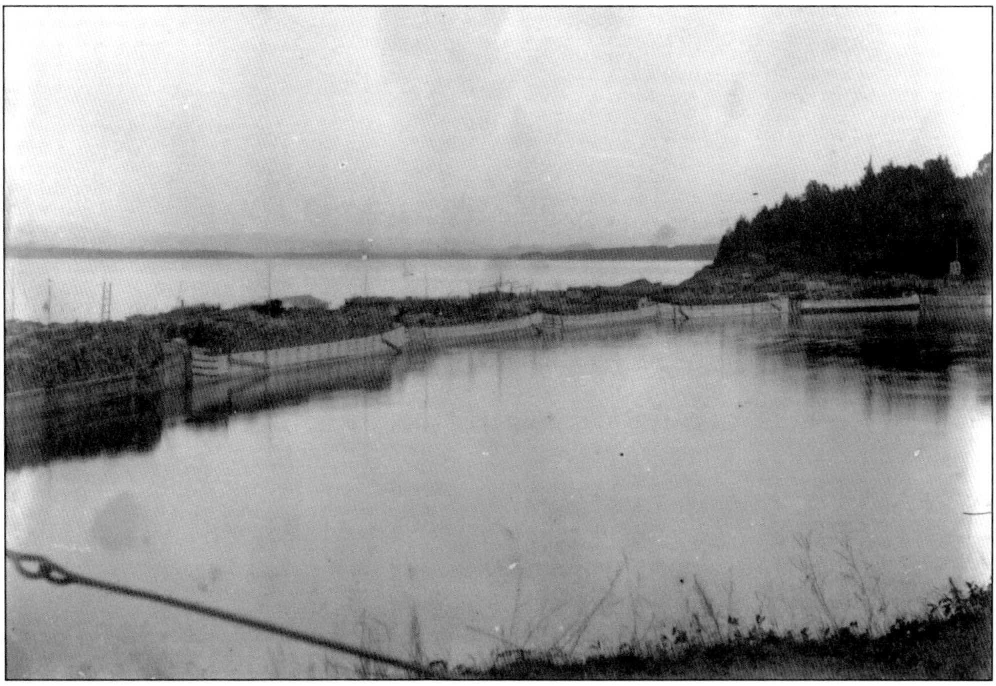

CANAL BOATS. Here is a fleet of well-filled canal boats at Essex. Forestry products could be stored and shipped much cheaper than by land transportation. Gradually railroads and trucks became more economically competitive, and after the 1920s, few canal boats were left in regular use.

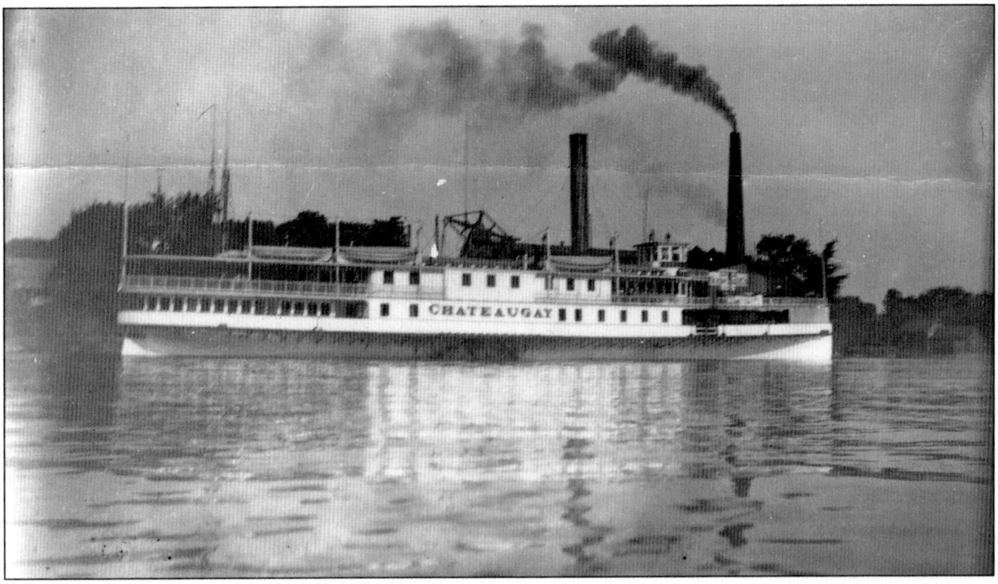

STEAMBOAT *CHATEAUGAY*. In 1809, a steam-powered boat, the *Vermont*, was constructed at the Burlington shipyards and was the second successful commercial steamboat in America after the *Clermont*. While the *Chateaugay* appears to have two smokestacks, the forward smoking chimney is actually attached to the Essex Horse Nail Company factory. A large coal bin was located on Shipyard Point to replenish the cavernous bins on the lake steamers.

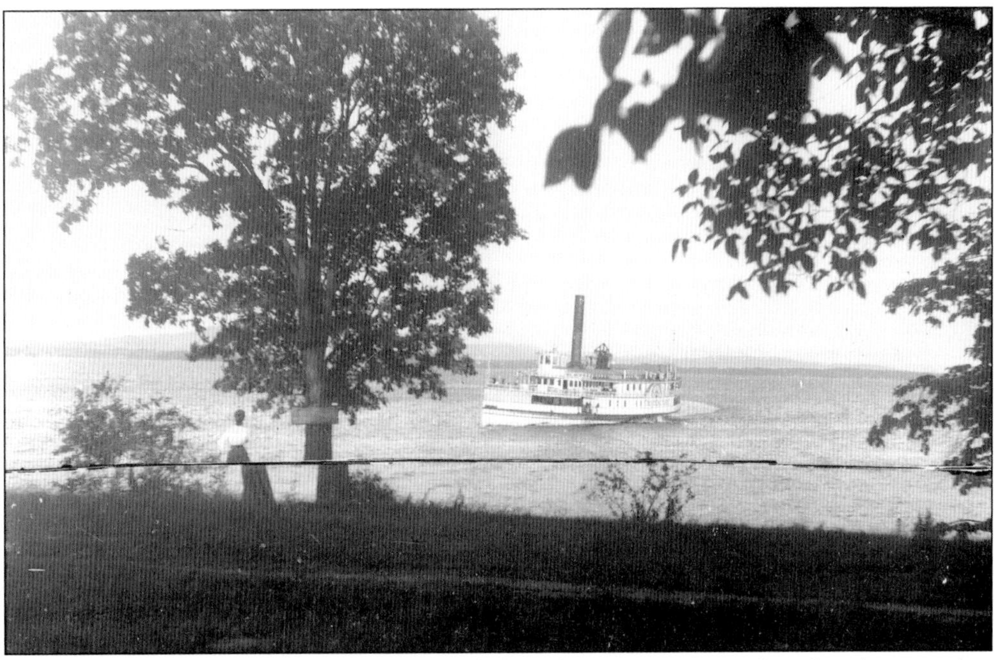

***CHATEAUGAY* APPROACHING ESSEX.** Original glass-plate negatives are often found wrapped in crumbling newspapers in an attic, as was the case here. They are vulnerable to breakage yet when developed and printed can still yield a valued image. This scene still from about 1890 details imagery of the steamer *Chateaugay* approaching Shipyard Point on a summer day.

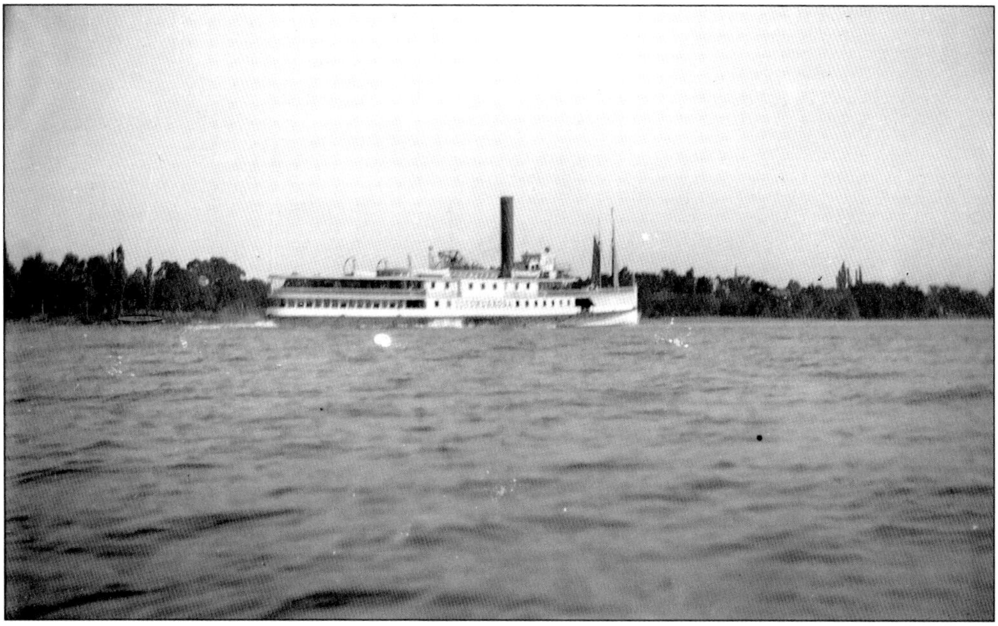

TICONDEROGA LEAVING ESSEX. The hardworking and much-admired *Ticonderoga*, or "Ti," was the only lake steamer to be preserved and one of the few remaining in the country of the walking beam type. The steamboat era finally ended entirely with the retirement of the *Ticonderoga* in 1954. It was preserved and in 1955 moved inland to the Shelburne Museum, and the story of it being moved is one of the highlights of touring the ship today.

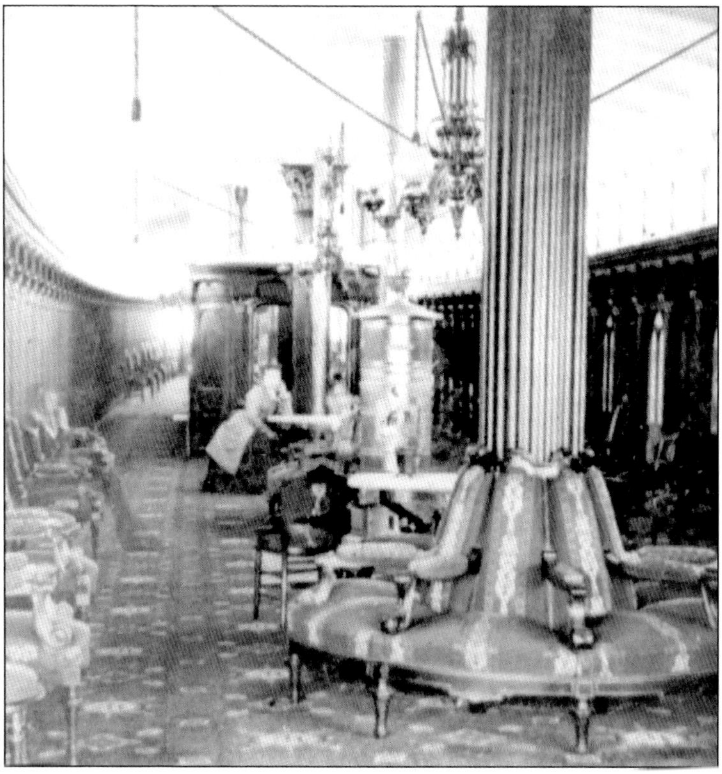

RARE STEAMBOAT INTERIOR. Prevailing Victorian interior decoration held sway in the main parlors, such as here in the Renaissance Revival mode. The 1870s popular taste expressed a preference for dark woods, specifically the black walnut used for chairs, sofas, divans, and other seating furniture. Upholstery was often in crimson hues with a medallion pattern. The oil lamp chandeliers were also in the Renaissance Revival style.

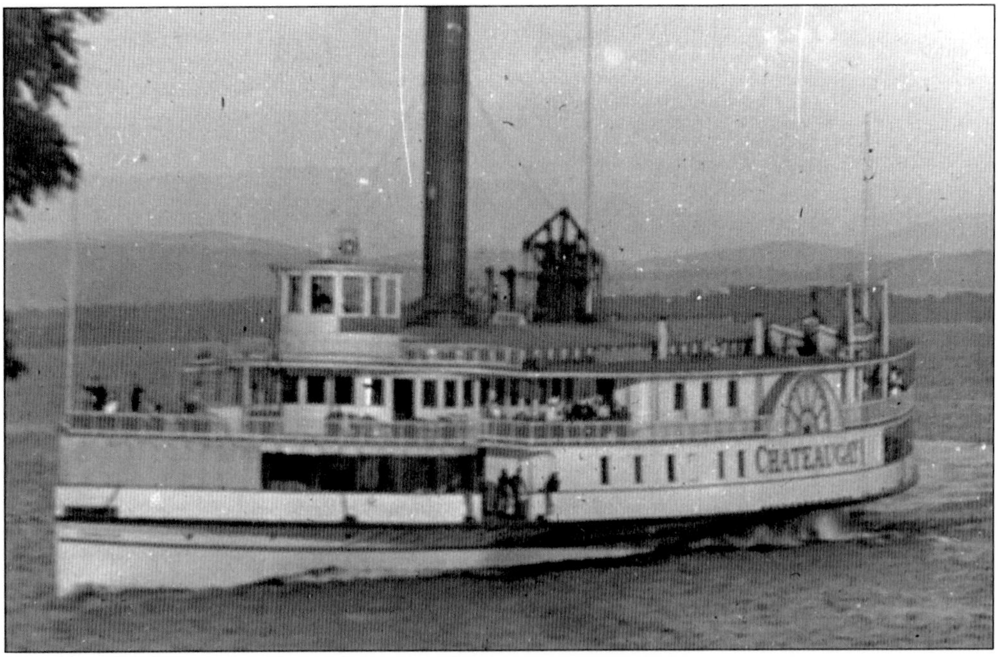

STEAMBOAT ERA. The side-wheeler *Chateaugay* was named after a small town and lake in the Adirondacks. The walking beam steam engine rises midship as it steams into Essex in the 1890s. Between 1807 and the last sailing of the side-wheeler *Ticonderoga* in the 1950s, numerous sizes and descriptions of steamboats plied the approximately 100-mile length of the waters of Lake Champlain.

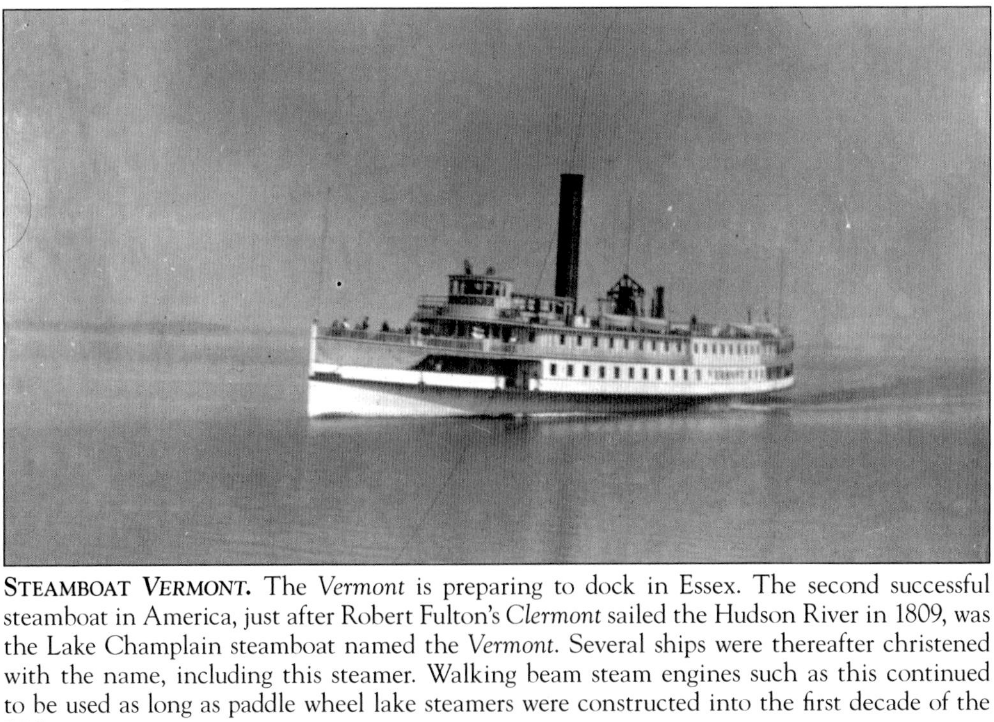

STEAMBOAT *VERMONT*. The *Vermont* is preparing to dock in Essex. The second successful steamboat in America, just after Robert Fulton's *Clermont* sailed the Hudson River in 1809, was the Lake Champlain steamboat named the *Vermont*. Several ships were thereafter christened with the name, including this steamer. Walking beam steam engines such as this continued to be used as long as paddle wheel lake steamers were constructed into the first decade of the 20th century.

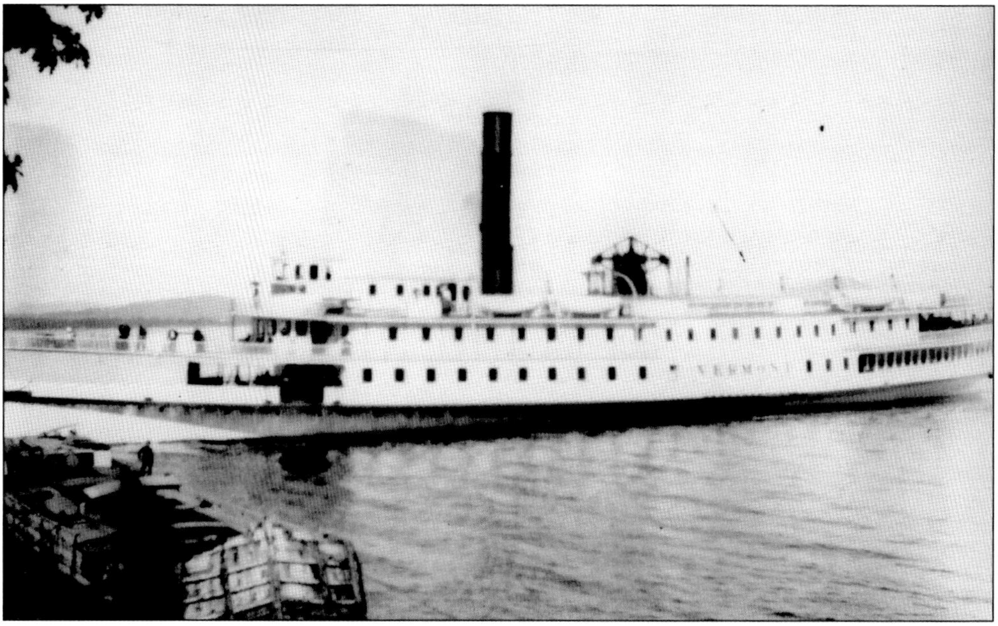

COMPARISON OF MOTIVE POWER. As with many active ports, the old and the new in shipping operated side by side. The derelict remains of an old canal boat are bypassed by a later-day version of the *Vermont*. Earlier the sailing canal schooner *General Butler* was constructed at the Essex shipyard in 1862 of a size and scale that responded to the recent widening of the Champlain Canal.

LAST *TICONDEROGA* EXCURSIONS. For a few years in the early 1950s, an attempt was made to operate the *Ticonderoga* as an excursion boat. The usual downfalls to steam operation eventually occurred: there were no longer any trained steam engineers or mechanics, and there was an inability to obtain new parts, as most American manufacturers had ceased producing steam engines of all types with the rise and quick domination of the petroleum fuel–burning marine diesel engine.

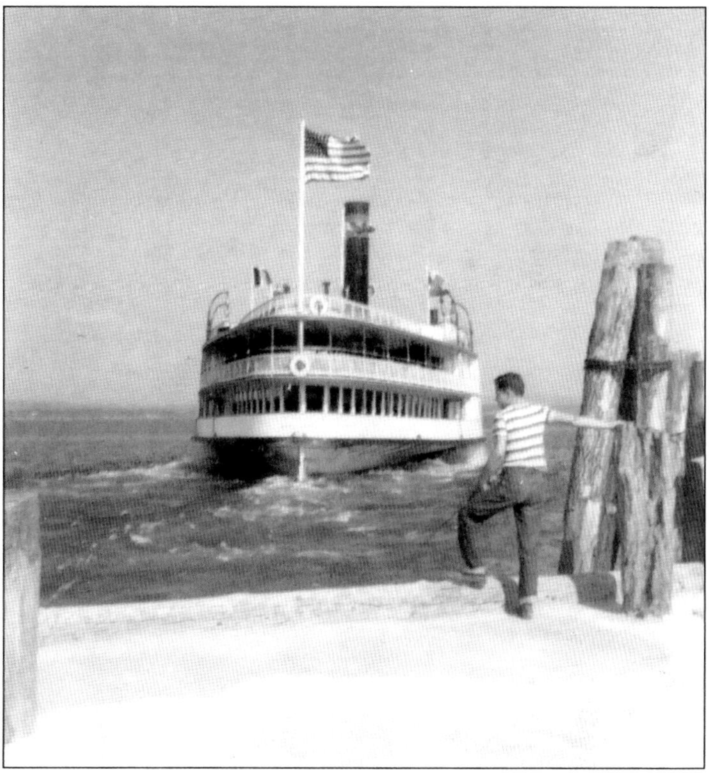

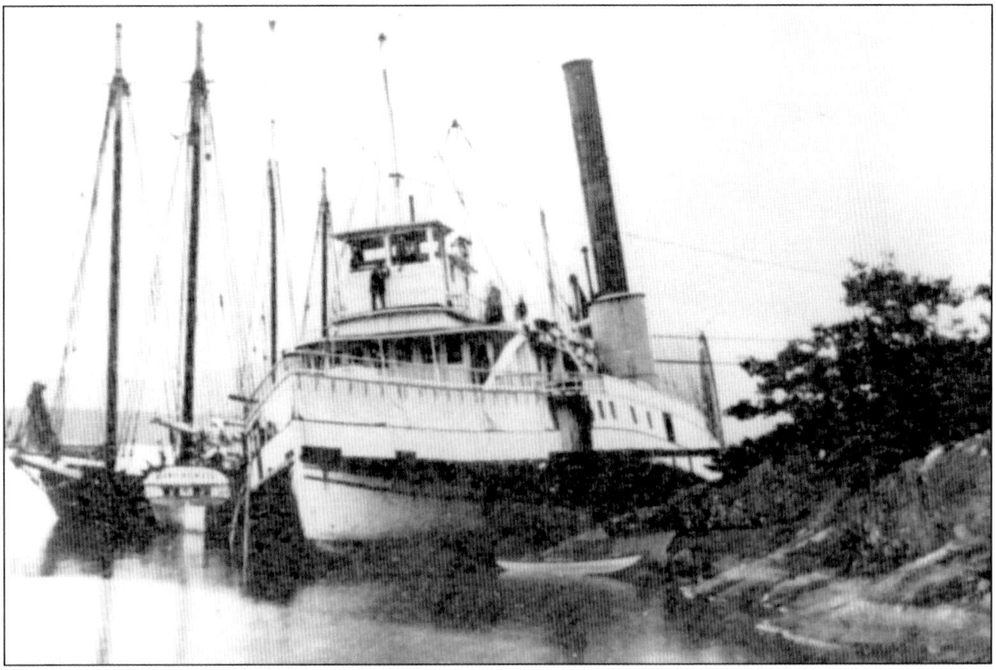

Wreck of the Steamboat *Champlain*. Perhaps the best-known tragedy on the lake was the wreck of the 258-foot steamer *Champlain* on the rocks of Steam Mill Point near Westport in July 1875. Remarkably, when the time came for salvage operations, the company wanted only the valuable steam engines. The local population was invited to take the rest, and they did. To this date, many parts and pieces of the *Champlain* are spread throughout Essex.

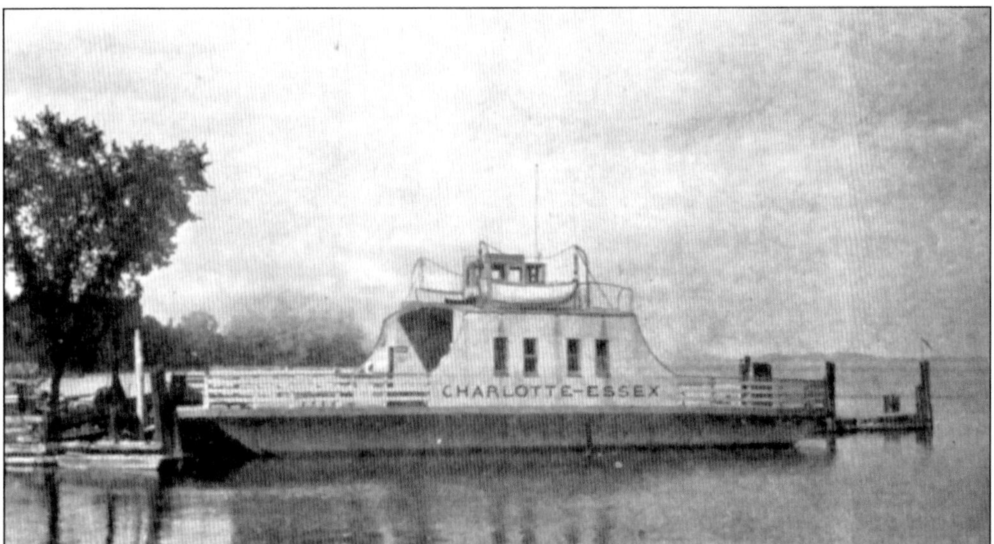

Double-Ender Steam Ferryboats. Also in demand were varying types of boats for the cross-lake ferry service. A ferry crossing has existed between the Essex coastline and the Vermont shore near Charlotte since 1791. The initial ferryboats were sloops powered by sail and had various spots to land, depending on the winds. Some were replaced early in the 19th century by a unique type of vessel, the horse-powered ferryboat.

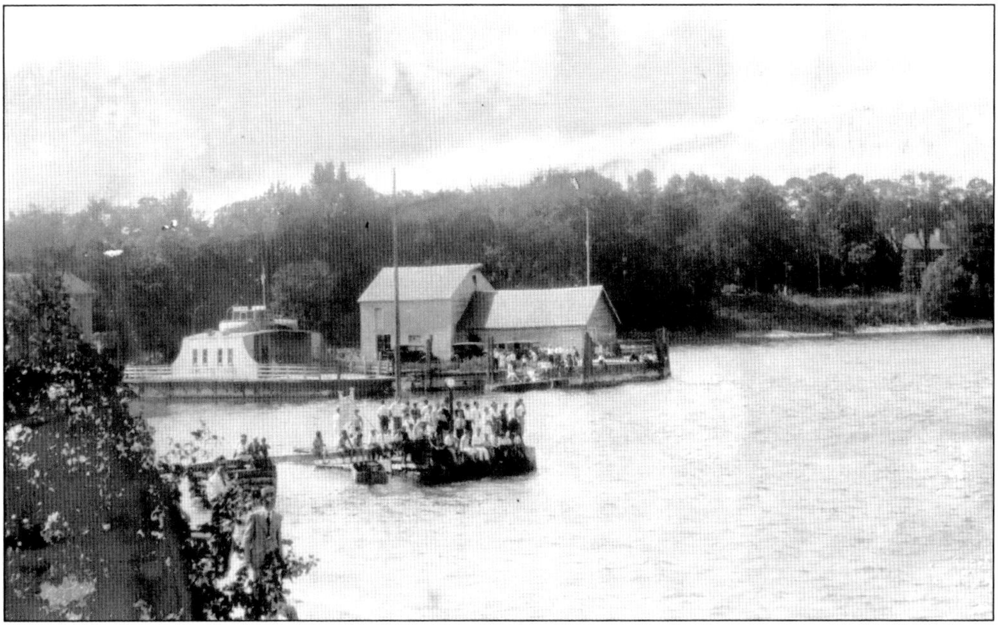

FERRYBOATS. Steam ferryboats soon plied the Essex–Charlotte route, and the Vermont crossing used vessels that were double-ended so they could dock straight on at both sides of the lake without turning around. Many ferry companies vied for the market through the mid-19th century. Especially in the 1920s, almost all ferries became capable of transporting automobiles on their lower decks. With the transition to steam, ferryboats docked on the side of the old dock.

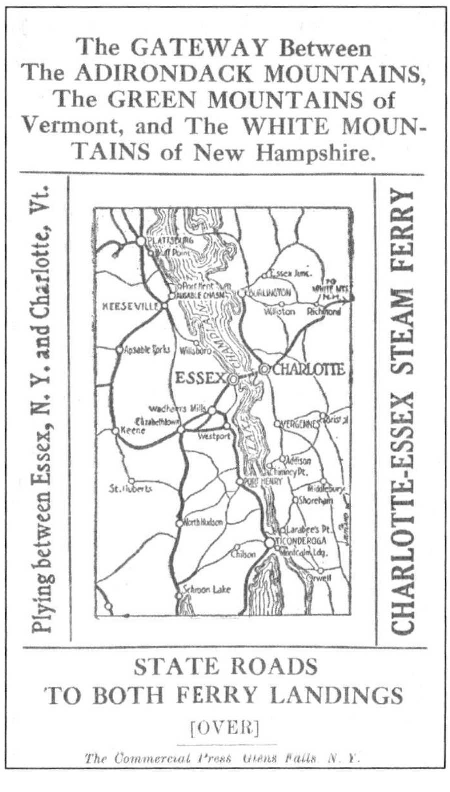

CHARLOTTE-ESSEX STEAM FERRY. Here is a ferry ticket from the 1920s promoting the region and the neighboring mountains as a tourist area. The market for cross-lake travel was cornered until 1929 when the first major bridge, the Champlain Bridge, opened at Crown Point. In addition, an independent cable ferry operates in the Fort Ticonderoga area.

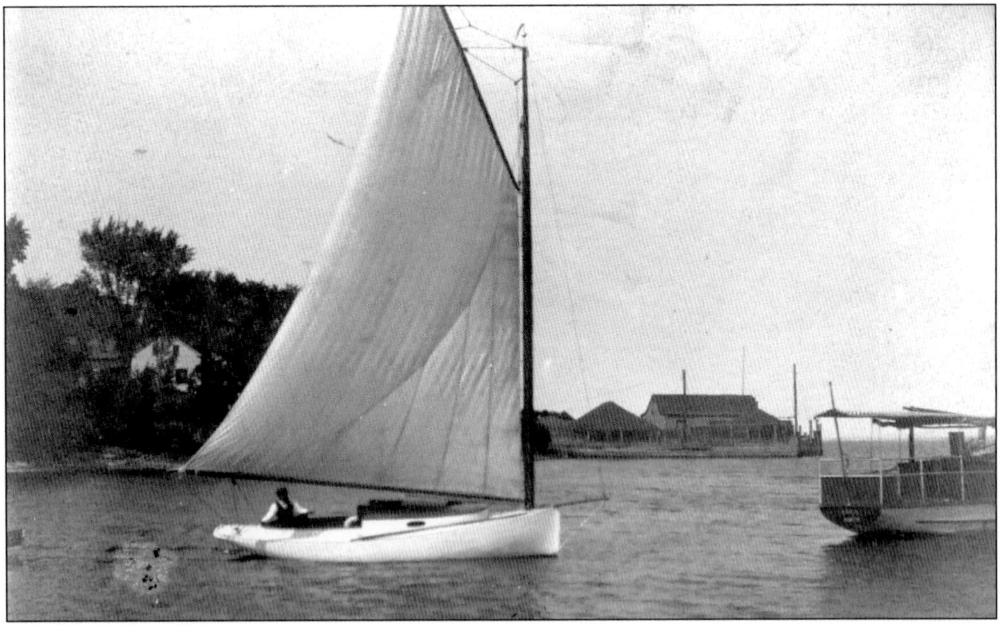

RECREATIONAL BOATING. Pleasure craft sailing on Lake Champlain came into its own in the 1890s. With tourism booming by the 1920s, boating on the lake became a preferred recreation. Watercrafts were moored in the Noble harbor and beside the Noble family dock. Canoes were seen on the only sandy beach in the hamlet limits. Since then, numerous regattas have been staged both in the harbors and at Whallons Bay.

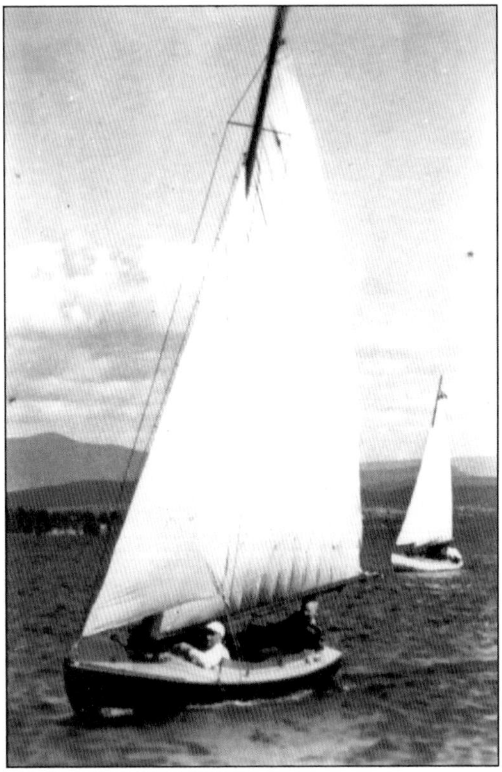

KNOCKABOUT. Koert Burnham, son of the famed nature writer and publisher John Bird Burnham, was a lifelong Essex resident. A type of pleasure craft known as a knockabout and named the *Mary G.* is sailed here by Burnham in about 1940.

WINTER ICEBOATS. Not to be neglected off-season, the occasional complete freeze of all Lake Champlain allowed for the sport of iceboating. These sleek, often locally made craft could cover the ice and sail over it all the way to Vermont. The frozen waves of water provided endless adventure, as seen here in front of Greystone.

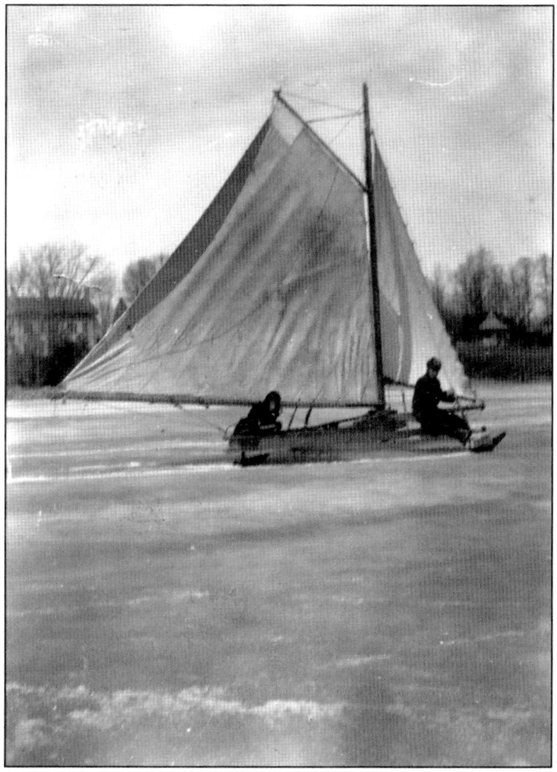

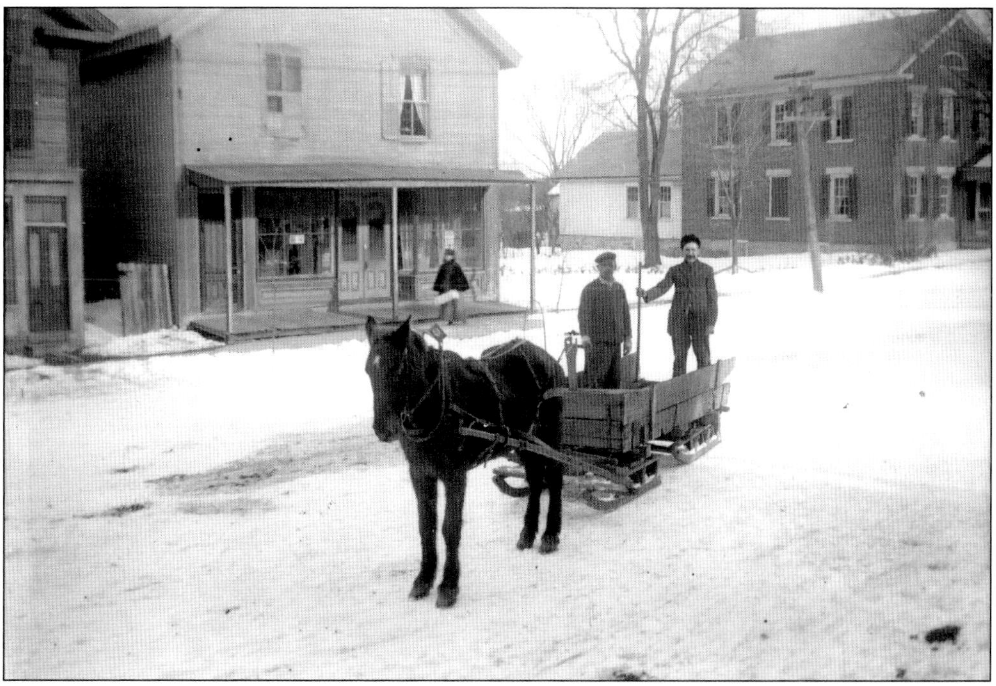

WINTER INLAND. The winter scene precipitated the switch from wheels to blades. The cutter shown here on Main Street in Essex could carry freight or workers waiting to load freight. The old general store is in the background, and the Manse is to the right.

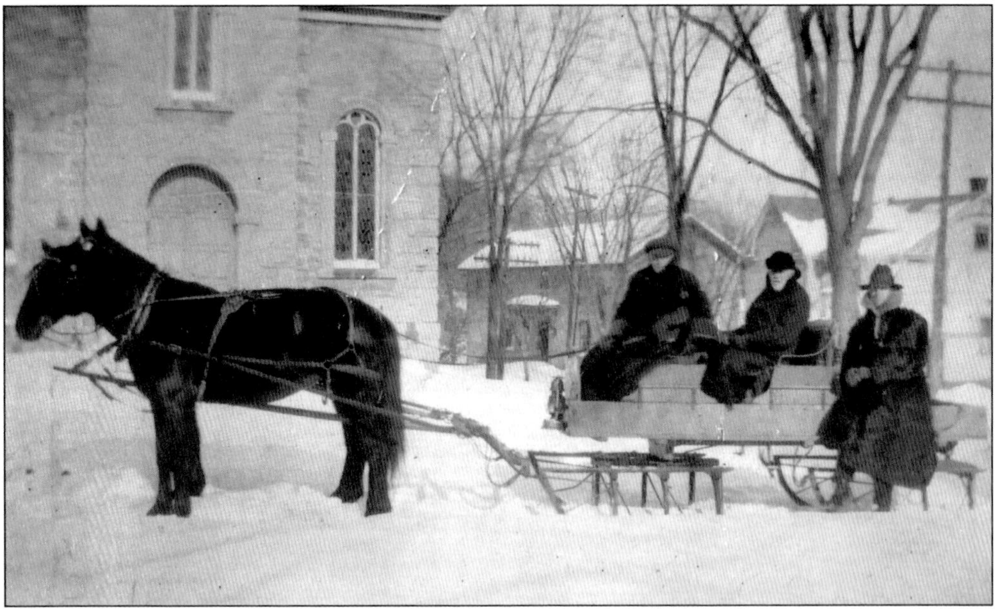

Passenger Transport. Passengers could also be accommodated in winter as this team of horses and three unidentified men pose in front of the Essex Presbyterian Church. The original 1850s windows are visible in the front facade of the church. The Noble warehouse beyond them has not yet been converted to a theater.

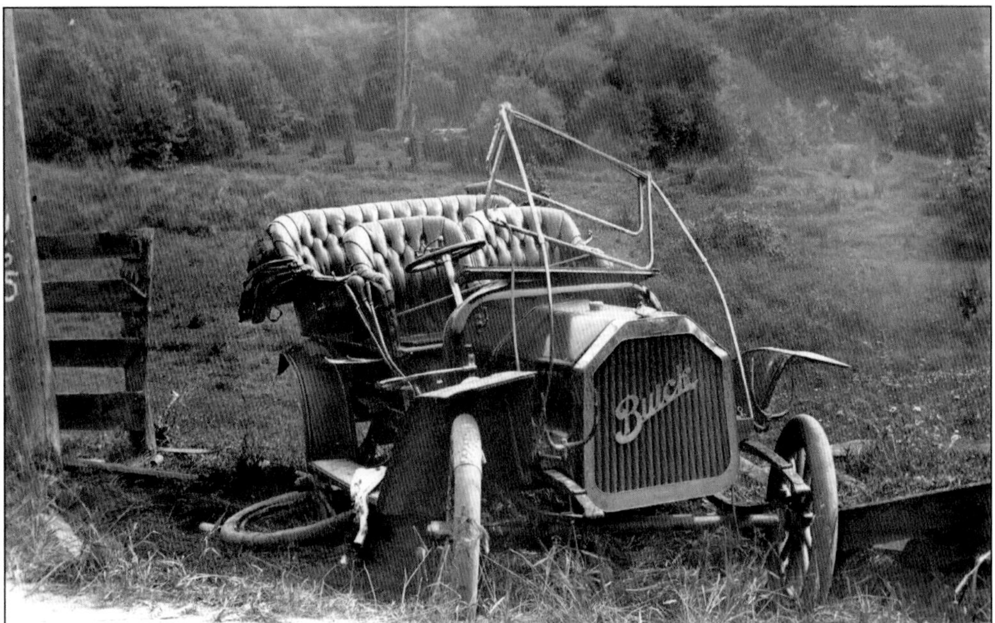

Wrecked Buick. Sometimes a cliché like "get a horse!" takes on a real-world urgency. Essex postmaster C. E. Van Ornam was the proud owner of the second car in the village, until one day in 1913 while motoring.

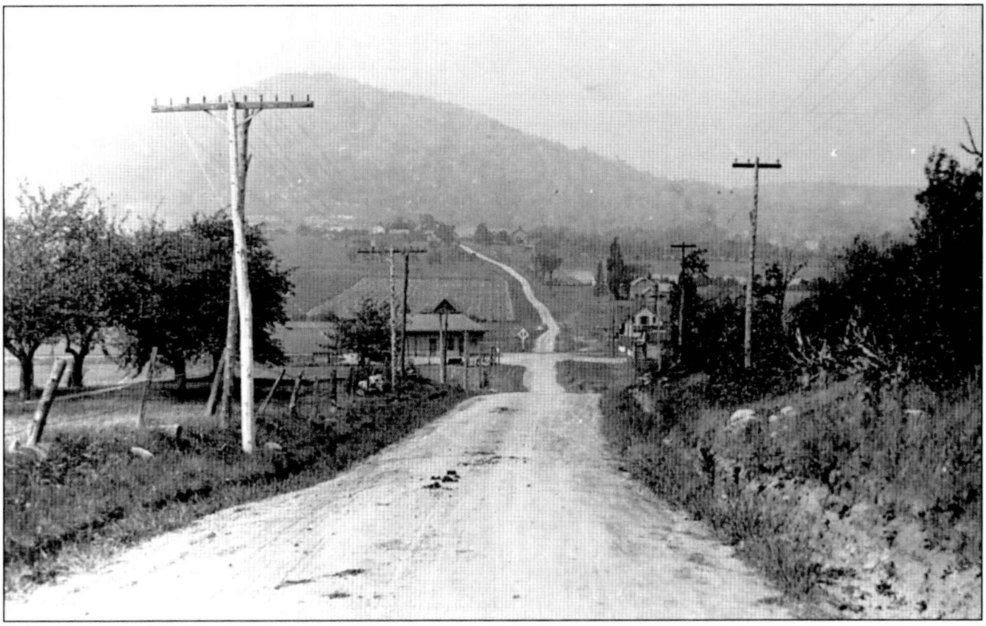

Essex Station. The Delaware and Hudson Railroad, stretching from Albany to Montreal, entered Essex in 1875. A station was not constructed until a decade later. By that time, the major natural resources of timber, iron, and potash had long been depleted or were available cheaper in the American West. However, there was still a significant business in farming and agricultural commerce, which continued for nearly the next 100 years.

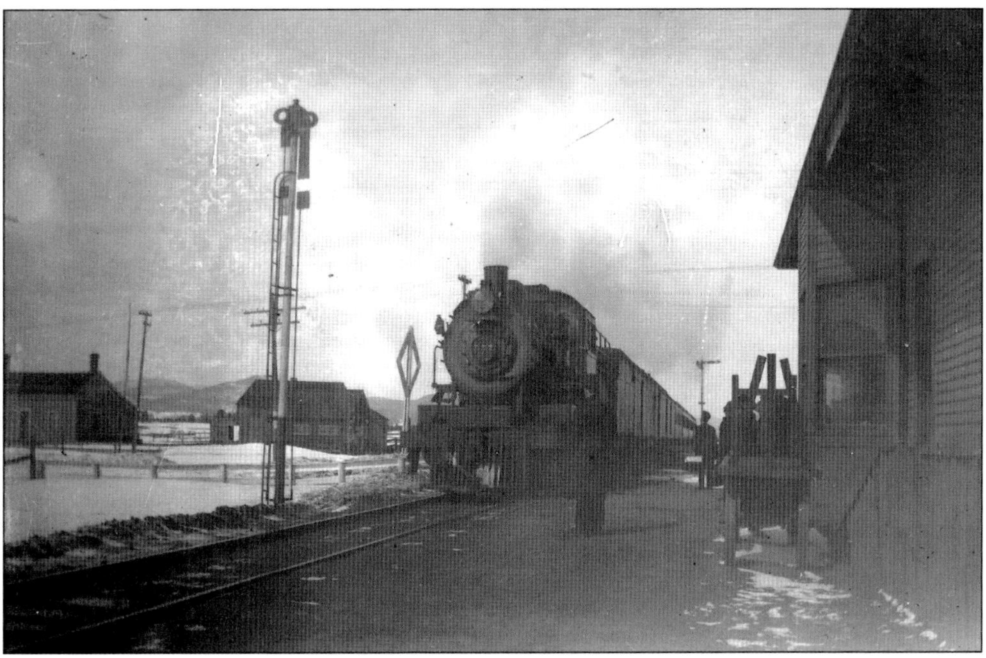

Locomotive at Essex Station. As steam locomotives were phased out in the 1950s, scenes that were common for more than a century started to disappear. The Essex station soon followed. Today the *Adirondack* passenger train managed by Amtrak still runs between New York City and Montreal, stopping just 20 minutes away from Essex in Westport.

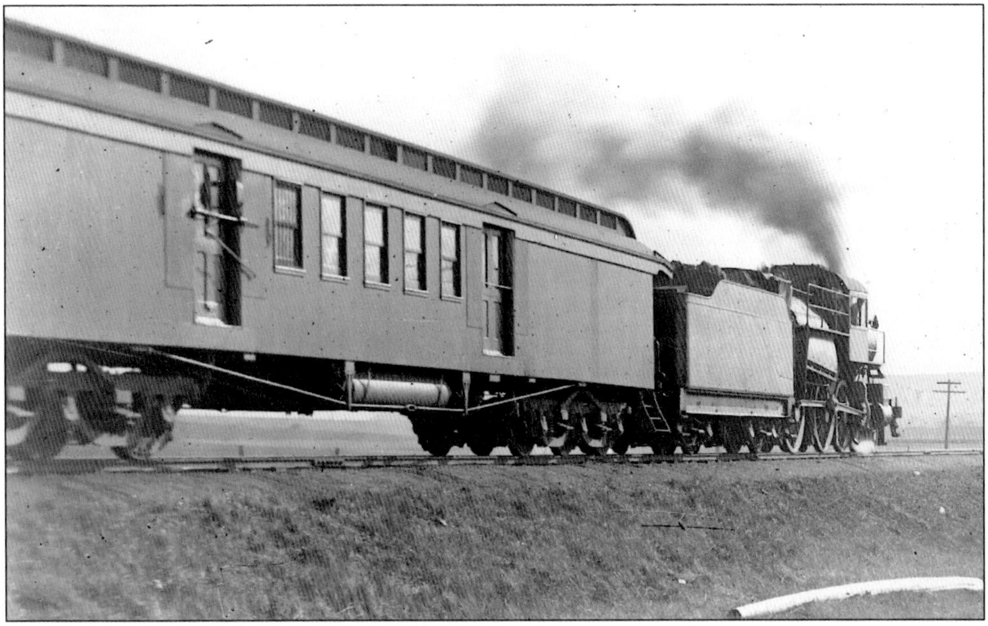

CAMELBACK LOCOMOTIVE. By the 1920s, direct service on the railroad was regularly scheduled to New York City, and one could commute there by train, as a few Essex residents did on a regular basis. The Delaware and Hudson Company was famous for its camelback steam locomotives, with the engine cab located midway astride the boiler. Presumably this allowed for better visibility for the engineer.

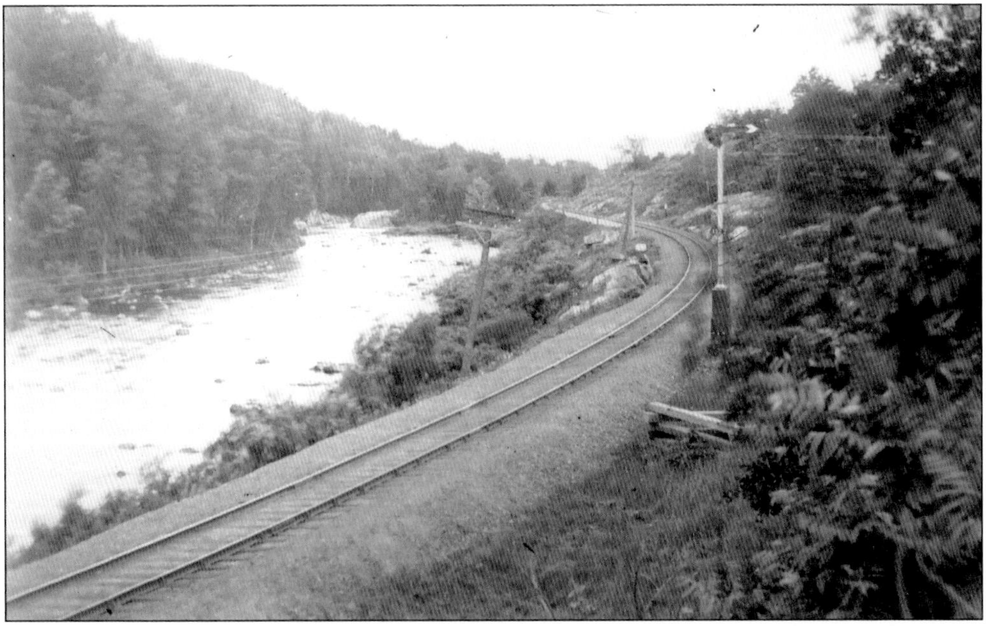

DELAWARE AND HUDSON MAIN LINE. The Delaware and Hudson maintained the same single-track main line for over a century. The successor company, Canadian Pacific Railway, today continues to use the same roadbed built along the path of the Boquet River. Only in the early 21st century have the original signals become obsolete and endless miles of telephone lines abandoned.

Three

VILLAGE VIEWS

Street scenes in the village are important to record the design, condition, and front facade details of buildings in town as they appeared at a certain point in time. These views show not only the individual buildings but also the pattern of spatial dimensions between principal structures and fences, outbuildings, vehicles, and roads. Research dates the majority of Essex buildings, 84 out of 143, as being constructed between 1820 and 1860. By far, the vast majority, an impressive 60 percent, of the buildings in the village were constructed during this great Crystal Palace exposition era in the early to mid-19th century.

This was the period of prominence for Greek Revival architecture, when often the gable end of buildings faced the road and heavy cornice lines on the roof were prevalent. In fact in Essex, 46 percent or nearly half of the hamlet's buildings can be clearly recognized as Greek Revival in design. Of the total buildings, 34 percent are of the gable-front style, and 12 percent have the long side of the building facing the road. So 75 percent of all the Greek Revival buildings have the gable end of the building facing the road. As one of the defining features of Greek Revival is the classical appearing pediment, Essex had nearly one-third of all its buildings in this form. Few places left in America have this much of the built environment exclusively from one period.

Closely aligned with Greek Revival is the building style that immediately preceded it, often termed the Federal style. As expected in a town that began its boom in the early 19th century, the second-largest number of buildings in Essex is in the Federal design at 22 percent of the total. Essex's first period of prosperity and growth centered on the shipbuilding industry for the War of 1812, which was the height of the Federal period. When the similar classically derived Federal style is counted in with the Greek Revival, a full 70 percent of the buildings in Essex still standing are in the neoclassical mode.

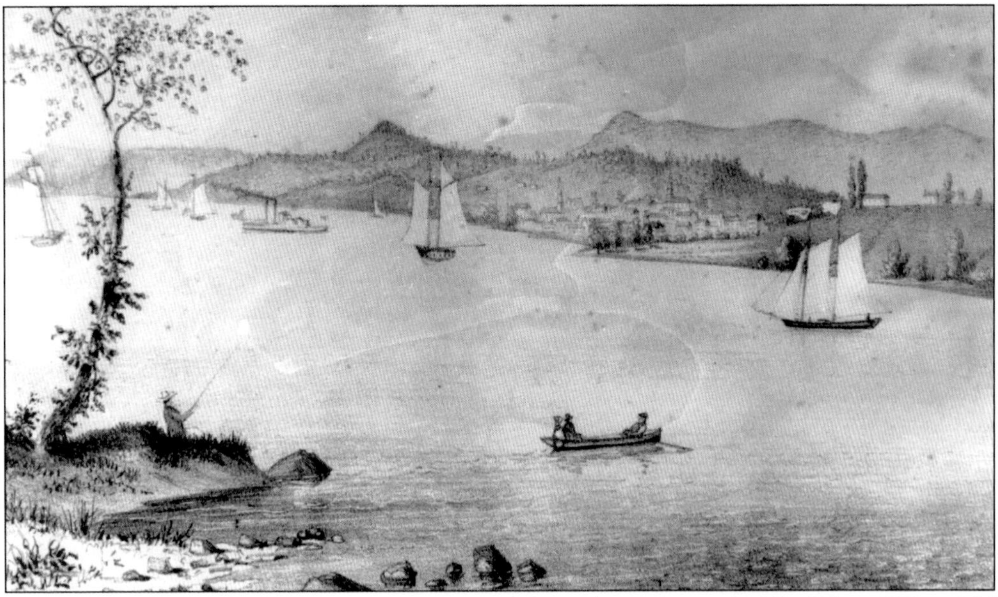

EARLIEST PICTURE OF ESSEX. An engraving of Essex from about 1846 by Edwin Whitefield (American, 1816–1892) is seen here. When William Gilliland settled the region, he laid out rectilinear street patterns in the grid form. This cultural tradition carried over from his familiarity with the New York town plan without a village green. The roads paralleled the lakeside and created a strong north–south circulation pattern. This orientation is still predominant, exemplified regionally by the Delaware and Hudson Railway and the Adirondack Northway highway.

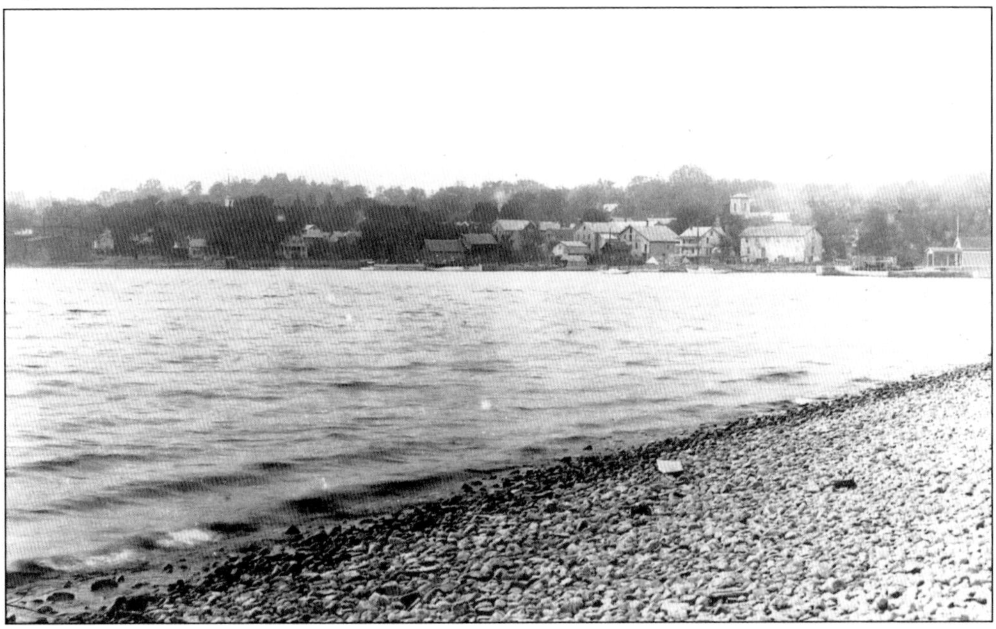

SANDY POINT TOWARD ESSEX. Essex is seen here from the lakeshore known as Sandy Point. Visible is the north harbor and the cluster of Noble buildings near the wharf. Many Noble buildings were limestone. Despite the fact that a stone quarry has long existed in Essex and nearby Willsboro, only 12 out of 142, or 8 percent of the buildings, are made of stone. Nearly all are of the local limestone, popularly called Essex bluestone.

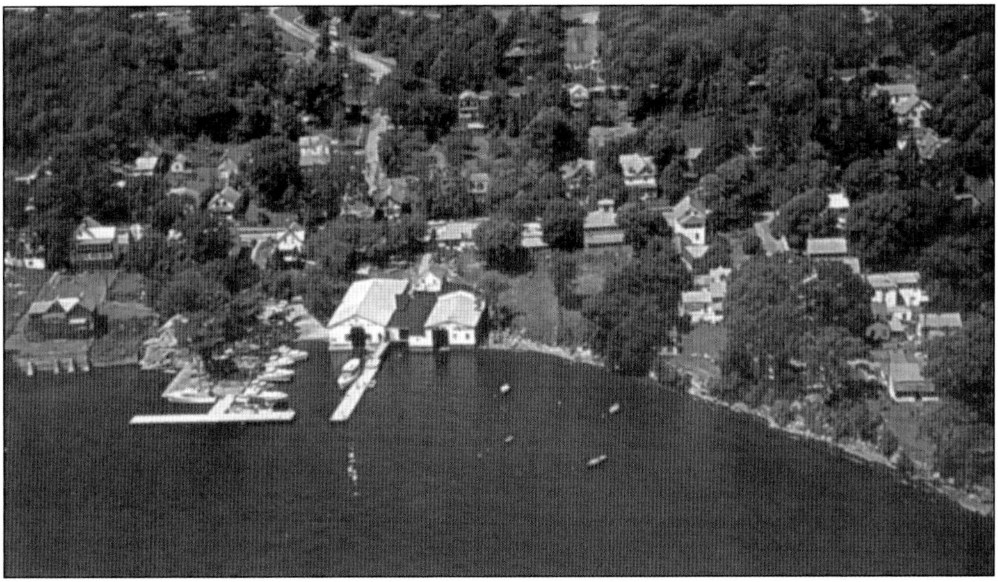

AERIAL VIEW. Attempts at attracting tourism began to undergo a change by the early 1970s. The recently formed Essex Community Heritage Organization (ECHO) made early attempts to promote what is now understood as heritage tourism. This aerial picture of the village near the waterfront reveals the sloping topography and the natural harbor. The uniformity of the simple classical architectural style is also evident from the air.

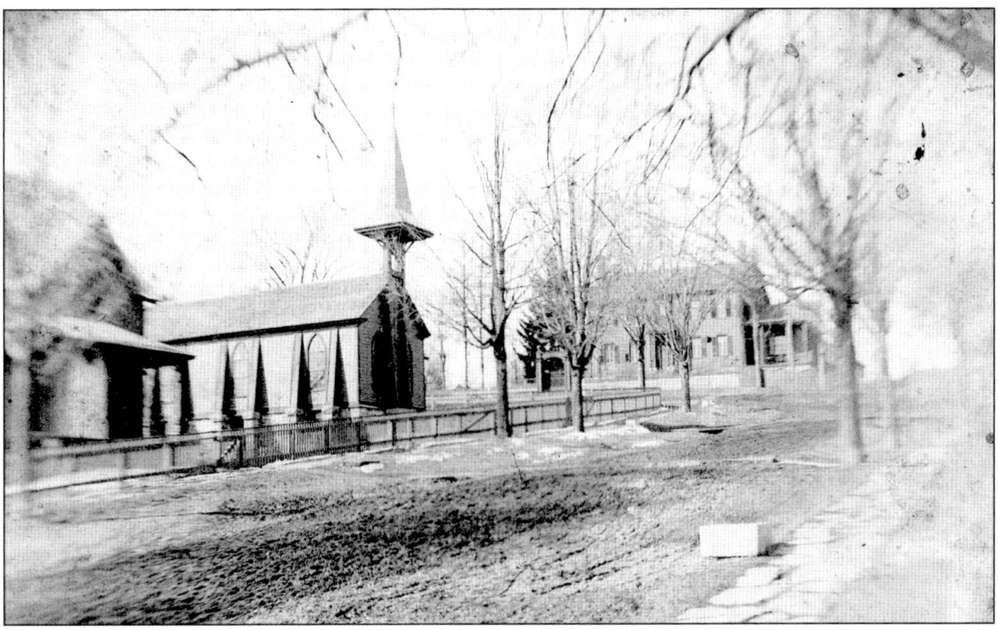

LIMESTONE SIDEWALK. Here is a view of St. John's Church looking west toward Hickory Hill with the original limestone sidewalks in place. Small-scale elements in the Essex landscape are exemplified in these sidewalks and in the numerous limestone hitching posts and carriage blocks in their original locations throughout the village. Here a carriage block is evident, marking this as a residential entrance. (Courtesy of Tilly Close.)

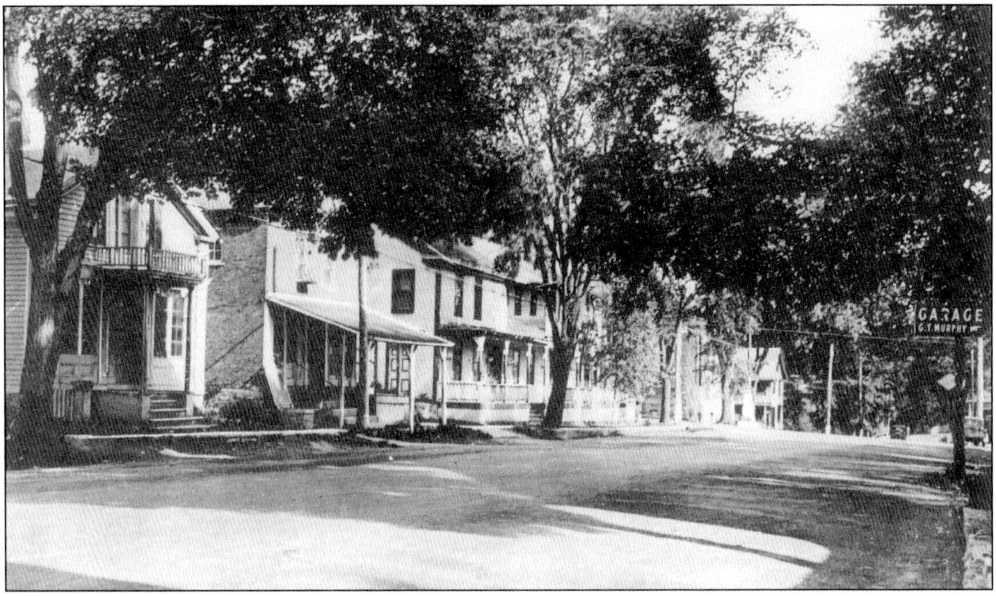

WEST SIDE OF MAIN STREET. Main Street on the west side is pictured with a sign for Murphy's Garage. As is frequently quoted when proposing the rare state of building preservation in Essex, 70 percent of the buildings existing today were constructed prior to the Civil War (1860). This means that approximately 100 out of 140 buildings are in the 150-year-old range. Few American towns can make such a claim.

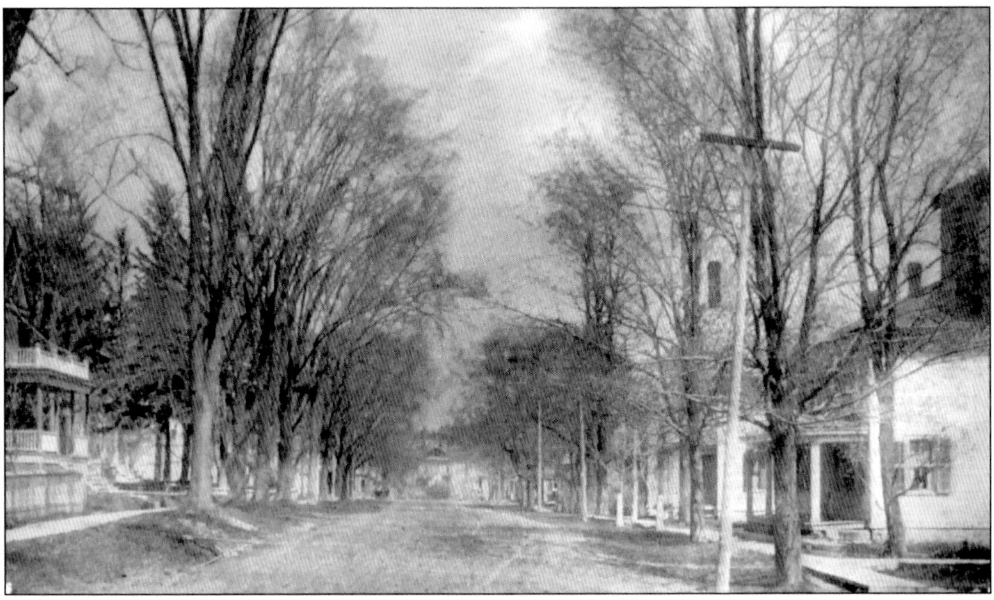

EXPERIMENTAL SIDEWALKS. Still looking north closer to the town center, one can see little but a canopy of elm trees and house porches. The sidewalks are an experimental mixture developed by John Burnham and laid about 1906. The concrete had a high crushed stone content, and much of it still exists in very good condition today, over 100 years later.

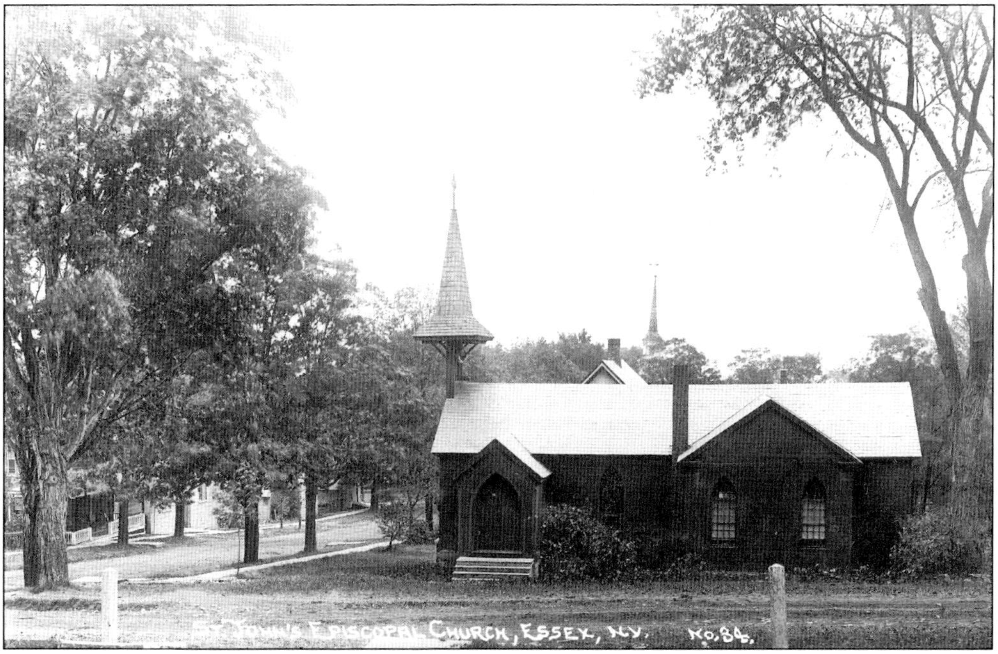

ST. JOHN'S STREET SCENE. This view shows the west facade of the Episcopalian church long before the parish hall of the 1980s addition was added and the church was painted white. Dark colors were preferred in the Victorian era, while painting churches white on the exterior became popular with the Colonial Revival movement of the early 20th century. Here the church is dark red.

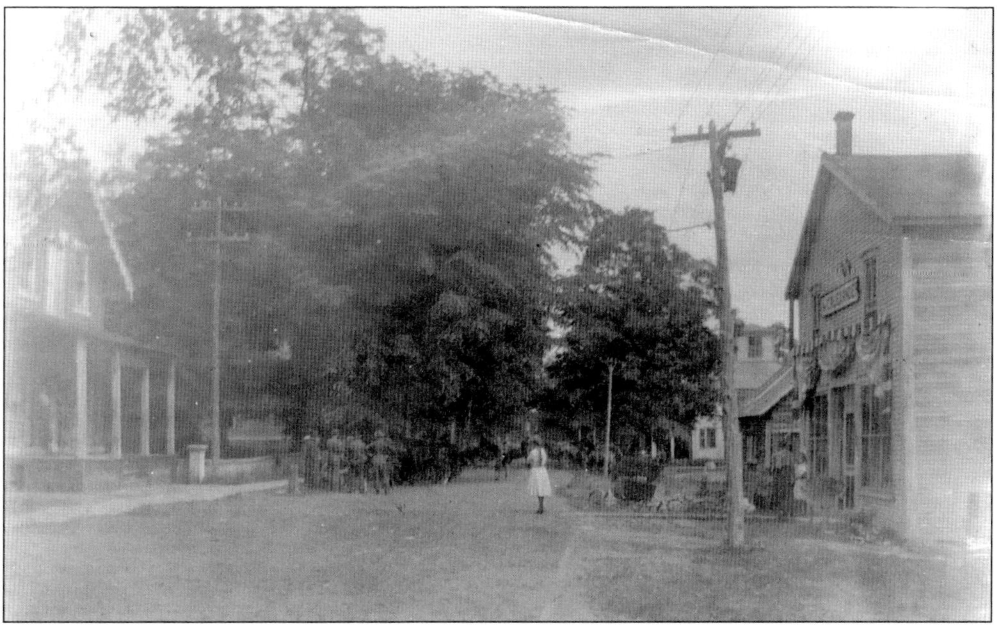

W. C. ALEXANDER STORE. These are probably soldiers in pre–World War I uniforms awaiting the start of a parade or celebration, as the bunting on the storefront indicates. The bunting, although festive, could have been black as a premonition for the loss a few years later of the building it is on. It became the site of the first gas station in Essex, which still stands today.

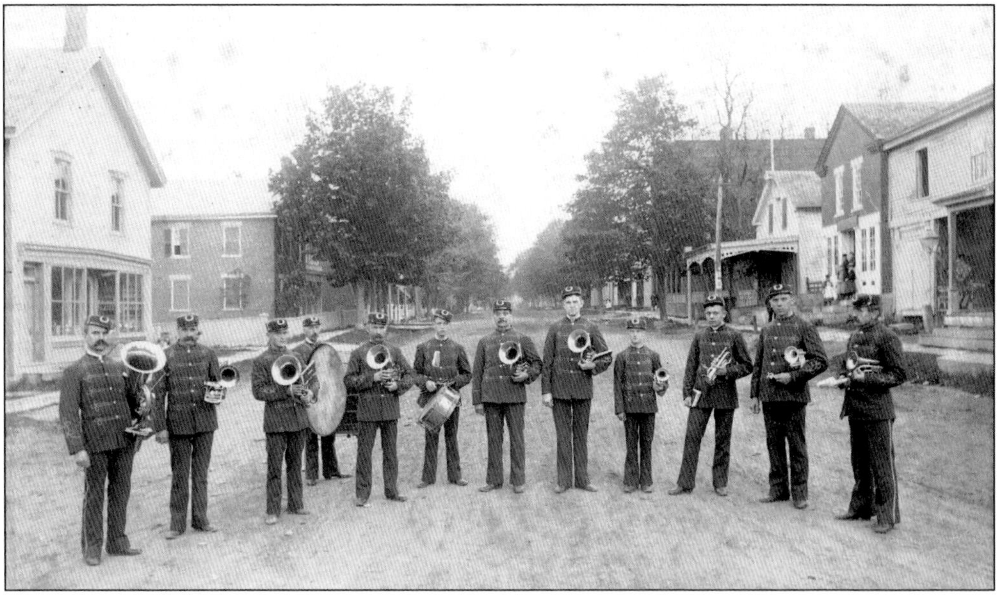

BAND ON MAIN STREET. These residents comprise the local musical ambitions in the era before any recorded music. Behind them on the left is a typical brick residence. Essex seems to have many brick structures prominent in appearance throughout the hamlet. Bricks, by oral tradition, were brought in as ballast on lake vessels or baked locally from deposits of clay. In total, brick structures account for 18 percent of the buildings, evenly distributed throughout the historic district. (Courtesy of Tilly Close.)

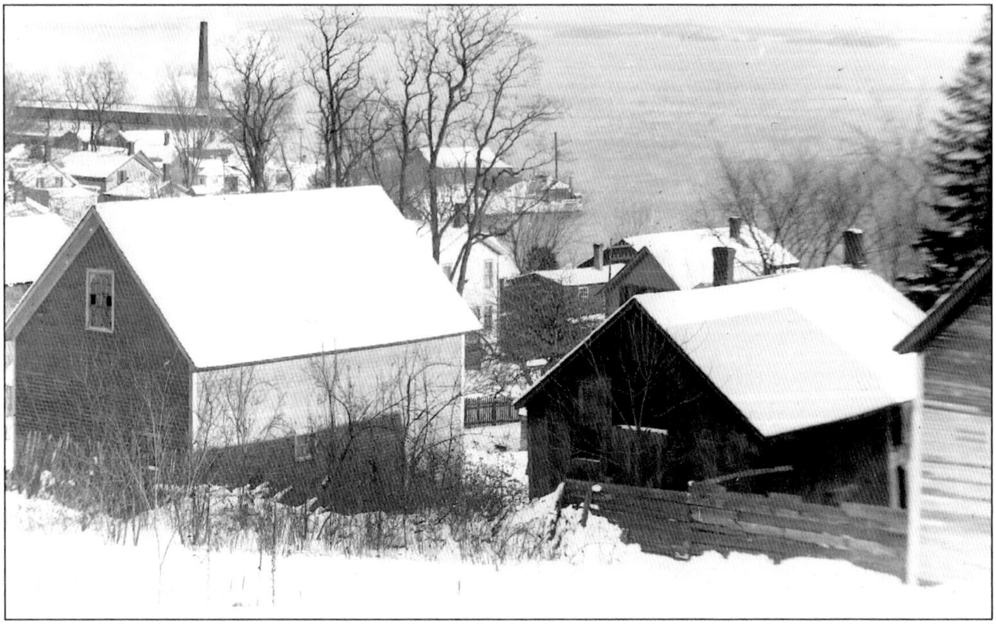

OVER BULL RUN. A wonderful photograph illustrates at a glance another important factor about Essex—the survival of so many outbuildings, such as barns, carriage houses, shops, garages, and storage sheds. Except for the large factory on the point, all these little structures are still extant today. This section was referred to as Bull Run, because of an old story about Irish ladies arguing with such gusto that it sounded like a herd of the beasts.

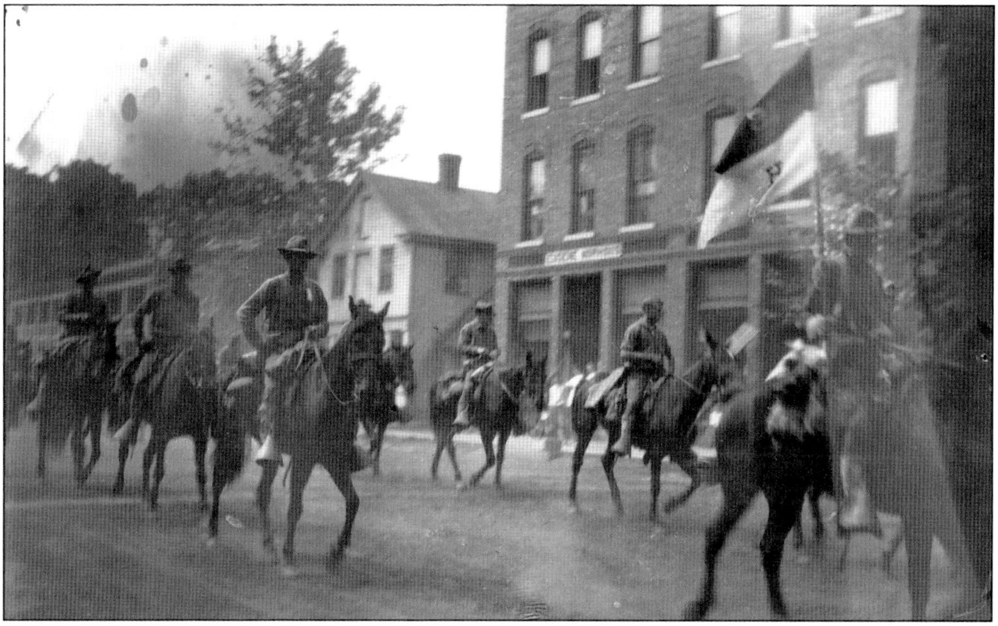

PARADE GALLUP NEAR THE BRICK BLOCK. According to research files, an estimated total of 30 buildings have been demolished in Essex since its founding. This includes the first Presbyterian church, the Baptist Church that burned in the 1940s, the Tart garage and diner that was demolished in the 1980s, and the Mason house replaced by a double-wide house. This represents only 15 percent of all buildings ever constructed in the village since 1765.

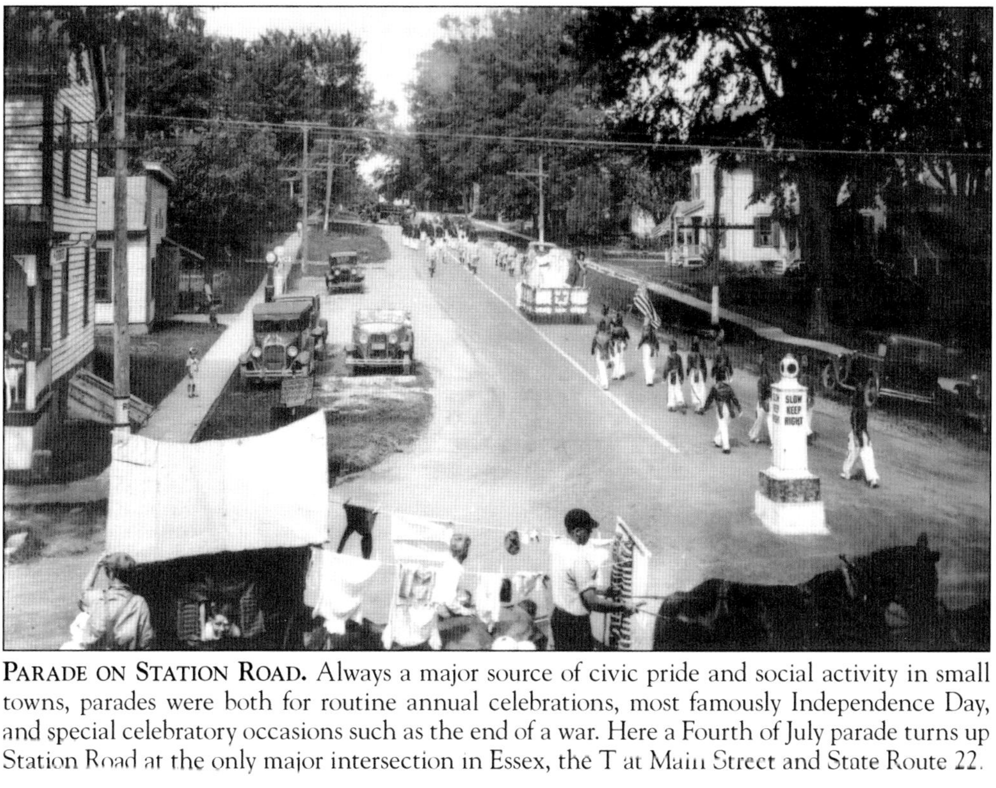

PARADE ON STATION ROAD. Always a major source of civic pride and social activity in small towns, parades were both for routine annual celebrations, most famously Independence Day, and special celebratory occasions such as the end of a war. Here a Fourth of July parade turns up Station Road at the only major intersection in Essex, the T at Main Street and State Route 22.

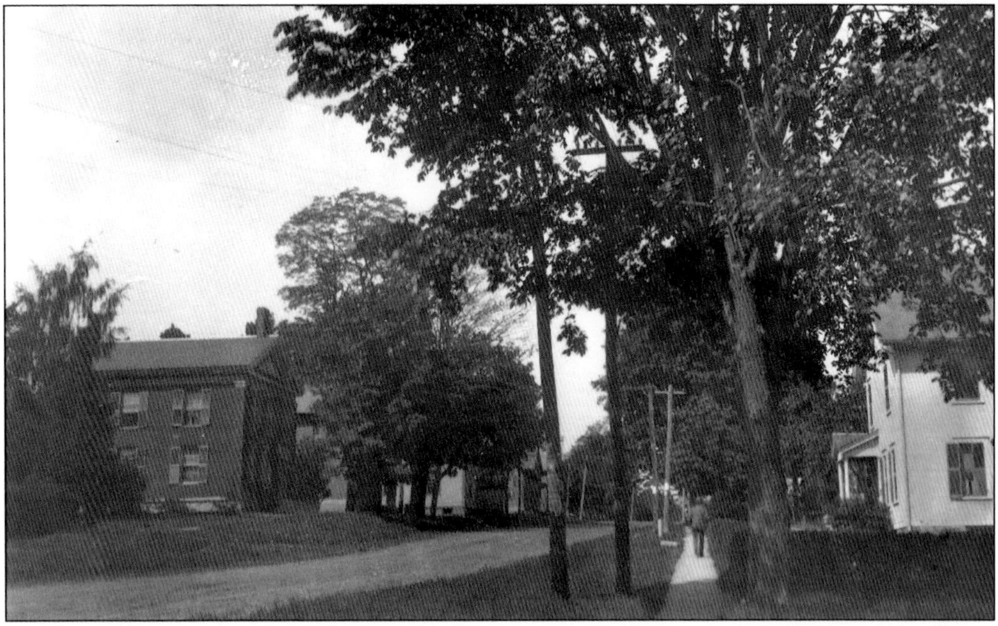

Cyrus Stafford House. The Stafford house is on the left, built around 1847 in the Greek Revival style with the gable end of the house facing the street. This allows the triangular pediment of the roof to appear as the entrance to a Greek temple. The house features a pattern book doorway design after Minard Lafever. The limestone stoop features carved scrolls with fluted terminals.

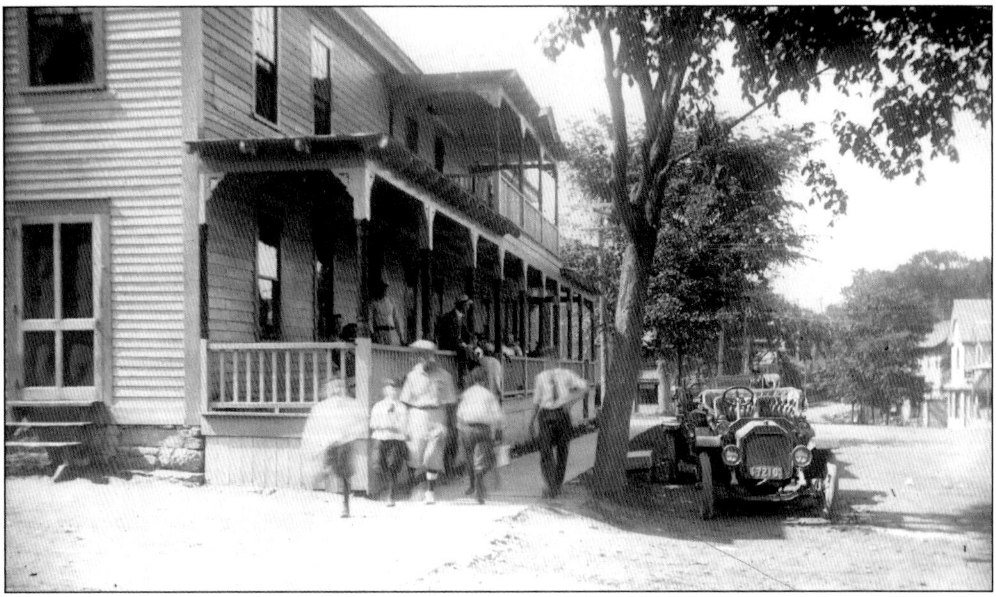

Adirondack House with Two Porches. As expected by its location near the Adirondack forest, wood is the principal construction material. The majority of Essex's first residents came from New England, where wood-frame construction was a long tradition. Unlike in their native England, New Englanders had ample forest products available. The need to clear the land produced a ready supply of wood, and the plentiful water supply was available to run sawmills and planing mills.

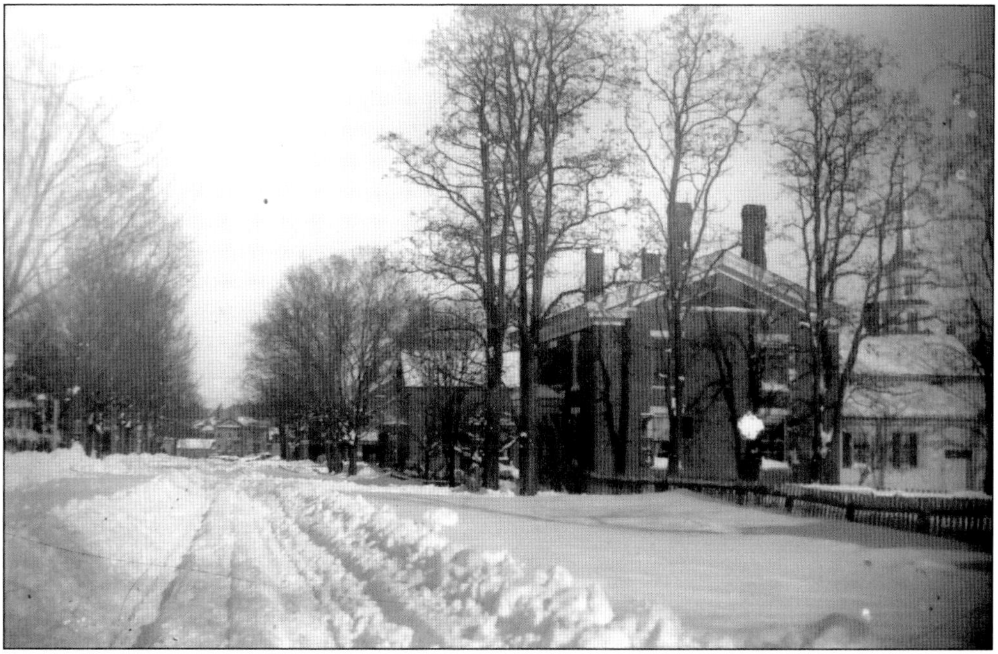

HENRY GOULD HOUSE IN WINTER. Winter is a far more successful time for looking at architecture. The Henry Gould house sits prominently in view with the steeple of the Baptist church rising behind it. The house is surrounded with black locust even today. Note Greystone visible to the north, presiding gracefully over the main street.

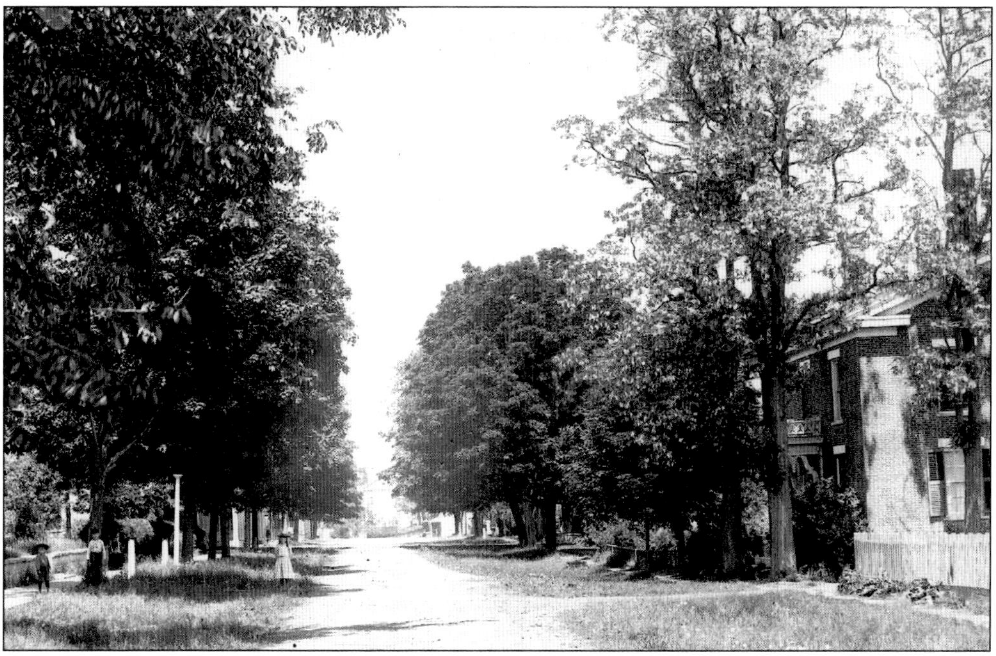

HENRY GOULD HOUSE IN SUMMER. Here is Main Street looking north with a little girl and two boys on the left. The narrow dirt, rutted road in the 1890s abuts front lawns. Lawn areas were not the manicured and chemically fertilized places they are today but rather any combination of green and low plants that were frequently grazed upon by the resident animals.

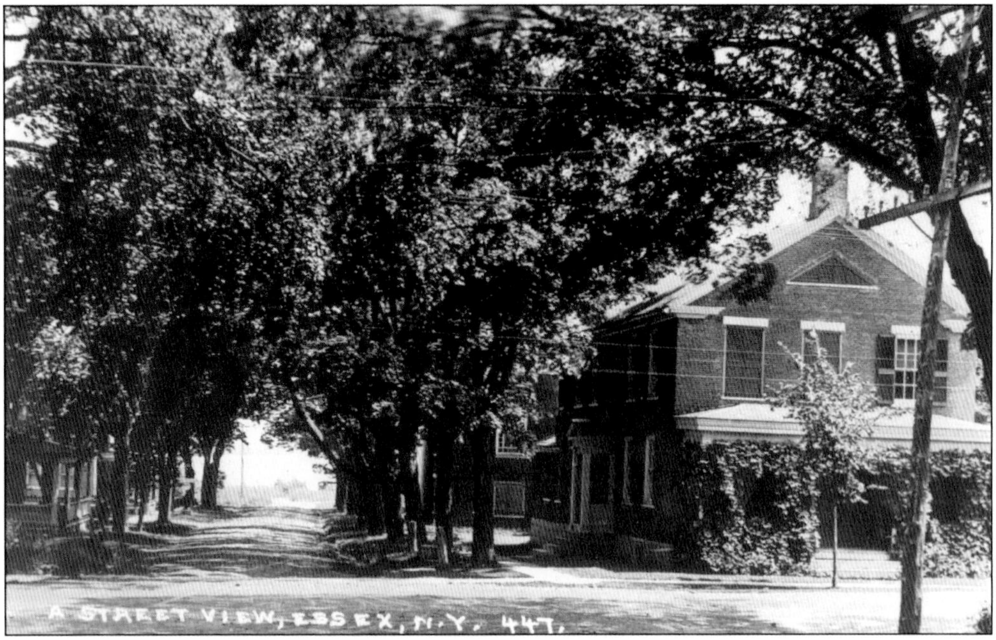

CHURCH STREET. On the formerly lower Church Street (now labeled as Beggs Point Street), a fine allée of trees prospered. On the corner is the brick house once owned by Tom Parkhill, with the gable end facing Main Street and a long, low, broad porch. In Essex, 80 percent of the buildings were constructed before the end of the 19th century. Only 25 buildings, or 18 percent, were added in the 20th century, and less than 10 were added since 1950.

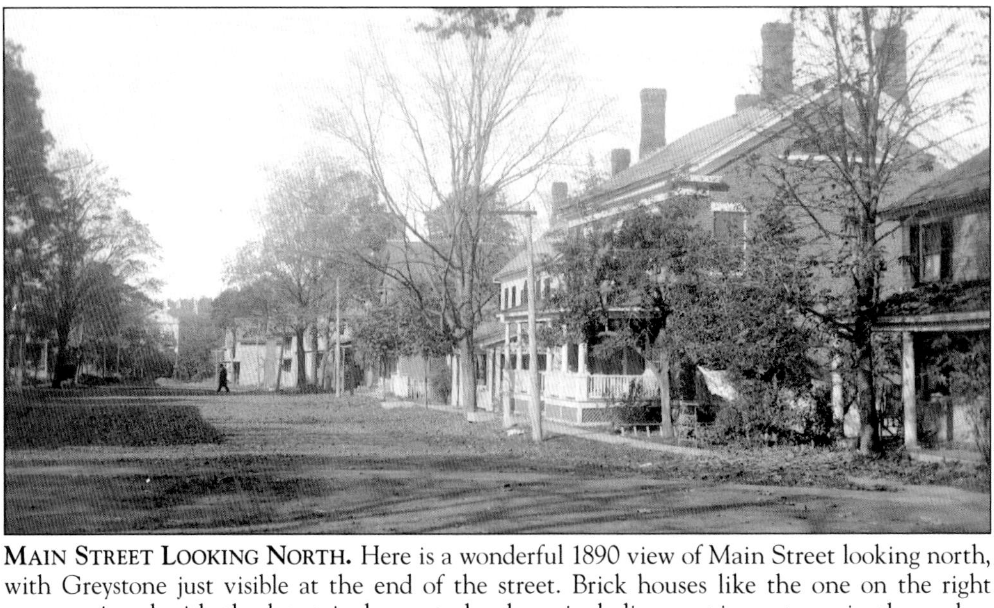

MAIN STREET LOOKING NORTH. Here is a wonderful 1890 view of Main Street looking north, with Greystone just visible at the end of the street. Brick houses like the one on the right were equipped with the latest in home technology, including cast-iron stoves in the parlors and coal-burning cookstoves in the kitchen. Water closets arrived with cisterns for water and plumbing.

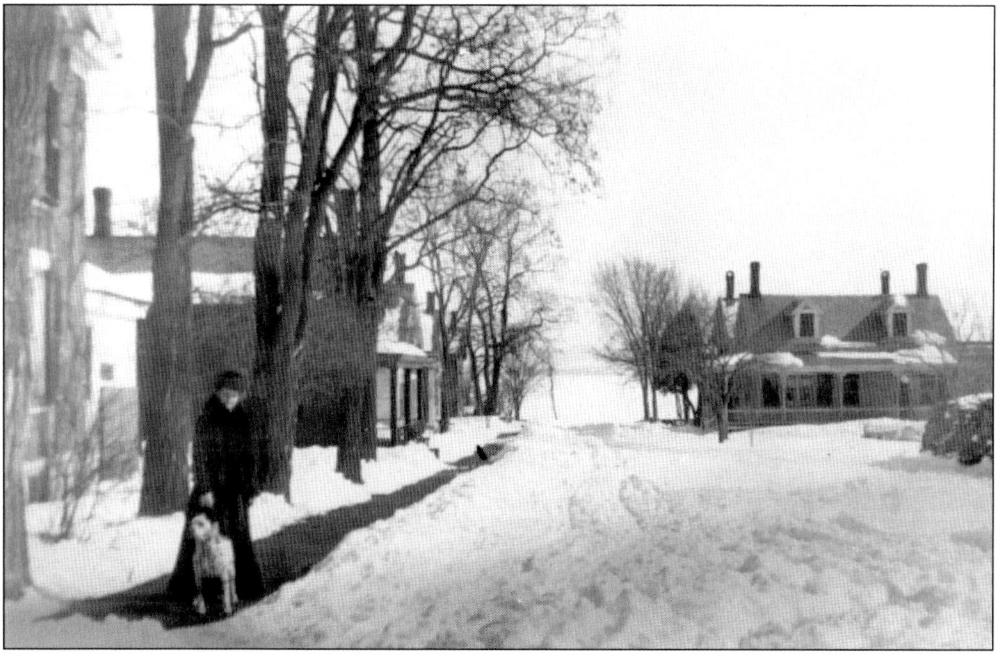

BLACK LOCUSTS. This close-up shows the black locusts and an unidentified lady with a dalmatian. It must have been cold but sunny, as the warm sunlight has melted the snow off the sidewalk. Snow was often rolled and packed by large horse-drawn iron rollers. This provided a smooth but compact surface for the cutters and sleighs.

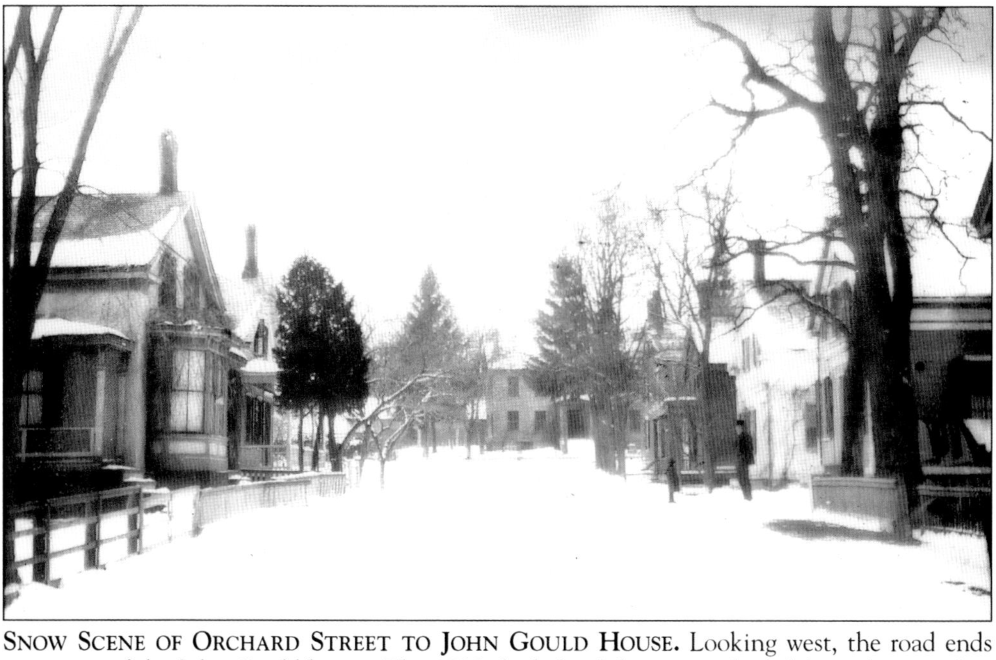

SNOW SCENE OF ORCHARD STREET TO JOHN GOULD HOUSE. Looking west, the road ends in a vista of the John Gould house. The 1830s little brick house on the left has a bay window that was probably added during the bay window craze of the 1860s. Thanks to the sensitivity to historic restoration by the current owners and with the addition of a few minor fences, the scene is identical in the early 21st century.

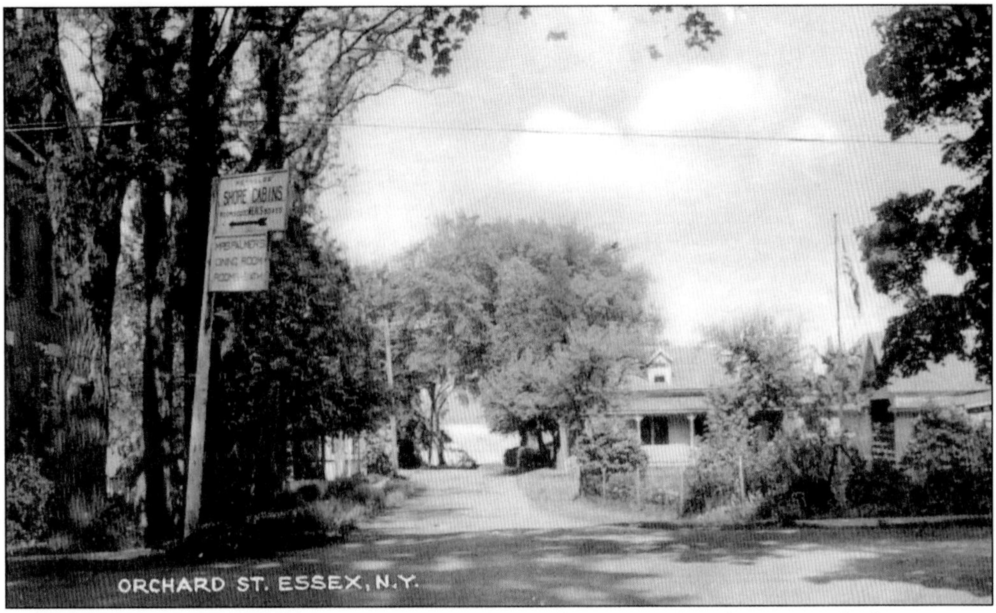

A View of Orchard Street Looking East. Within just a decade or two, the horses were banished to the farms, and the new automobile emerged. Streets were widened as the grassy shoulder disappeared, and traffic slowly began to increase. The livery stable on the right became a barn with openings for an automobile garage.

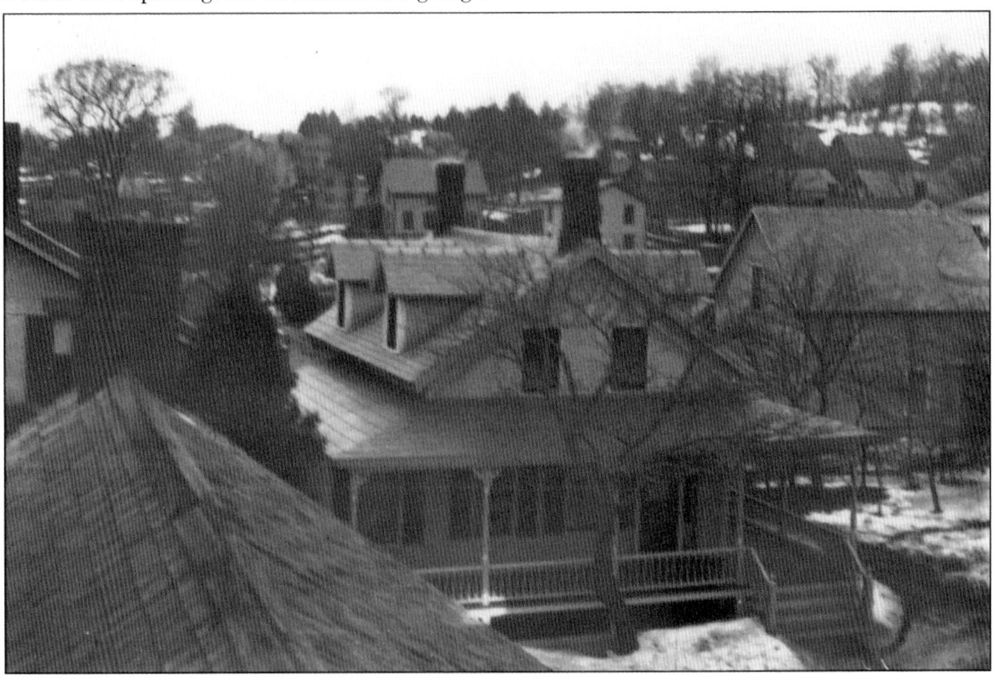

Orchard Street Rooftops. Rarely in early photographs is the perspective other than that of a linear street view. Most of the simple vernacular buildings in town are of wood. Thus 97 out of 142 buildings are wood framed with clapboard siding, which equals 68 percent of all buildings in town. They are scattered almost evenly throughout the village both on Main Street and the side streets.

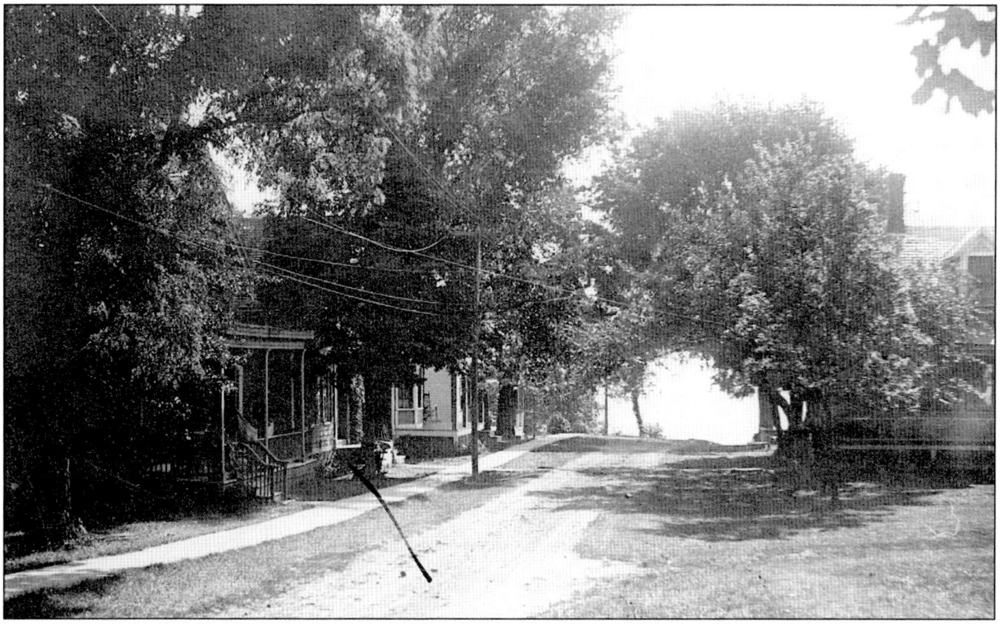

Orchard Street. The pedestrian-oriented component of a livable town was determinedly under attack in Essex in the late 1970s. Soon after, a key historic preservation battle fought successfully to retain the post office in the middle of town rather than have it move to a proposed suburban mall at the edge of the hamlet. Residents today can still walk into the village center to get their mail and meet their neighbors.

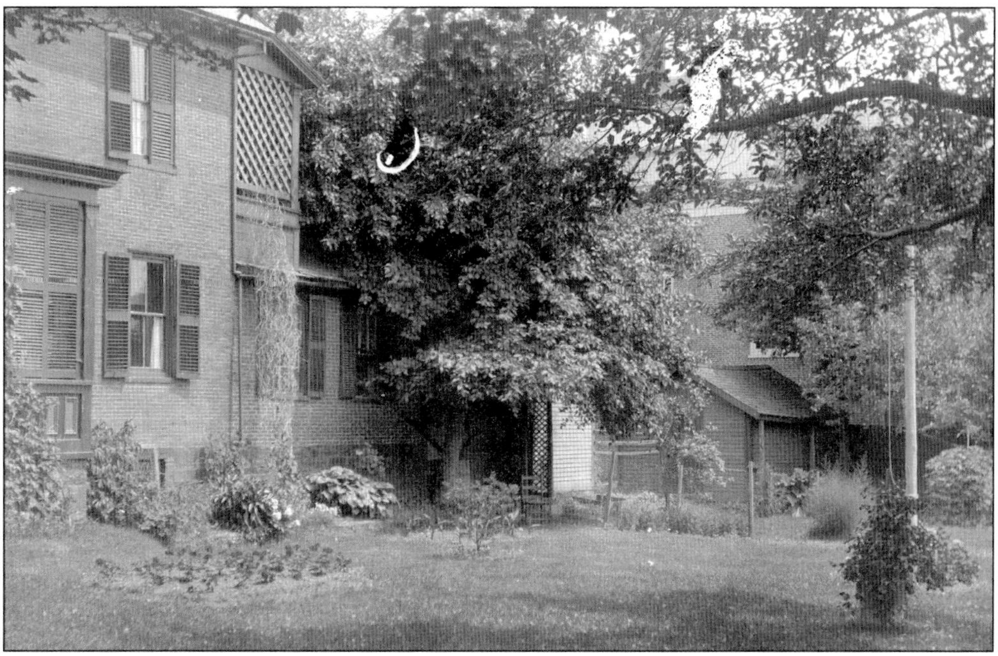

Private View. While formal street facades of houses are popular subjects for early photography, rarely are the rear garden areas photographed, especially in middle-class houses. The simple latticework screening covering a sleeping porch is still intact today, but the bay window on the left was removed during the 1990s for an enclosed sunroom.

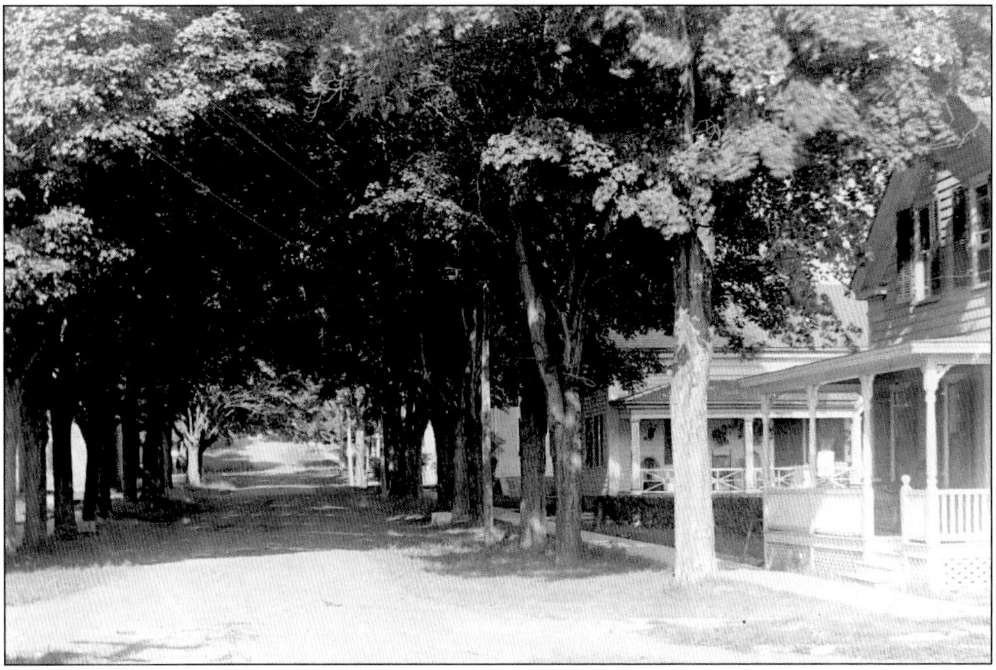

SUMMER BEGGS POINT WITH LOST HOUSE. Seen here is a canopy of maple trees that for so long defined small-town America. The second house back on the right has ornamental porch supports that now look out to the lake. The house closest was lost some years ago and was replaced by perennial gardens overlooking Beggs Point Park.

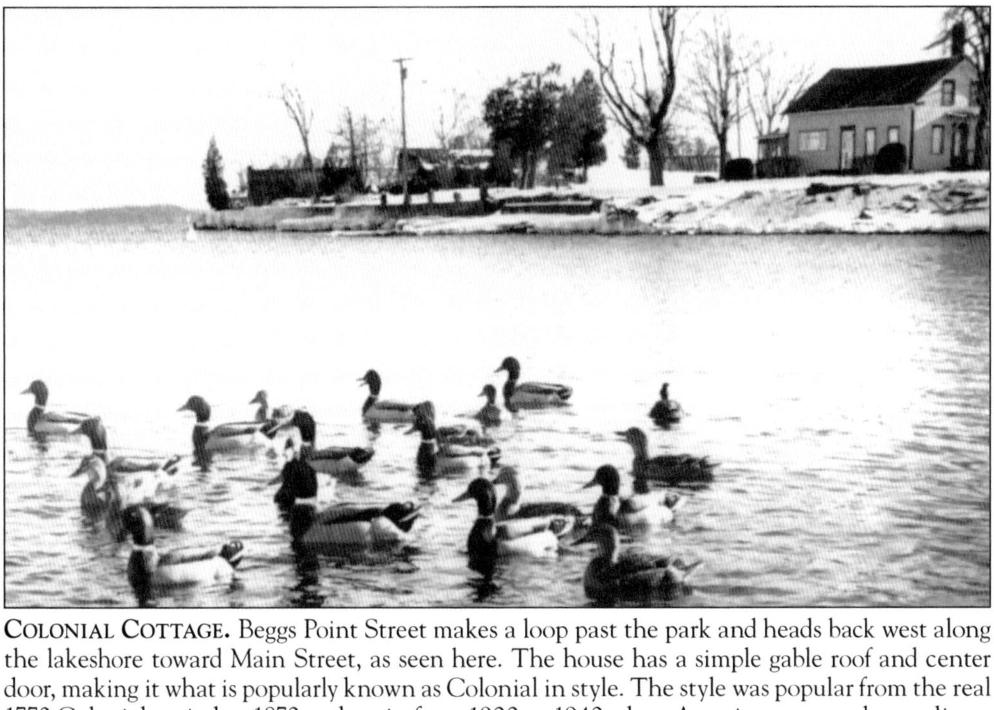

COLONIAL COTTAGE. Beggs Point Street makes a loop past the park and heads back west along the lakeshore toward Main Street, as seen here. The house has a simple gable roof and center door, making it what is popularly known as Colonial in style. The style was popular from the real 1770 Colonial period to 1870 and again from 1900 to 1940 when Americans wanted to replicate the homes of their ancestors.

Four

Business and Industry

The commercial center of Essex has remained unchanged for over 150 years. Of course, the type and nature of the businesses has changed, with the passing of owners and the fragile nature of investments. The core hamlet always retained the town businesses such as hotels, stores, eateries, and services like the post office, town offices, fire station, churches, and schools. The first early-18th-century settlers began necessary businesses such as the three taverns run by Amos Anson, Nathan Nichols, and Isaac Drew. Full-scale lodgings could be let at the hosiery establishments of Gen. Daniel Wright and Belden Noble. Ransom Noble established a tannery and then a store by 1818. Trade was brisk in iron ore, shipbuilding, and potash, and by 1810, there were three asheries in town that produced 200 to 300 tons of potash annually.

By the 1830s, the principal shop of the Nobles was selling tannery goods while the Rosses sold general merchandise in their stone store. Over the years, the Noble warehouse was converted to the W. G. Lyons general store downstairs. Upstairs, it held a shirt factory. In 1884, a feed store managed by W. W. Wilson sat on the lot to the south of the Noble warehouse. The Henry H. Ross stone store of 1812 had a general store on the ground floor and law offices on the second. Ross's brother William managed the general store and oversaw the adjacent dock house wharf operations.

Later 19th-century industry on Beggs Point included Essex's only factory building, first occupied by the Essex Manufacturing Company to 1877, then by the Lyon and Palmer blind and sash manufactory until 1879, followed by the Essex Horse Nail Company Limited from 1880 to 1918, which in 1885 employed 60 or 70 hands.

Commercial business architecture tended to cluster along the single Main Street and was typically a two-story building with a store and shopfront below and a residence above. Thus the commercial, residential, and public buildings are very closely intermeshed and occur in close proximity. Often the owners lived upstairs, as the original merchants did a century before. This pattern is occasionally seen even today in the small shops remaining in town.

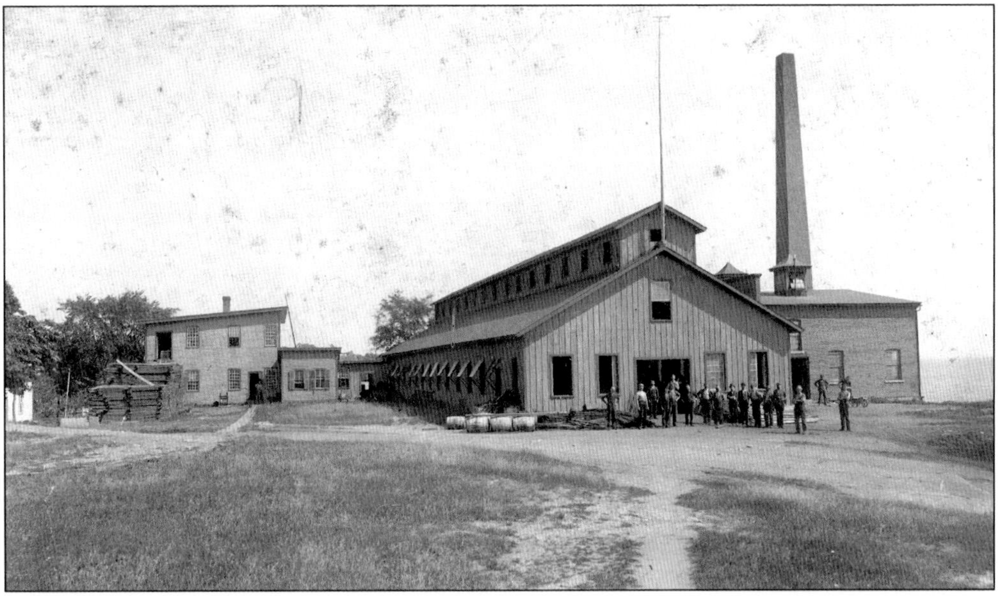

ESSEX HORSE NAIL COMPANY LIMITED. The first industry on the point was shipbuilding, culminating in the Hoskins, Ross and Company shipyard. The Essex Manufacturing Company then made wood sash and blinds there until 1877, when Lyon and Palmer bought out the concern. This manufactory took advantage of the ample availability of a local natural resource, the Adirondack timber supply. Finally, this two-story structure became the Essex Horse Nail Company Limited in 1880.

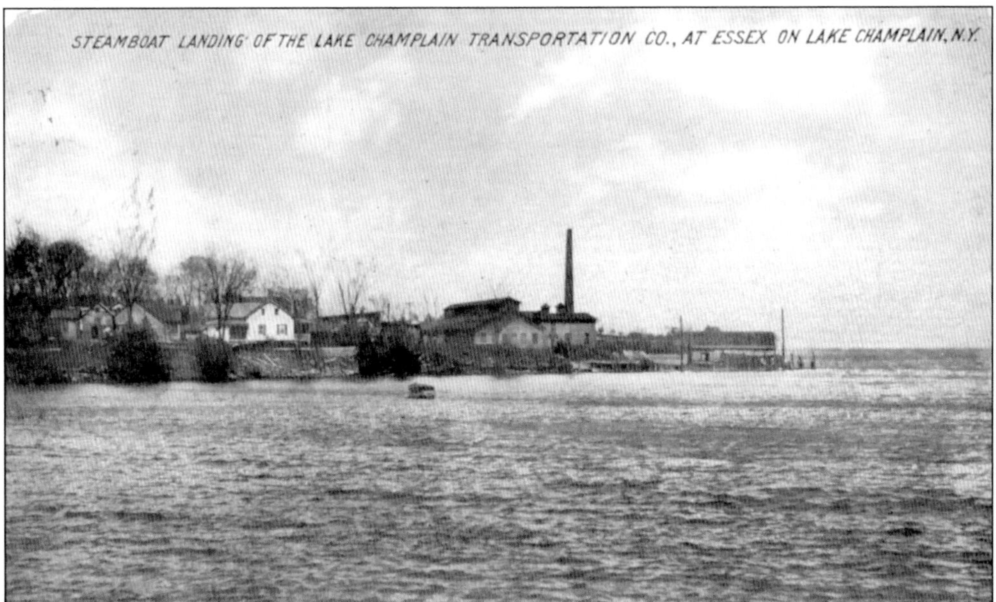

STEAMBOAT LANDING OF LAKE CHAMPLAIN TRANSPORTATION COMPANY. The use of locally mined iron ore to hammer into nails was also a booming business in the late 19th century. Iron mined in the Adirondack Mountains was forged at Noble furnaces in Willsboro and Lewis. Horses were a primary means of transportation, and the nails needed to shoe horses became as vital as tires to trucks.

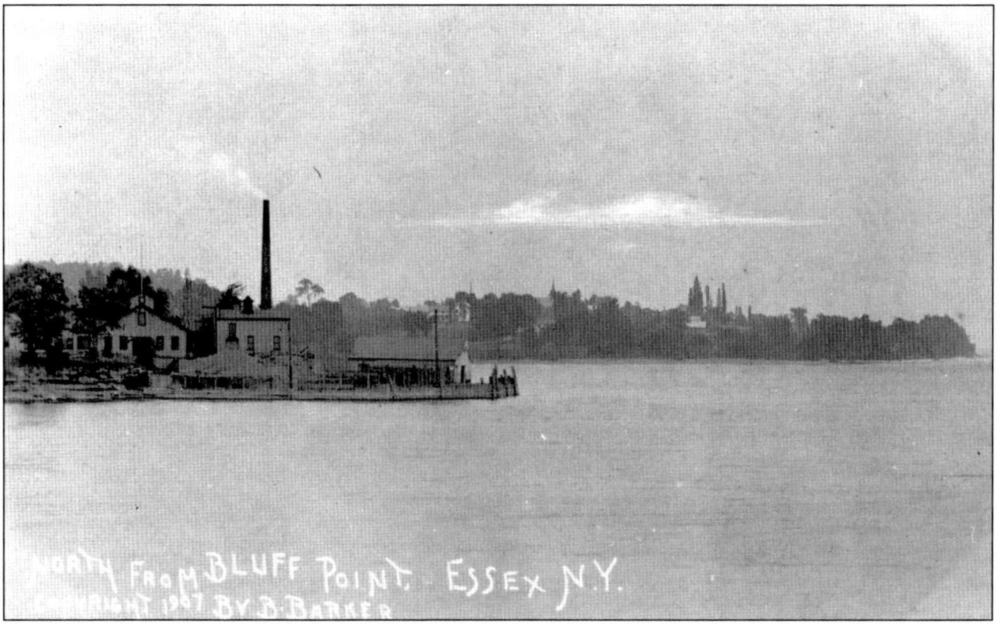

Steamboat Landing and Coal Dock. This view looks north from Bluff Point toward the piles of coal on the wharf at the steamboat landing. The former blind and sash factory, now the horse nail company, is in the background. The image is signed by the ubiquitous B. Benton Barker, who produced an important series of photographic postcards of many towns along Lake Champlain. His studio and publishing house was in Burlington, Vermont. This example was taken in 1907.

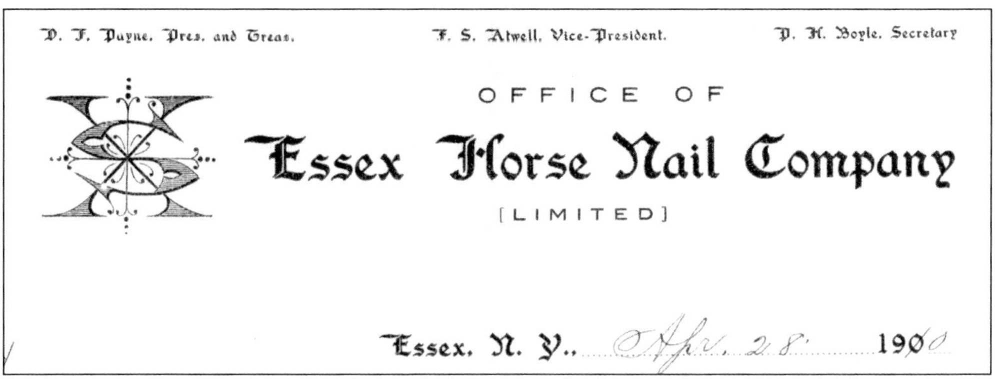

Logo. The Victorian Eastlake style, with its geometric precision and incised machine decoration, was ideal for creating colorful insignia. The Essex designers fashioned this worthy example as a billhead for the Essex Horse Nail Company Limited. In the 19th century, clever villagers discovered that if one pronounces the letters *sx*, it sounds just like Essex is pronounced. Frequently the town is thus referred to as SX in print.

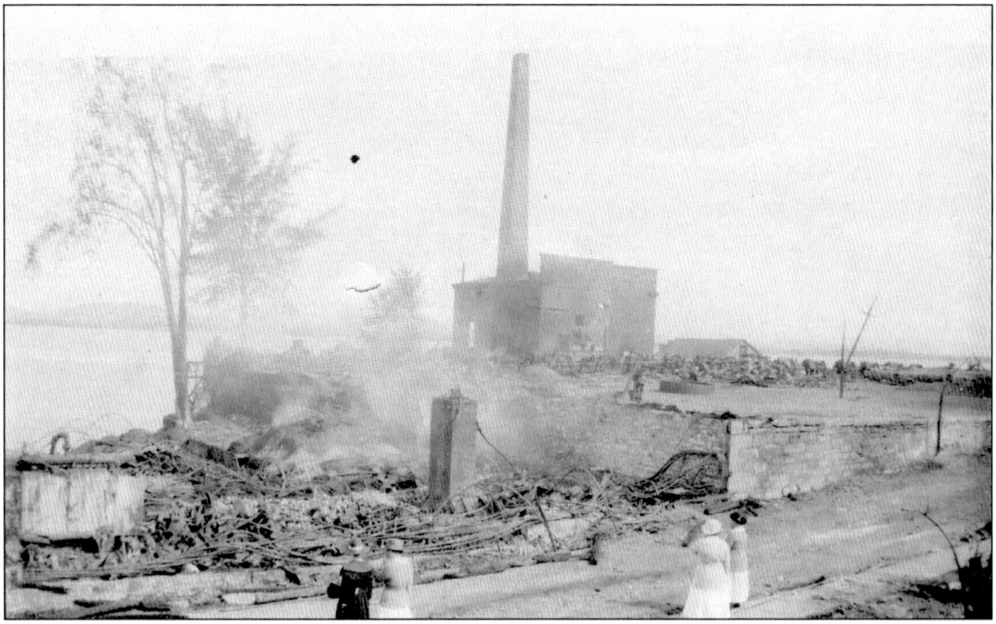

GREAT FIRE. In the fall of 1918, the Essex Horse Nail Company factory was completely destroyed by a spectacular fire. In the 1920s, creative Essex villagers relandscaped the area into a park, using the former stone foundation as material for stone walls along the cliff by the coast.

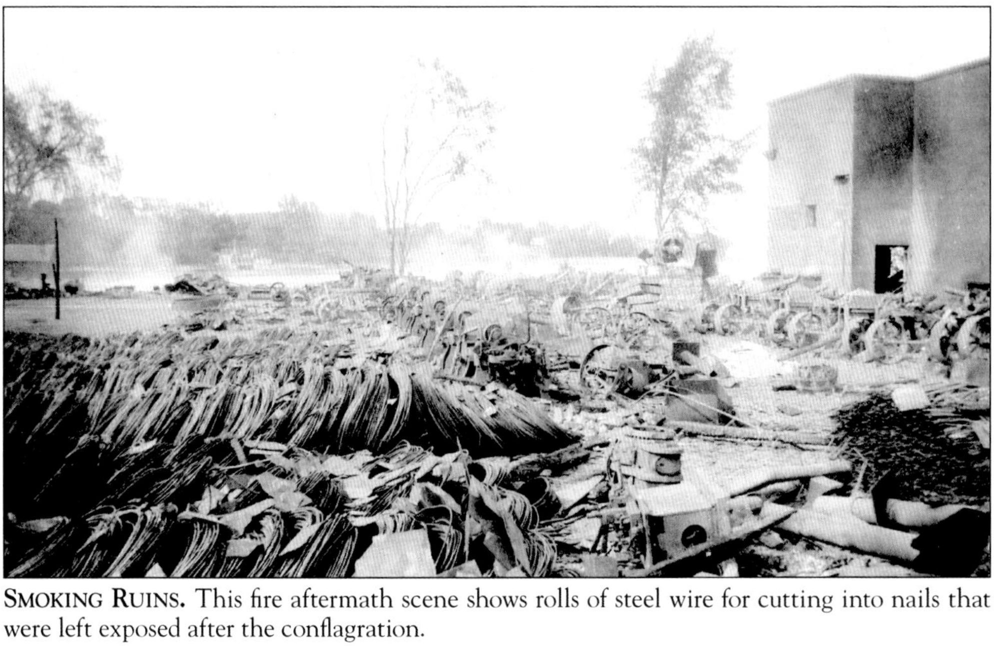

SMOKING RUINS. This fire aftermath scene shows rolls of steel wire for cutting into nails that were left exposed after the conflagration.

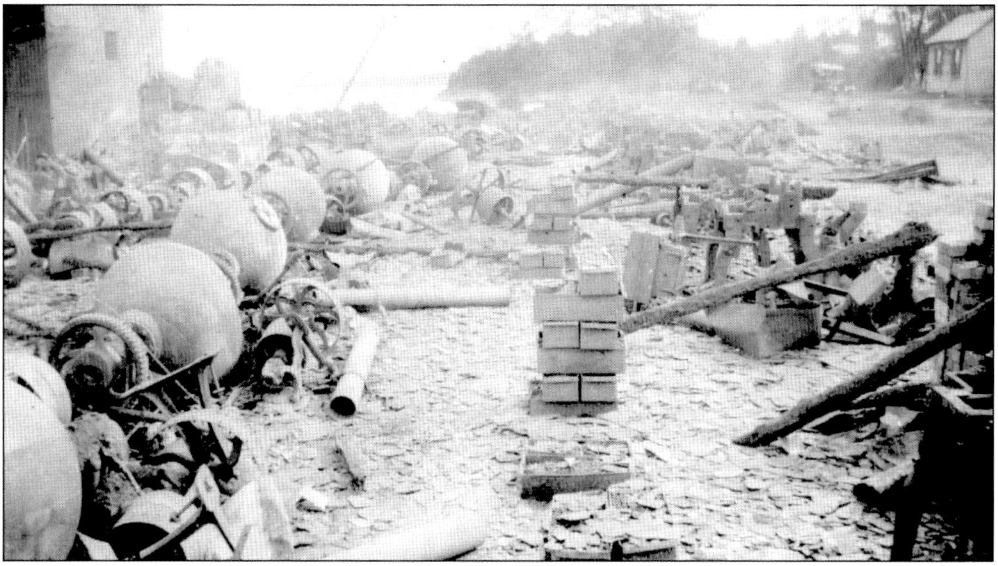

FIRE AFTERMATH. As in many towns and cities of the era, fire was always a major threat yet also a major event. Villagers came from far and wide to view the aftermath, and newspapers reported extensively on the blazes.

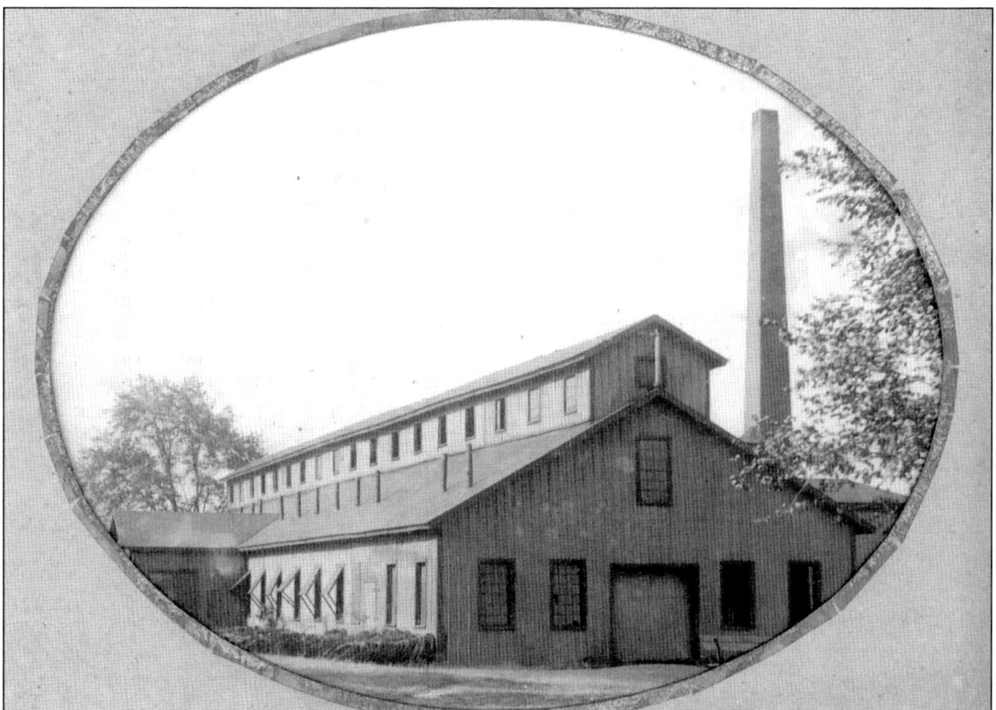

OVAL HORSE NAIL. Photographers created images of losses in multiples that found a ready market in the surrounding community. The careful framing and reverential hanging in parlors can be viewed as a memorial, although there is no known record of any loss of life in this case.

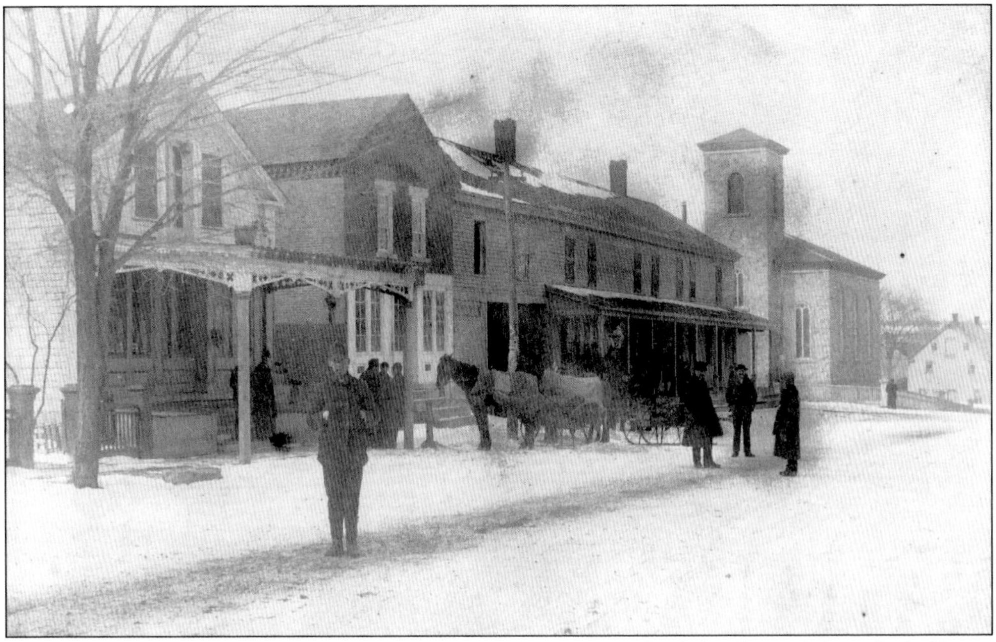

West Side of Main. The square opening at the near end of the long Adirondack House building was a drive-through that allowed horses and carriages access to the stables on the other side. On the far right is the "Beehive," demolished by 1900. (Courtesy of Tilly Close.)

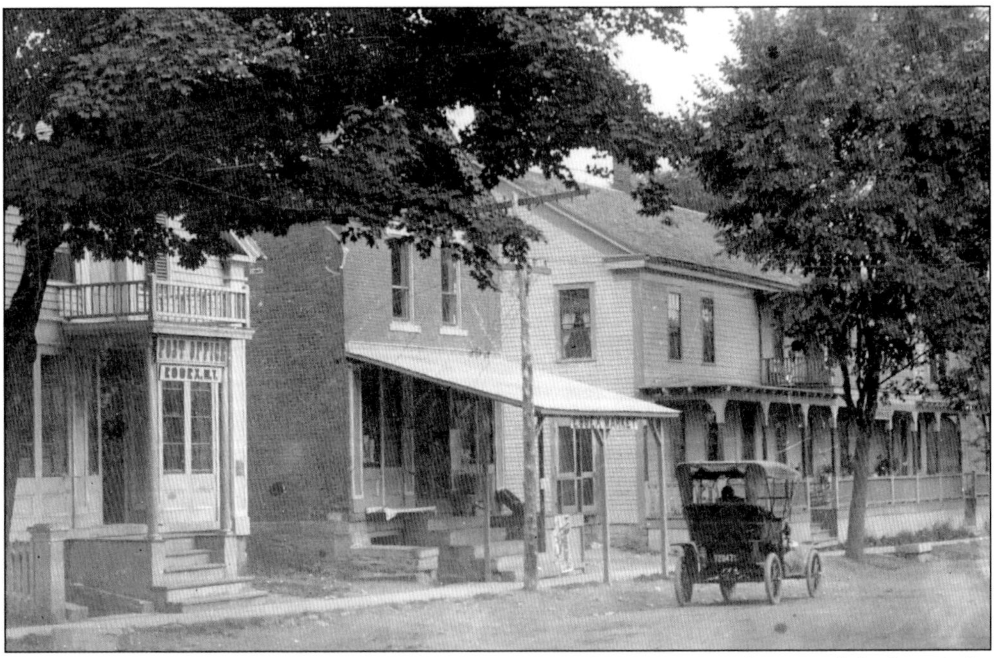

Horseless Carriage by Essex Market and Post Office. Note the use of shed roofs for sidewalk overhangs to shelter patrons. The 1905 Main Street view could be re-created today with just the addition of a few fences and porches, much the same as it could be all over Essex. The market was known for its vegetables. C. E. Van Ornam was appointed to post office director in Essex in the 1920s.

THE SOUTH VIEW DOWN MAIN STREET. Unchanged since the early 1800s, this 1980 view would be recognized as documented by the *Gazeteer* and published in 1836 by Thomas Francis Gordon: "The post village of Essex lies upon Lake Champlain and upon a handsome and gently inclined plain, and contains about 50 dwellings, 1 very fine Presbyterian Church, 3 stores, and 2 taverns. The buildings are generally good, many of them brick and limestone, surrounded with gardens, which gives the village an extent of three miles."

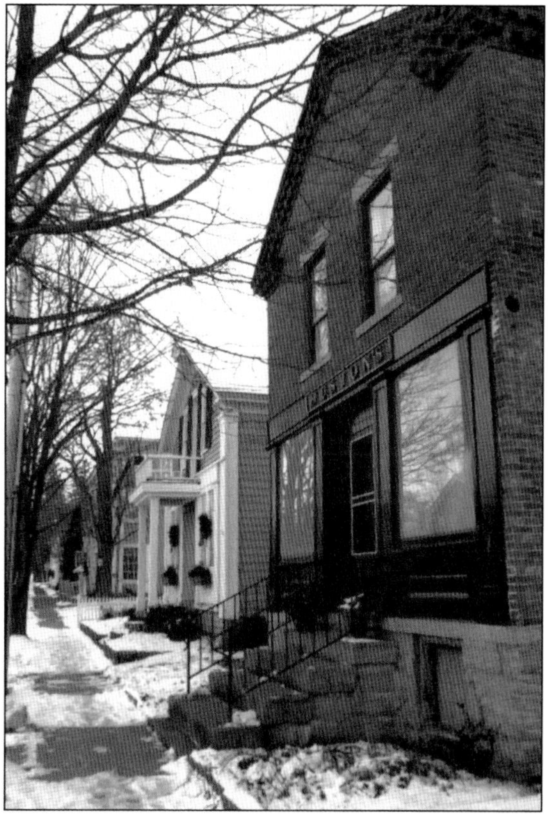

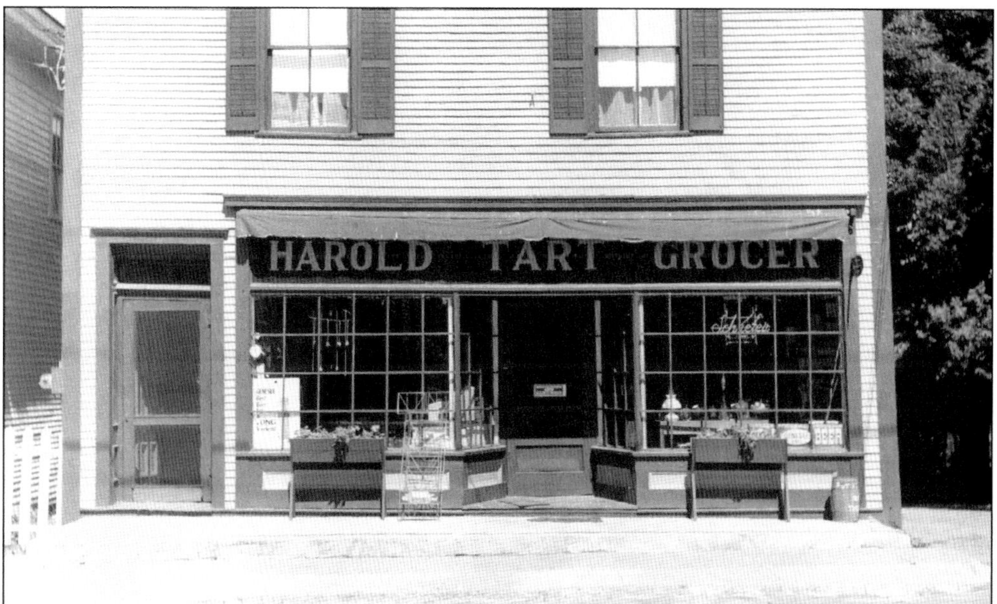

TART GROCERY. This store prospered in this location during the mid-20th century right up to the 1970s. The storefront remains in the Greek Revival style with small paned shop windows and inset wood panels beneath. The trim is darker than the body color, following Victorian taste.

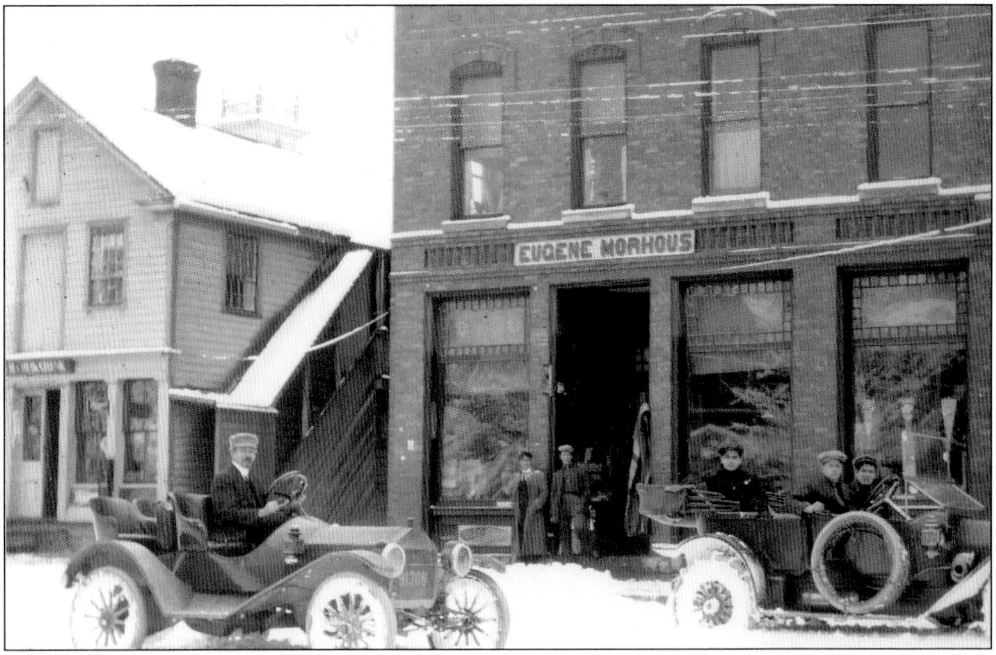

THE BRICK BLOCK, BUILT IN 1874. The brick block contained, as stated in the sign, a store operated by Eugene Morhous. In front of the store on a winter day is the 1913 Buick of Ralph Stafford leading the Chevrolet of Dr. John Stafford. The block burned in 1924, and the earlier Greek Revival store to the left was eventually lost also, leaving an empty space on Main Street.

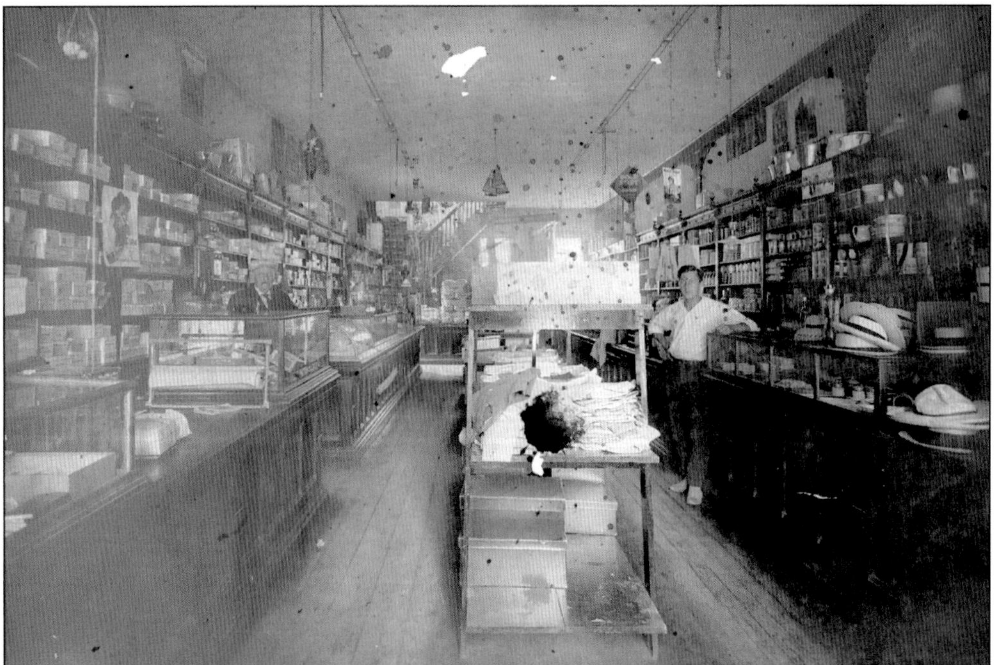

EUGENE MORHOUS. Morhous kept a tidy mercantile shop in the brick block on Main Street. He is seen here presiding with an assistant posed amid the organized shirts, collars, and straw hats. All was lost when the fire occurred in 1924.

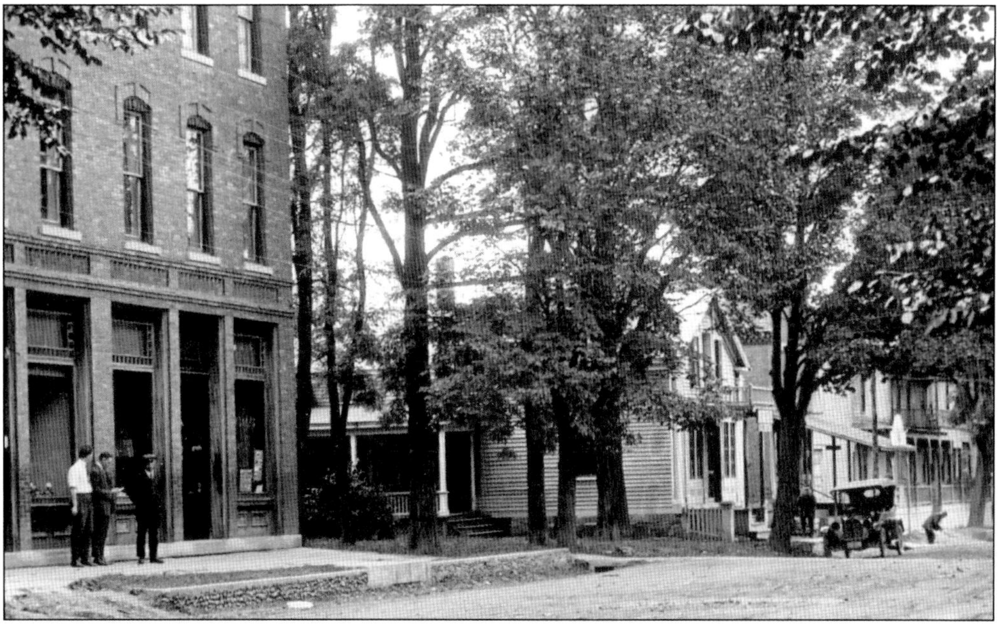

Brick Block Replacement. After the old brick block burned in 1924, nothing was put there until 1937, when the present structure was built. The present building took over four years to build; the post office moved in there in 1937. Gerry Van Ornam moved into the present structure after World War II with unfinished work still going on. The theater attached to this building opened on Thanksgiving Day in 1940 with the film *Third Finger, Left Hand*.

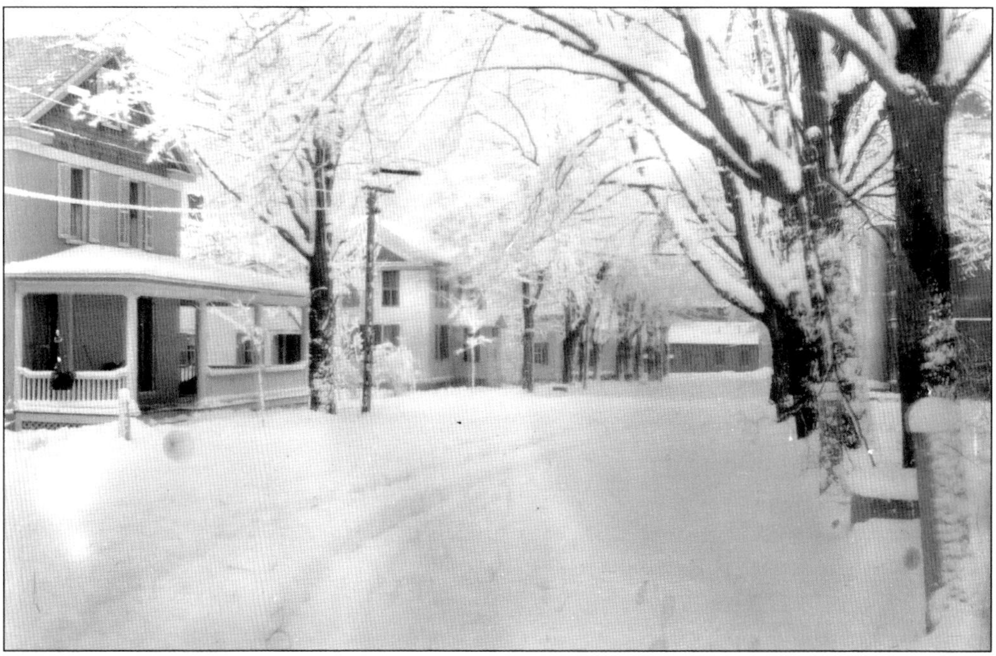

Snow Scene on Beggs. Winter on the former lower Church Street before 1918 saw the horse nail office at the east end of the street before it was a park. The house on the left was already updated from a simple gable-front Greek Revival to a shingle gable and American Foursquare front porch.

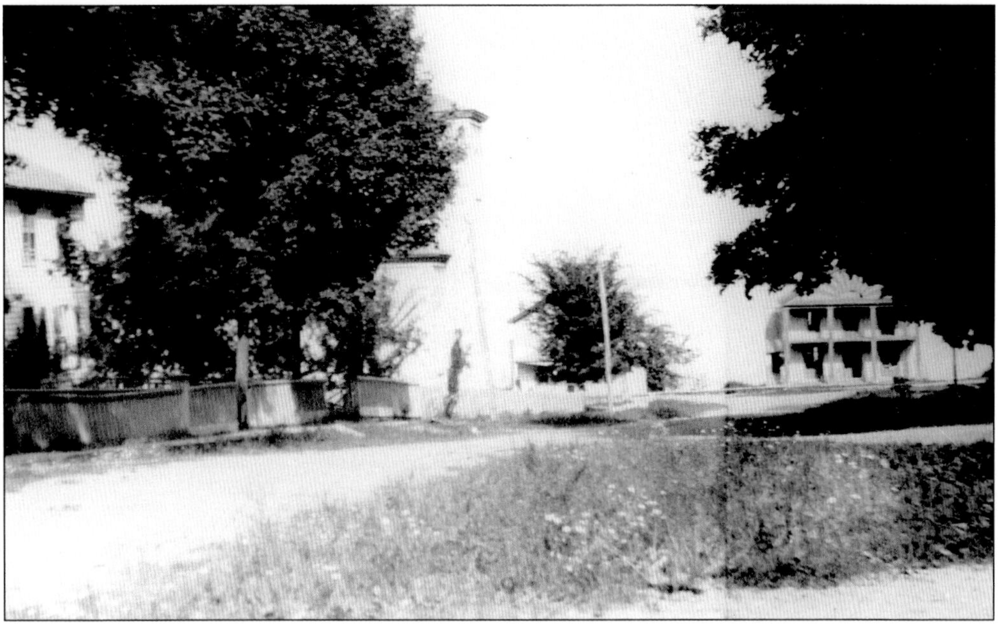

STATION ROAD. Here is a charming view looking east toward the lake with the former Henry H. Ross stone store revealing the distinctive sunburst motif in the pediment over the doorways. Essex has adopted the sunburst motif as its logo, and it can still be seen on buildings all over town. Now State Route 22, for years this was named Station Road because it left town heading west toward the Delaware and Hudson Railway station.

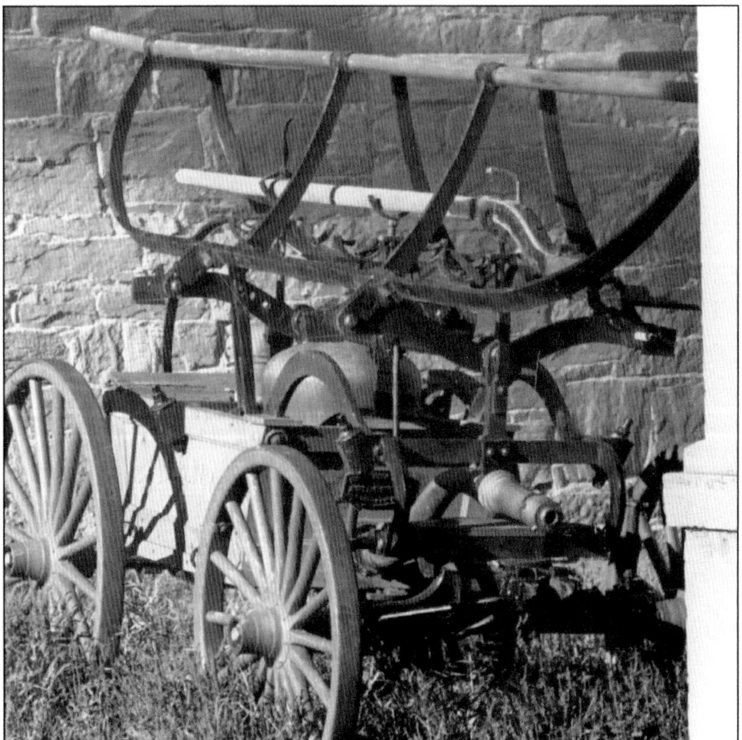

THE ETHAN ALLEN. The Essex Volunteer Fire Department proudly maintains relics of the past just as in most other towns. The hand-pumped fire engine, like all land vehicles, used horse-drawn power. Fortunately this Essex specimen never witnessed a major conflagration. Only after World War I, long after the arrival of the motorized fire engine, did Essex suffer any major downtown fires.

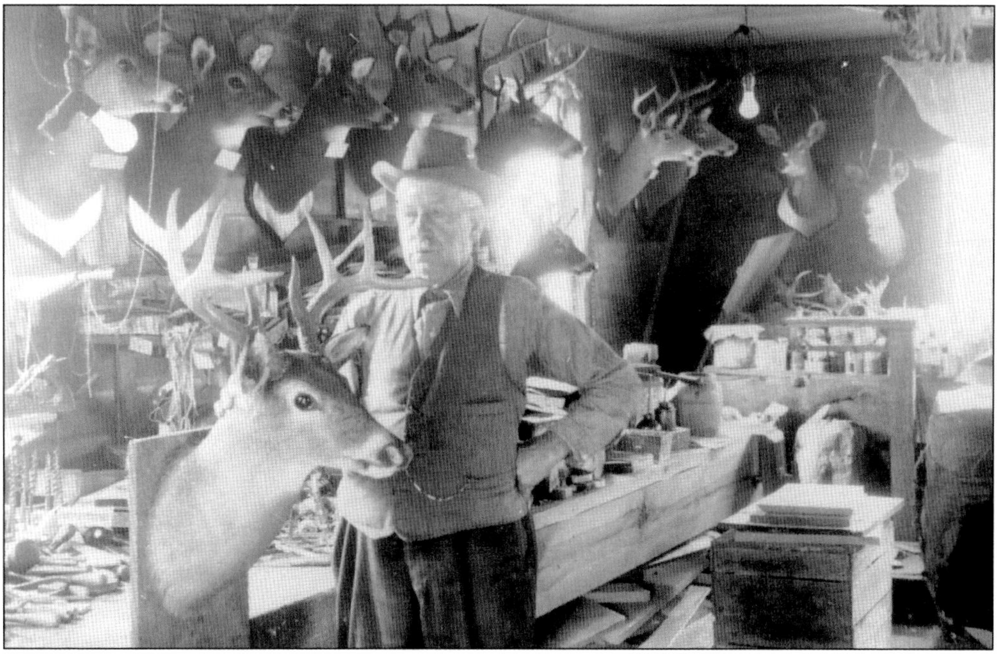

MORSE TAXIDERMY SHOP. Ever wonder why there are so many mounted deer heads for sale in antique shops? Long before the Adirondack rustic style was again popular in the 1990s, a century earlier, many local hunters wanted to preserve their specimens. Soon they were creating numerous antler chandeliers. The shop was located on Station Road.

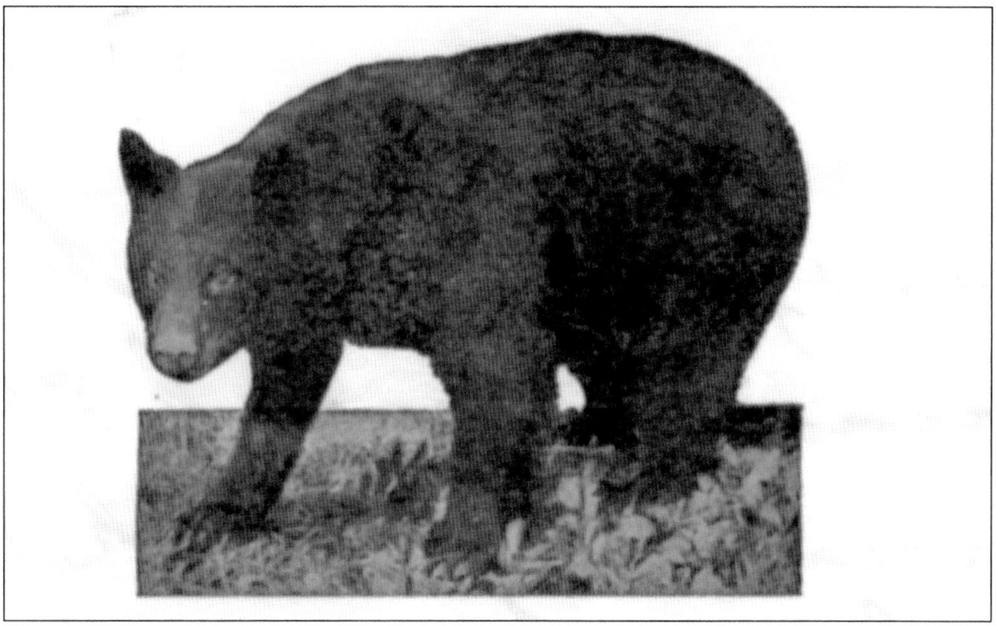

TAXIDERMY LOGO. What was more appropriate a logo for Frank Morse's taxidermy shop than the image of the indigenous black bear? Bear cubs were often captured and trained by caretakers and taught simple tricks to amuse the populace. Many ended up stuffed and mounted. However, some mounts got the last laugh, as toxic arsenic was used and to this day may rub off on the skin of unsuspecting humans.

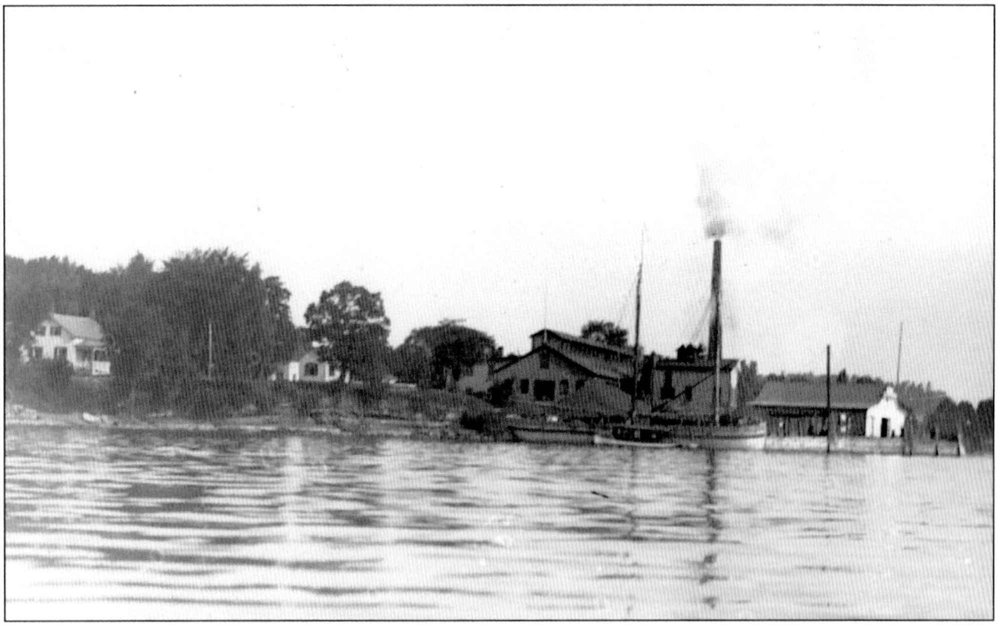

STEAMBOAT POINT LANDING. A sailing canal boat is docked at Shipyard Point. The packet boat was a form of canal boat designed with two long galleries along the sides to accommodate passengers. The trip on the lake was far more comfortable and safe for passengers than the alternative transportation of a carriage trip in the wilderness. The larger canal schooners continued to carry bulk products, such as cut stone from quarries, until well into the 20th century.

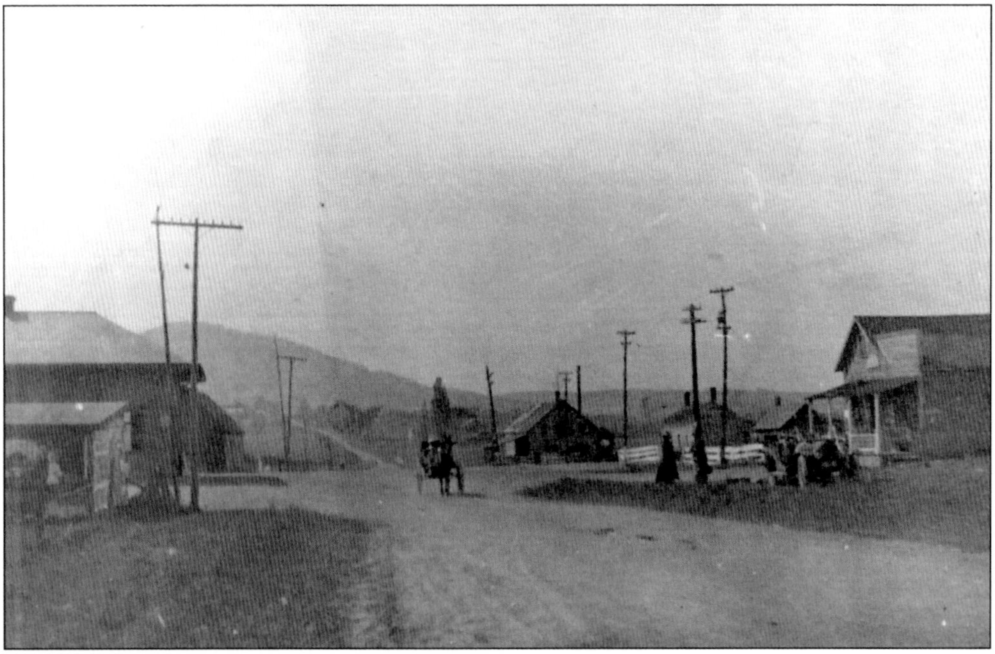

RAILROAD CROSSING. Significantly, unlike most towns, Essex never grew out to meet the railroad. Warehouses, brick industrial buildings, service structures, and so on, with only a few exceptions, never grew past the town boundary of the 1860s. The result was, and is, a rare rural boundary to the town that forgoes suburbs and melds seamlessly into the surrounding countryside.

Five

Civic Life in Public Buildings

Despite all the activity of commerce and mercantile businesses, Essexonians still made time for the important Victorian values expressed in civic life. Churches and schools were dominant in this life, as they were in most towns. The surviving written documentation shows that major families maintained ties to several of the local church groups. For instance, while the Noble family largely funded the construction of the Essex Presbyterian Church by giving the land and several major donations, it also gave many memorials to St. John's Church in later years. Indeed, one of the loveliest colored glass windows of St. John was given in memory of William Belden Noble after his death in 1896. The Noble family later donated the old warehouse to the town as a summer theater and the old tannery store as the town library. Noblesse oblige was taken seriously by Essex patrons, and their role in the town civic life created many institutions that survive to this day.

Churches and schools are also some of the few buildings in town that are not predominantly in the Greek Revival style. The strong association of the Gothic style with medieval architecture meant that at least some details or features were in this design. Indeed, lancet or Gothic arch widows line the sacristy of both St. John's and the Methodist Episcopal church. The Boquet Chapel is entirely in the Gothic style. The Essex Presbyterian Church is in the rarer form of Italianate, more in the Renaissance tradition. Only the lost Baptist church presented any Greek Revival influence, with its large pair of columns in the entrance portico.

The immense 1867 Essex Union Free School is firmly in the Greek Revival tradition, with its large pediment and simple quoins. However, the same could hardly be claimed about the earlier 1785 schoolhouse or the later 1909 high school. Both of these are brick structures in the vernacular Georgian and American Foursquare traditions, respectively.

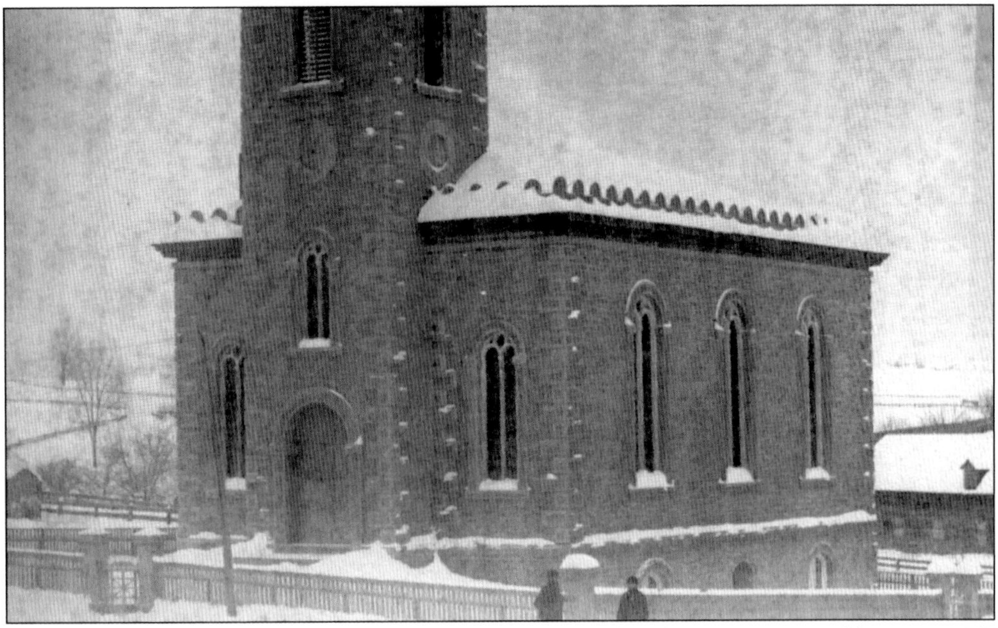

ESSEX PRESBYTERIAN CHURCH. The Essex Presbyterian Church was constructed between 1853 and 1856 on land donated by the Noble family. The ladies of the church created a framed memorial manuscript that included the names of all the donors and the amount they donated. Belden Noble, who was to be married in the church as soon as it was completed, donated the largest amount at $400. Iron cresting emphasizes the roofline.

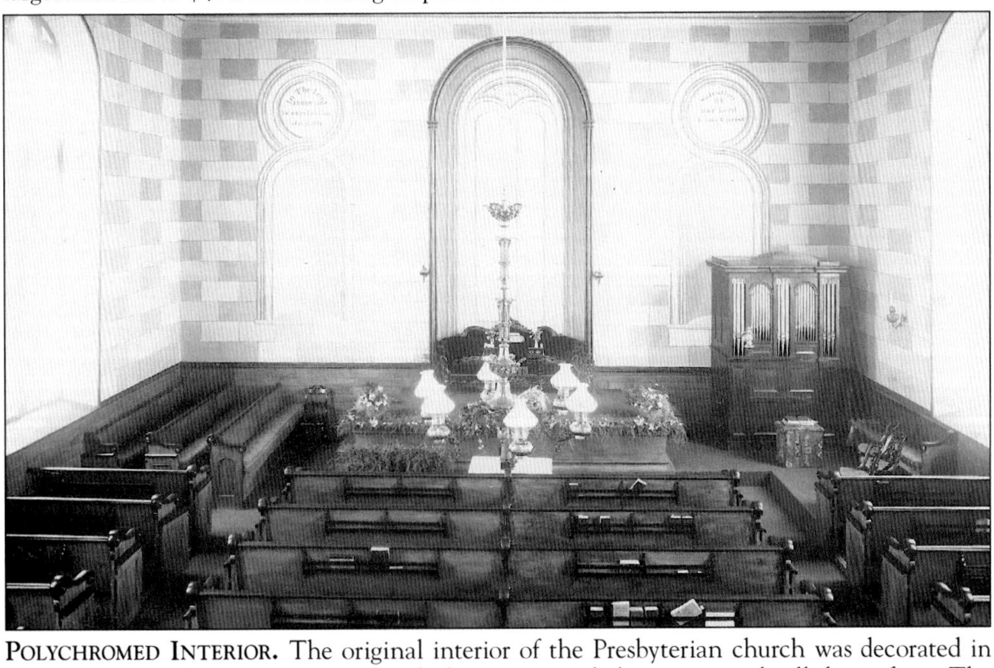

POLYCHROMED INTERIOR. The original interior of the Presbyterian church was decorated in the Renaissance fresco manner, with polychrome painted plaster on nearly all the surfaces. The ashlar-painted walls were designed to look like stone block. The ceiling had a trompe l'oeil effect to make it appear to have a Renaissance dome. The Renaissance Revival was the most fashionable decorative style of the 1850s when the church was completed.

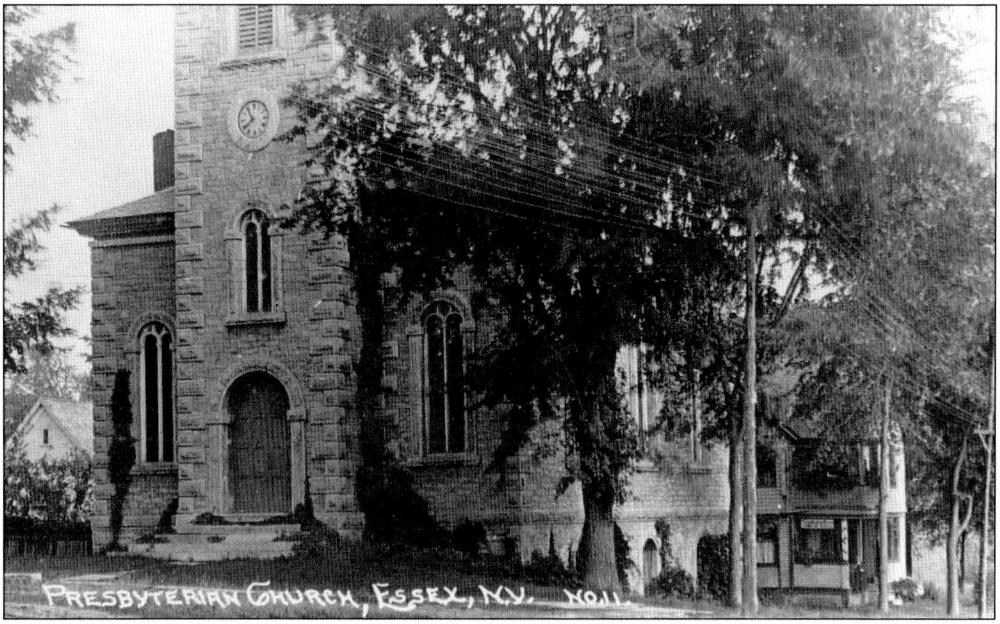

RUSTICATED LIMESTONE. Architect T. S. Whitby designed the rusticated exterior of the Essex Presbyterian Church to give the impression of a small but sophisticated church in an Italian village, thus satisfying the mid-Victorian sentiment for the exotic and faraway. Also listed on the church record were the names of the stoneworkers, masons, and carpenters, many who are documented to have worked on other projects in the village.

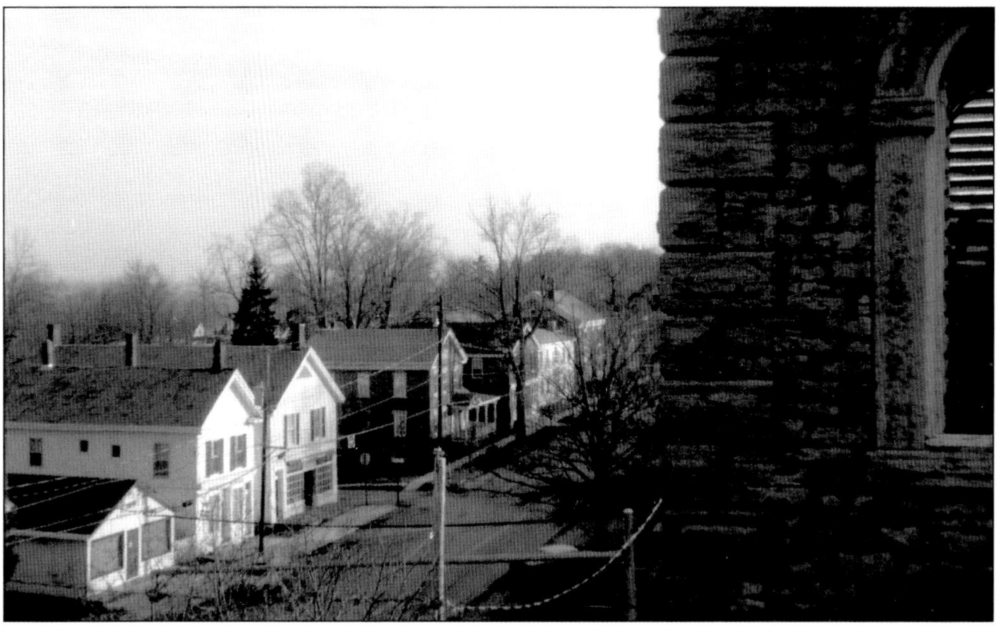

VILLAGE IN SCALE. Here is an unusual view taken from the roof of the Presbyterian church around 1970. The early-19th-century scale and continuity of the two-story classical houses and commercial buildings is apparent on the east side of Main Street. The view from the steeple illustrates how even a small church, when scaled to its surroundings, can still appropriately dominate the village scene.

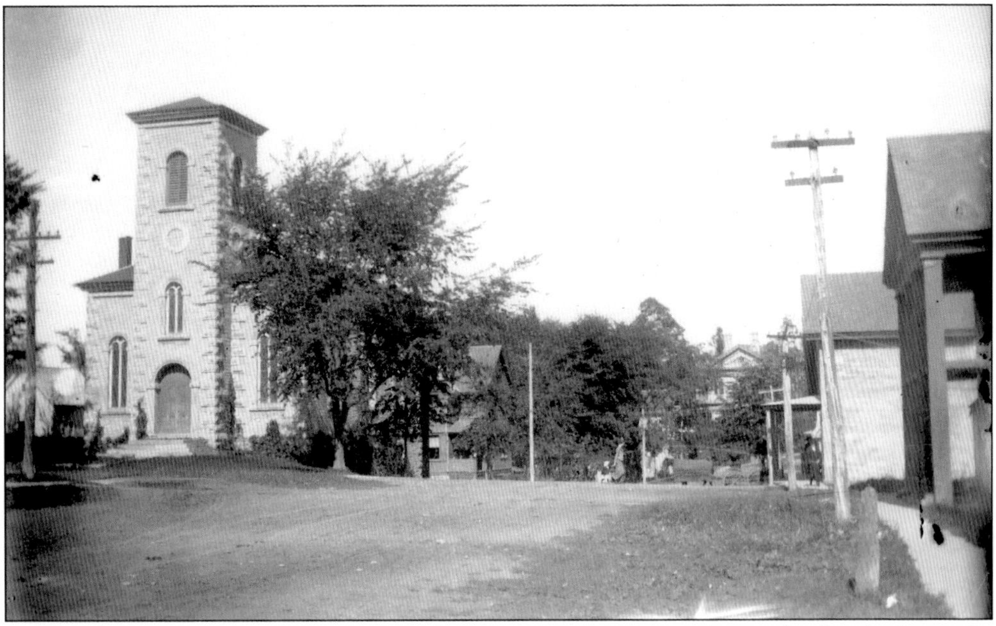

NORTH VIEW. Apparently the stone in the tower was cut out on three sides for the faces of a clock, when constructed. However, it was not until 1911, with the death of Adeline Noble, that Justice James S. Harlan and Maud Noble Harlan donated the funds to have a clock and bell installed. The clockwork mechanism is still operating and has to be wound weekly by hand. Early-19th-century stained-glass windows were comprised most often of small geometric panes.

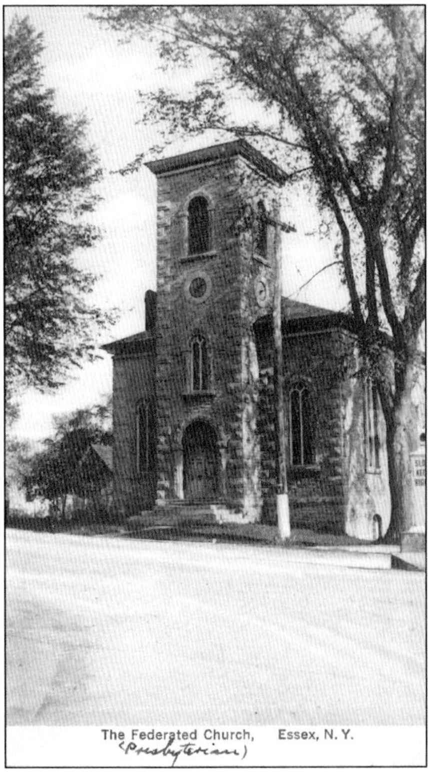

VILLAGE FENCES. Originally a wooden fence connected the Essex Presbyterian Church, later the Federated or Community Church, to the great houses to the north owned by the Nobles. As with so many early-19th-century rural communities, Essex once had fences surrounding most of the village properties. While the more substantial ones (of cast iron) remain at Greystone and Sunnyside, typical wooden ones have long been removed.

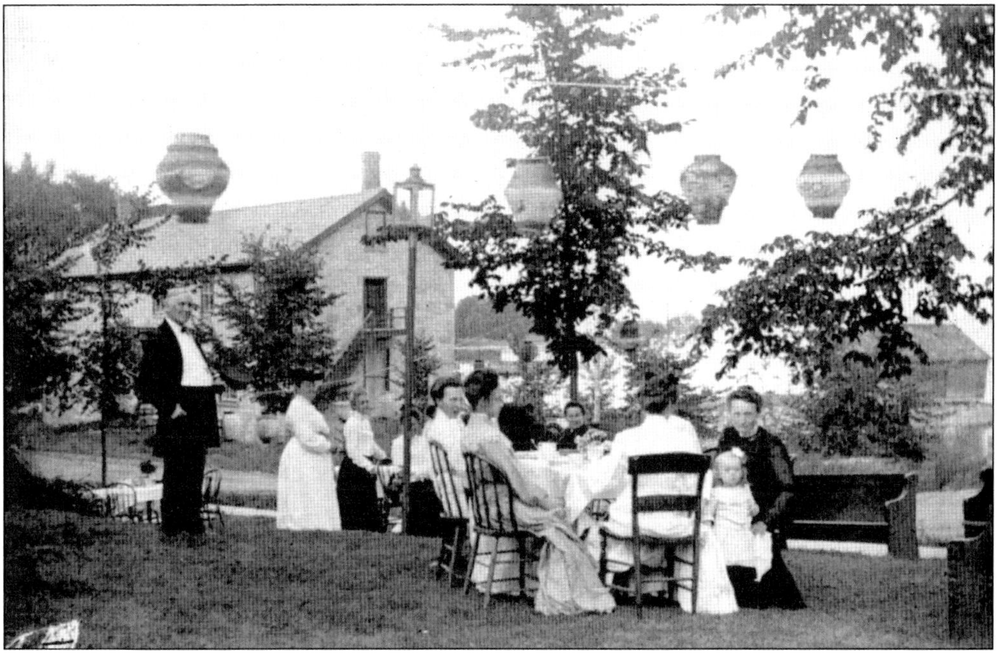

CHURCH SOCIAL, EAST HALF. Typical of churches everywhere in the 19th century, social events were held in the summer season both to entertain parishioners and to fund-raise for the church. This 1890s event on the front lawn of the Presbyterian church was photographed in two parts, the second image being only recently discovered.

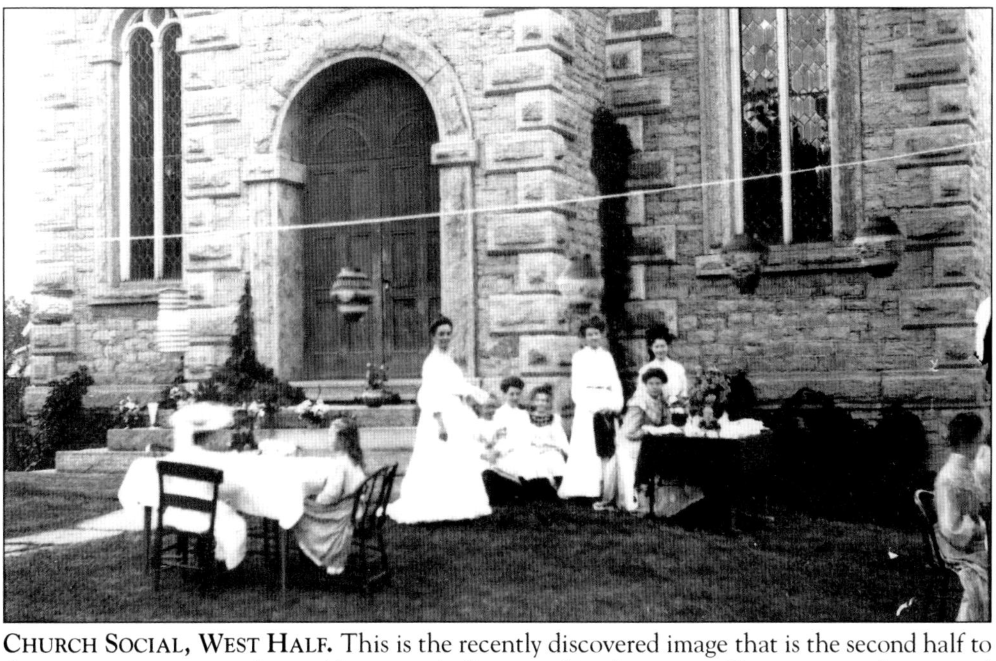

CHURCH SOCIAL, WEST HALF. This is the recently discovered image that is the second half to the summer event seen above. Also recently discovered in the attic at Greystone are the original Japanese lanterns that are in fair condition and still awaiting another summer fund-raising event. As there was no commercial gas available in Essex, the original chandelier inside the Presbyterian church formerly held oil-burning lamps.

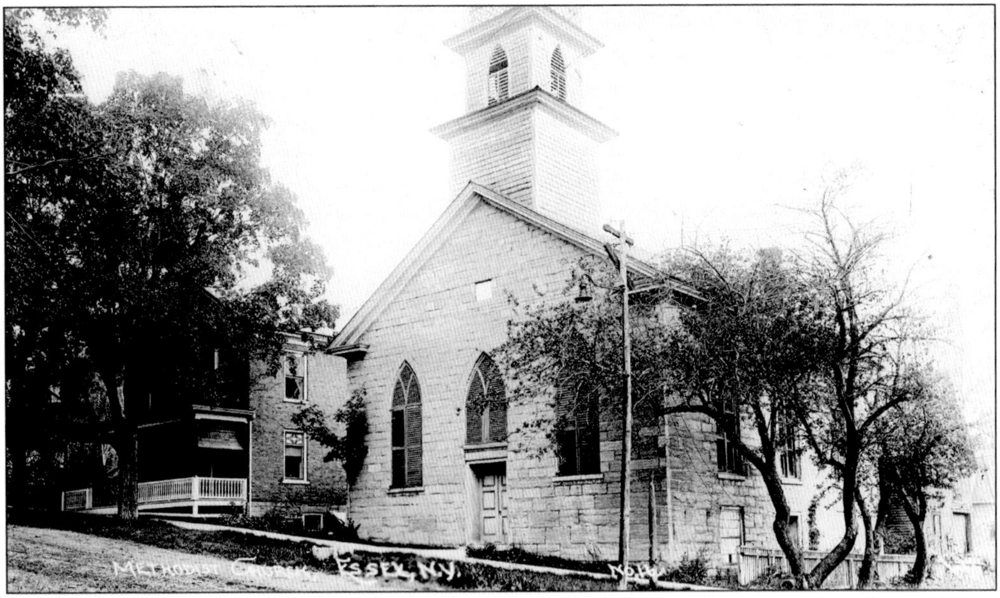

ESSEX METHODIST CHURCH. The Methodists constructed this cut limestone church in 1835, as a marble plaque inset on the front gable attests. Inside the front door is a vestibule then a divided staircase on both sides up to the raised sanctuary. The simple Greek Revival–style steeple was lost more than 50 years ago and has yet to be reconstructed. The lancet arch windows add an early Gothic note to this essentially Greek Revival structure. In 2007, the building was given to the town in order for a restoration grant administered by Historic Essex to proceed.

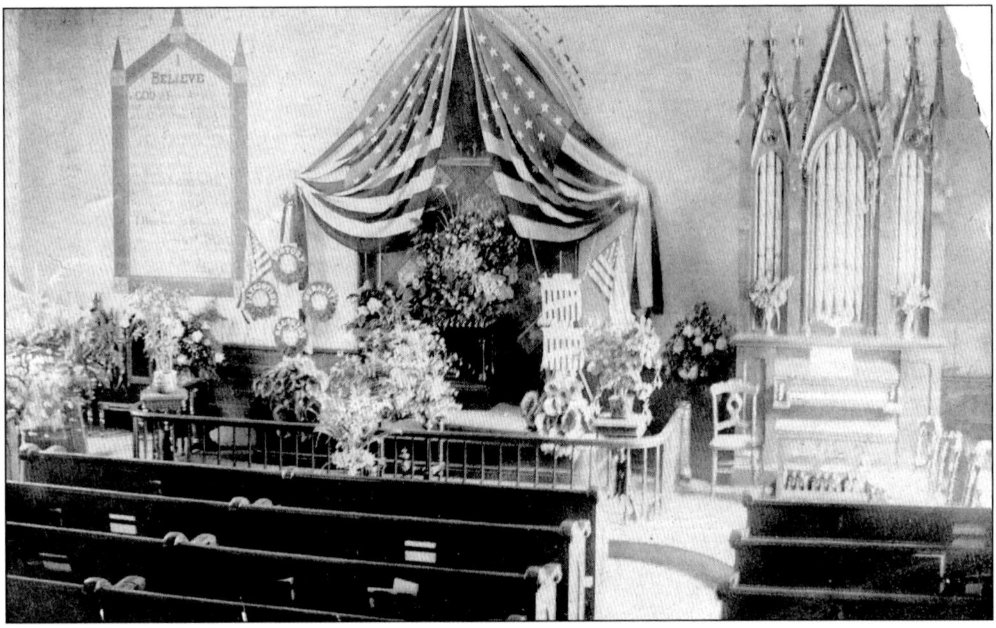

INTERIOR VIEW. Special occasions such as weddings, funerals, holidays, and commemorations were often recorded on film. The interior of the Methodist church is festooned in flags and flowers for such an event. The center ceiling medallion with carved plasterwork retains its blue and silver 1850s color scheme. Further improvements occurred when the church building was extensively improved in 1876 and again in 1884, the last time at a cost of about $1,000.

ESSEX BAPTIST CHURCH. Perhaps the most traditional-appearing church in town was the 1842 brick Essex Baptist Church with its prominent front Doric columns and New England–type steeple. The Baptist congregation prospered in the late 19th century; it had 105 members at its peak in 1885. The Baptists had long since dwindled and decamped, and the Masons arrived by the Depression in 1931. A fire destroyed the building in 1943, removing a prominent steeple from the Essex skyline.

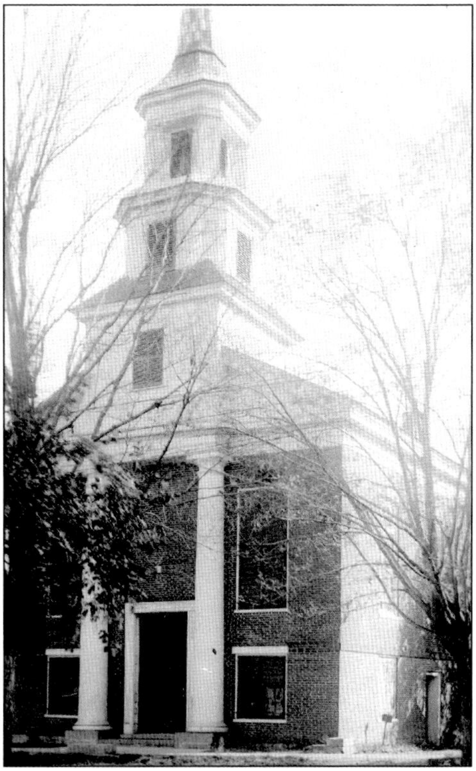

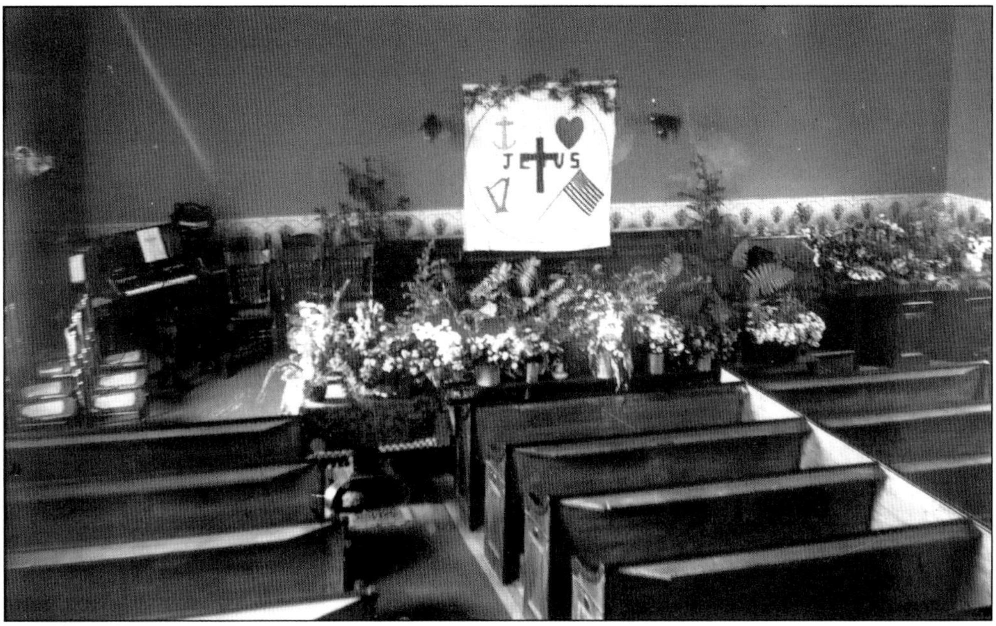

INTERIOR LIGHTING. Essex was too small a community and too far removed from urban areas to provide a supply of natural gas. So like its fellow congregations, the Baptist church burned oil lamps. In addition to the visible sidelights there was a large circular hanging lamp possibly made by the I. M. Frink Company in New York City, which specialized in lighting for community halls, churches, and assembly chambers.

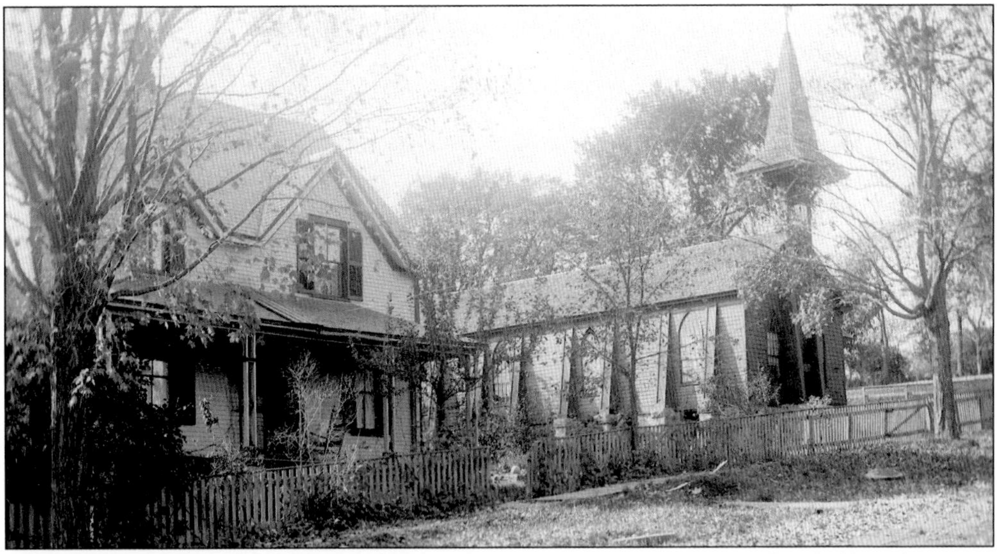

ST. JOHN'S CHURCH. St. John's Church was founded when services were first held in the 1850s. The Ross family had constructed a schoolhouse around 1835, and from 1853 to 1877, services were held there. In 1877, the church purchased the building and lot, removed the old building to its present site, and reconstructed it in its present form, using designs by the Reverend John Henry Hopkins. In the same year, the rectory in the foreground was built.

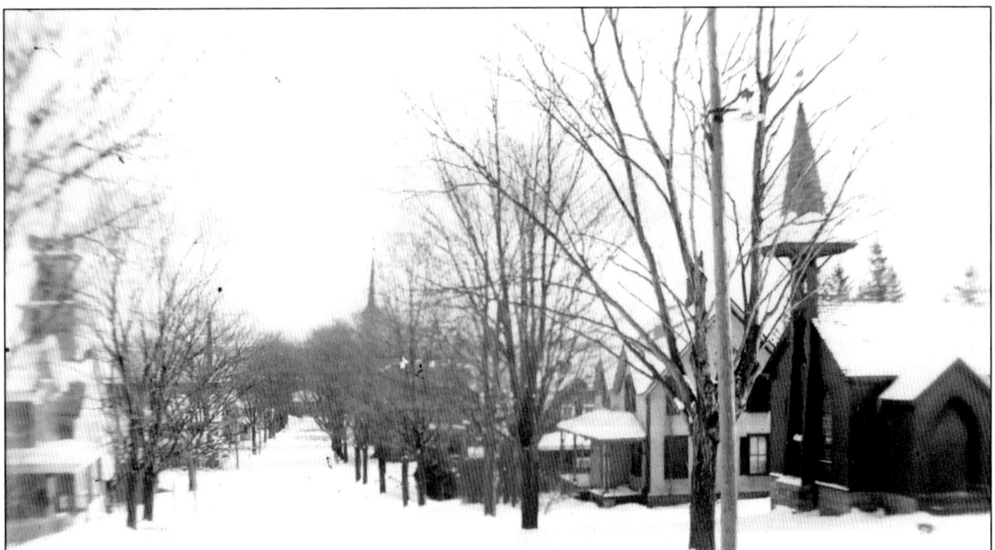

CHURCH STREET STEEPLES. Here is Church Street with the Methodist steeple visible at left. St. John's Church was built in the spirit of the country English Reform Gothic, with a steeple containing the bell from the 1875 wreck of the lake steamer *Champlain*. The church is a frame building supported by buttresses on the sides, with a wing for the organ chamber and vestry room and a bellcote at the north end. A parish hall was added as a new west wing in 1984.

THE RUSTIC INTERIOR OF ST. JOHN'S. Functioning year-round as a parish church during this period, Christmas was celebrated with lots of local greenery, particularly native spruce and white cedar boughs. The congregation has been both seasonal and year-round, depending on the number of parishioners and the availability of clerics. The St. John's congregation had 90 members in 1885. (Courtesy of St. John's Church.)

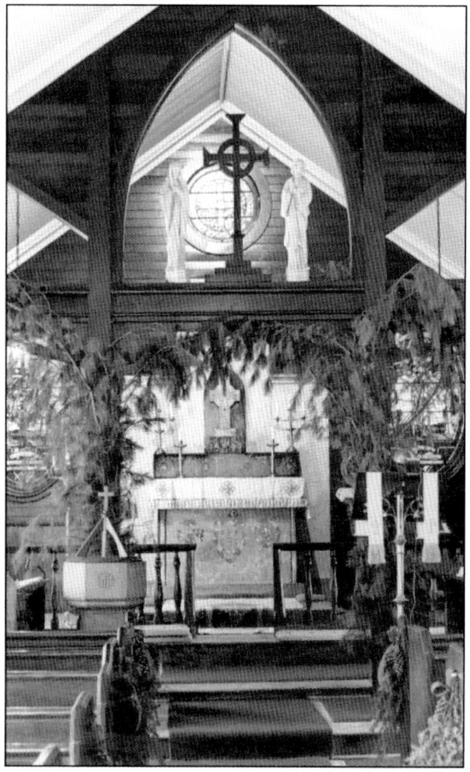

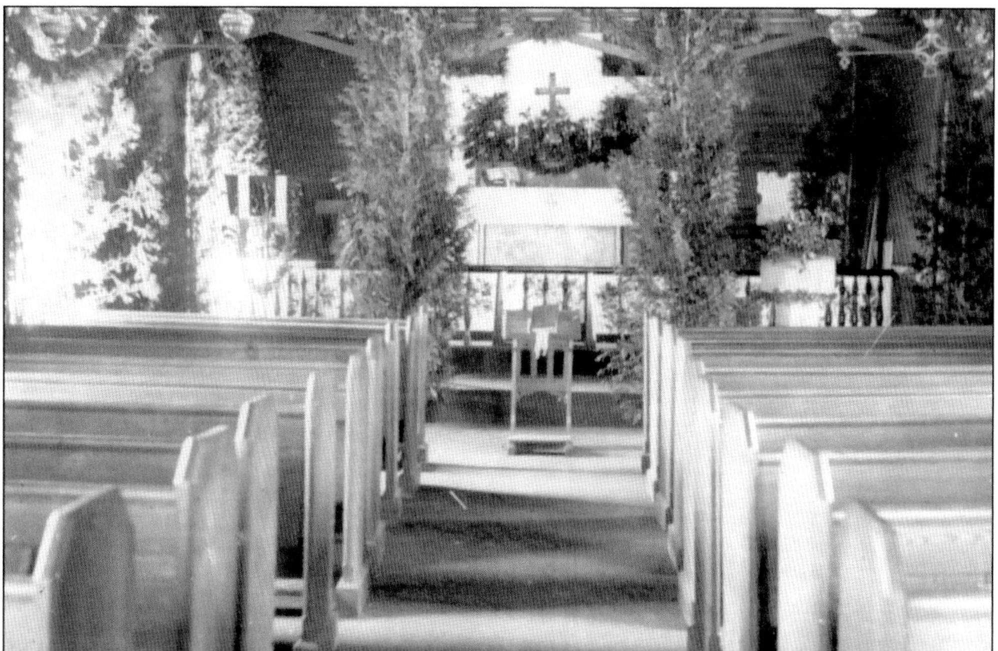

OIL LAMPS. Church structures such as St. John's also had to be illuminated without the benefit of a local gas supply. Manufacturers made simple chandeliers that were fitted with oil lamps, typically two connected by an ornamental rod. (Courtesy of St. John's Church.)

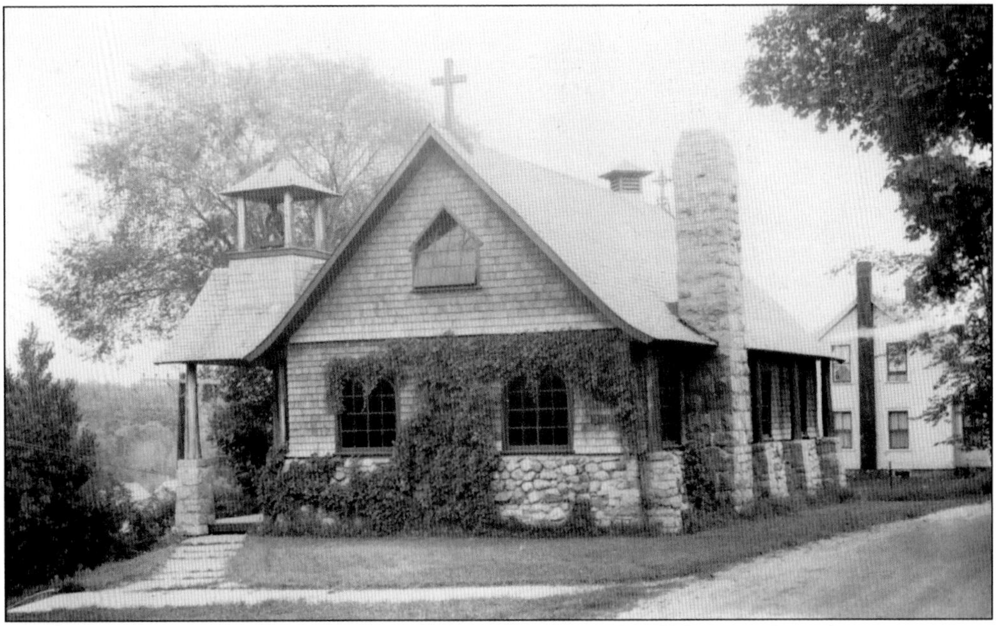

St. Mary's Chapel. Located in the neighboring town of Willsboro and sited in a spot once known as North Hill, St. Mary's Chapel was a mission church of St. John's Episcopal Church of Essex. The shingle-style structure still stands but is no longer in use as a church, having been converted to a commercial use.

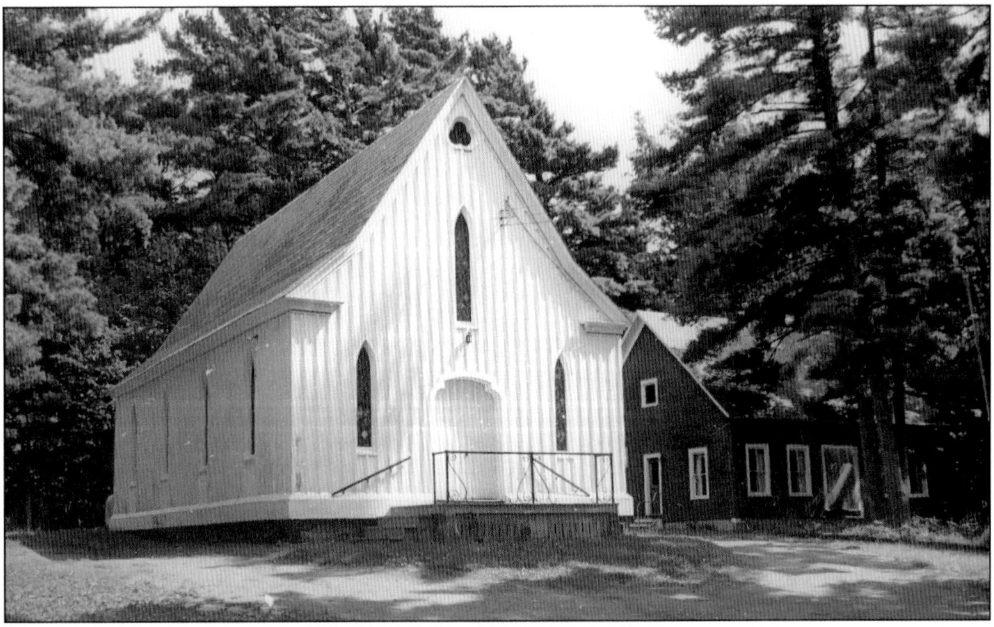

The Boquet Chapel. The Boquet Chapel appears to be the product of a pattern book design, specifically *Rural Architecture*, written in 1852 by New York architect Richard Upjohn (1802–1878). Upjohn designed several notable buildings, including Trinity Church in New York City. Here the vertically soaring Gothic Revival style is achieved by the board-and-batten siding and a steep gable roof. It was listed on the National Register of Historic Places in 1973.

FITTED WOOD INTERIOR. The wainscot interior woodwork has been varnished but left unpainted in its original form. The wainscoting is decorated with applied graining. The effect created is one of darker wood interior punctuated by bright window openings. The striking contrast produced is a hallmark of the romantic movement with its interest in atmospheric effects. The Victorians loved the dichotomy of light and dark, good and evil, and life and death, which prompted parishioners to dwell on spiritual matters.

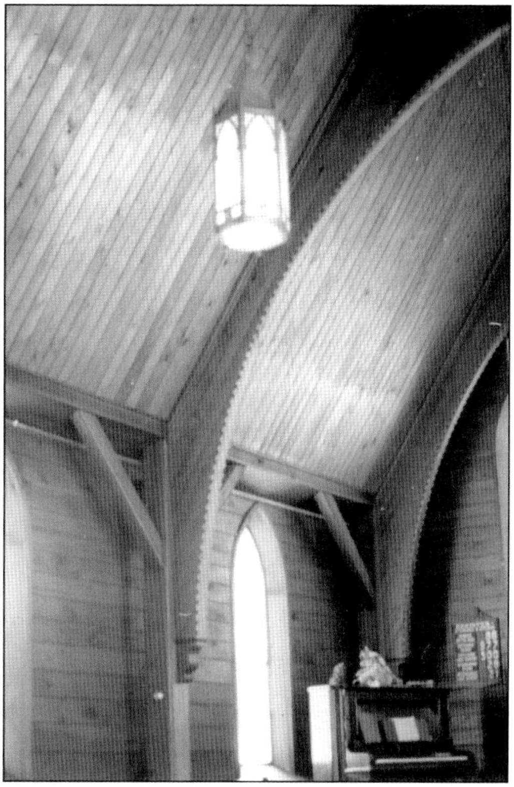

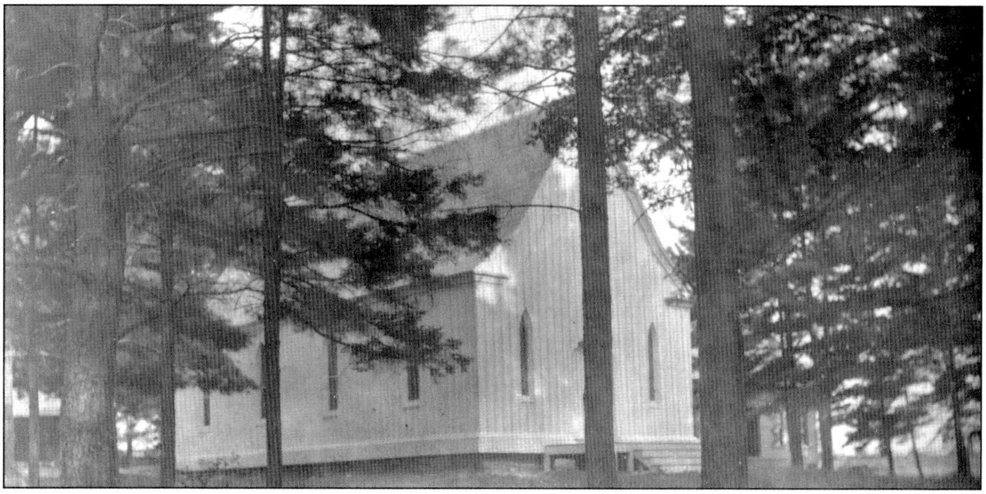

NATURALISTIC LANDSCAPE SITING. Historic siting in a pine grove around the Boquet Chapel demonstrates the importance of setting to the Victorians. By the 1850s, such landscape proponents as Andrew Jackson Downing promoted the naturalistic, romantic style in gardening. Curvilinear roadways, tall pines, specimen trees, and glimpses and partial views were all considered essential to the romantic genre.

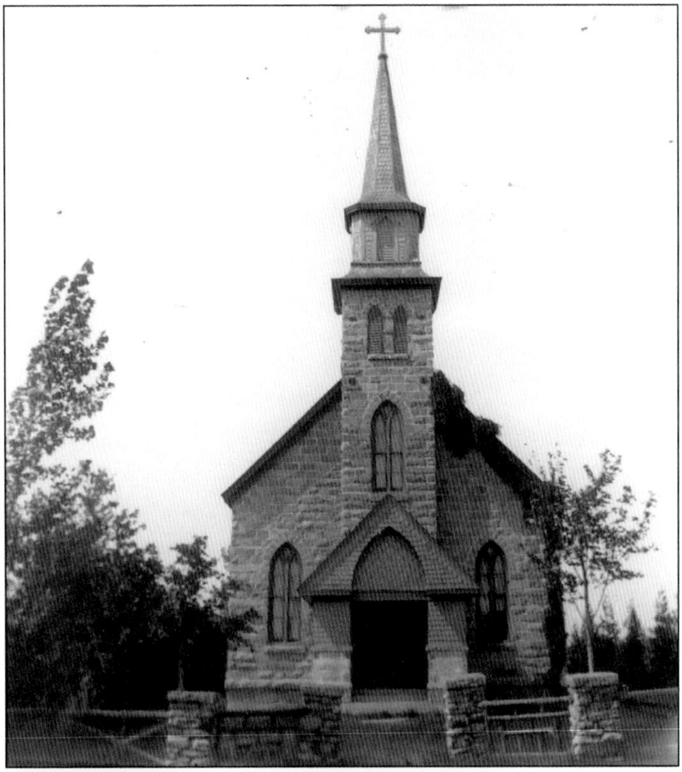

St. Joseph's Church. This Roman Catholic structure was begun in 1872 and finished in 1873 at a cost of $9,000. According to H. P. Smith, the congregation numbered 100 families in 1885. Local myth held its location out of town was because the existing religions in the hamlet did not want the Catholic church nearby. In fact, it was built to serve the congregations of two towns and was thought to be located conveniently in between. The rustic fence in front was lost to road widening.

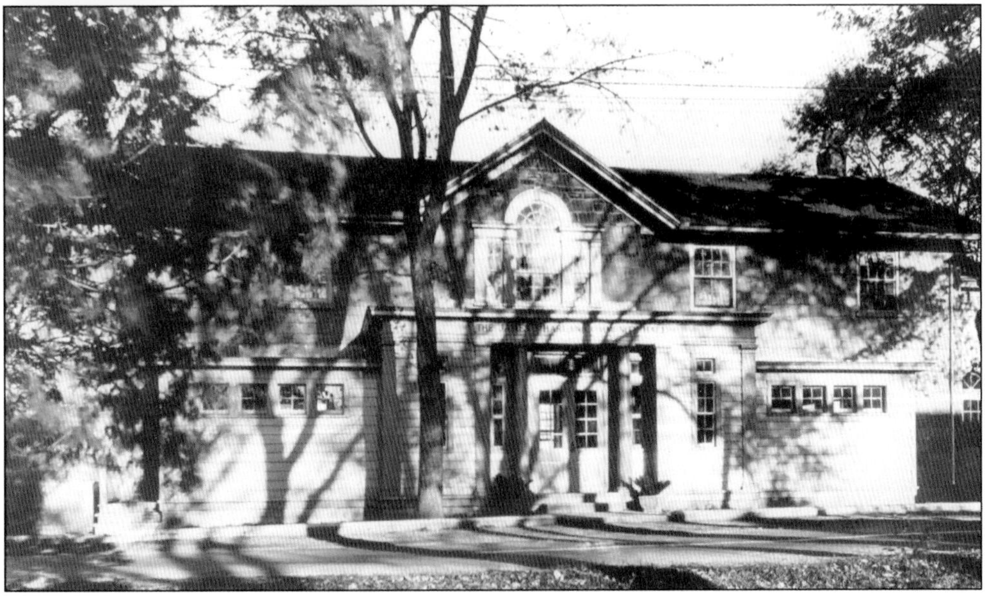

Noble Warehouse. As the Noble family began to control maritime shipping on Lake Champlain, it soon constructed a wharf and a warehouse. Later Maud Noble hired an architect to transform the warehouse to a concert hall. Detailed Colonial Revival features were added, such as a three-part Palladian window and clapboard neoclassical entranceway. Inside, a balcony and full stage allowed such genteel entertainment as members of the Boston Symphony Orchestra to perform in the summertime.

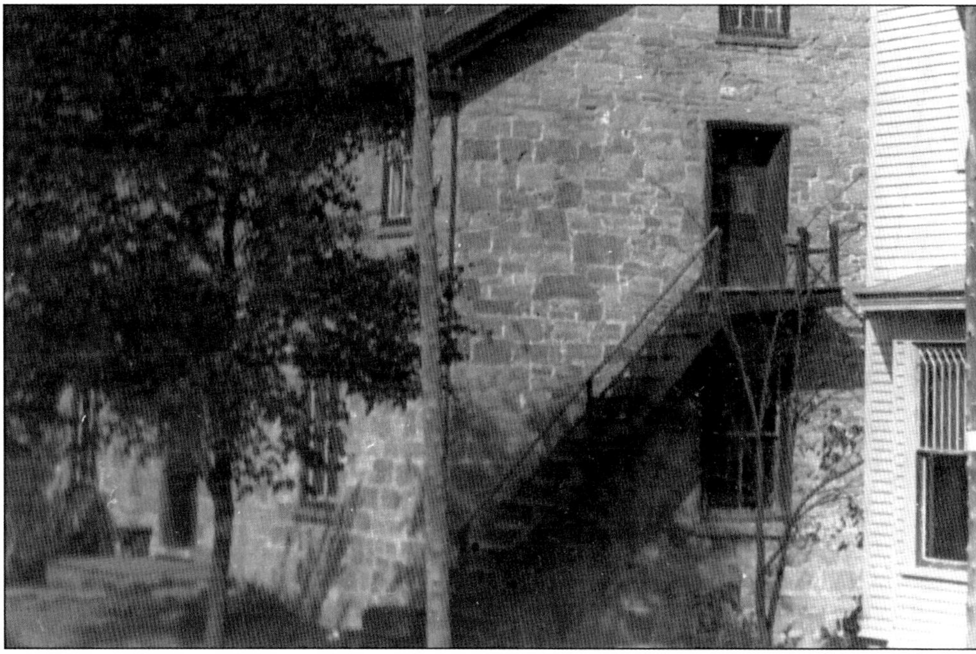

NOBLE DONATION. The Masons occupied several former churches throughout town before being donated the old Noble warehouse by Noble descendant Cornelia Hand Baird. Historic Essex has assisted recent restorations by acquiring public grants to do roof work and repoint the exterior stone. In the summer, it is used by the Essex Community Players, founded in the 1920s.

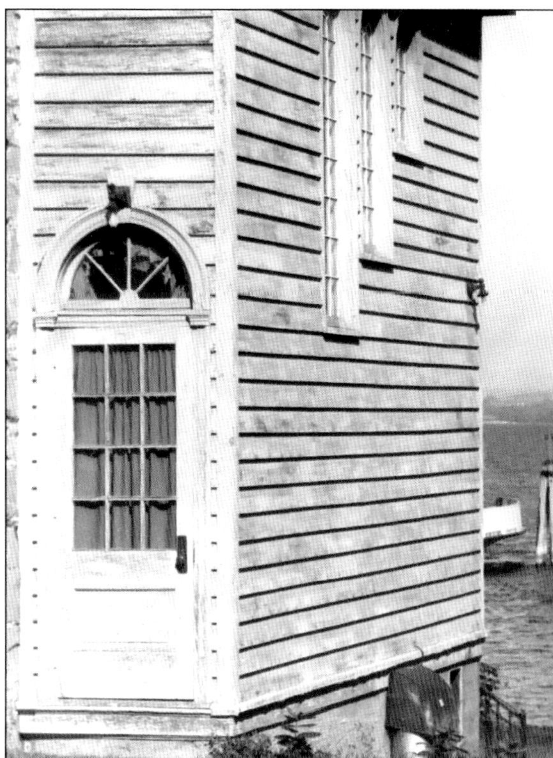

WAREHOUSE TO CONCERT HALL. The transformation from industrial warehouse to concert hall is apparent in the enclosure of the exterior staircase to the former second floor, now elegant balcony seating. The Colonial Revival details continue in the fanlight over the doorway and in the three small round-headed windows used to illuminate the stairway.

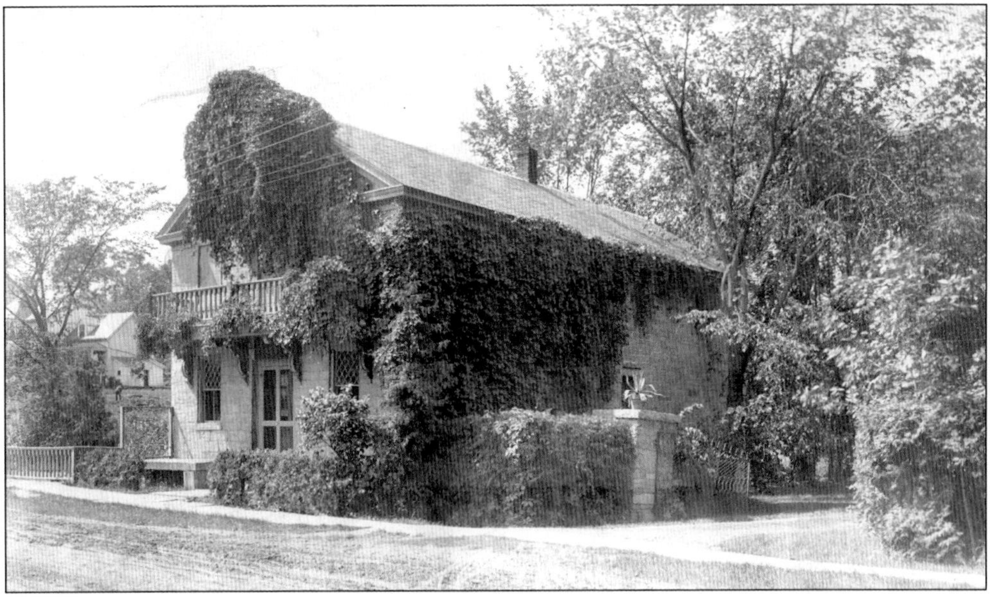

TANNERY STORE TO LIBRARY. In a similar fashion to the Noble warehouse, the former Noble tannery store was made obsolete. A tannery is a noxious use. In fact, the first zoning laws in America in the 1860s were promulgated to restrict their locations. Adeline Noble used the tannery store space to house a private library, with privileges extended to family, friends, and staff. A charter was granted by New York State, and the town accepted the now public library as the Belden Noble Memorial Library in 1899.

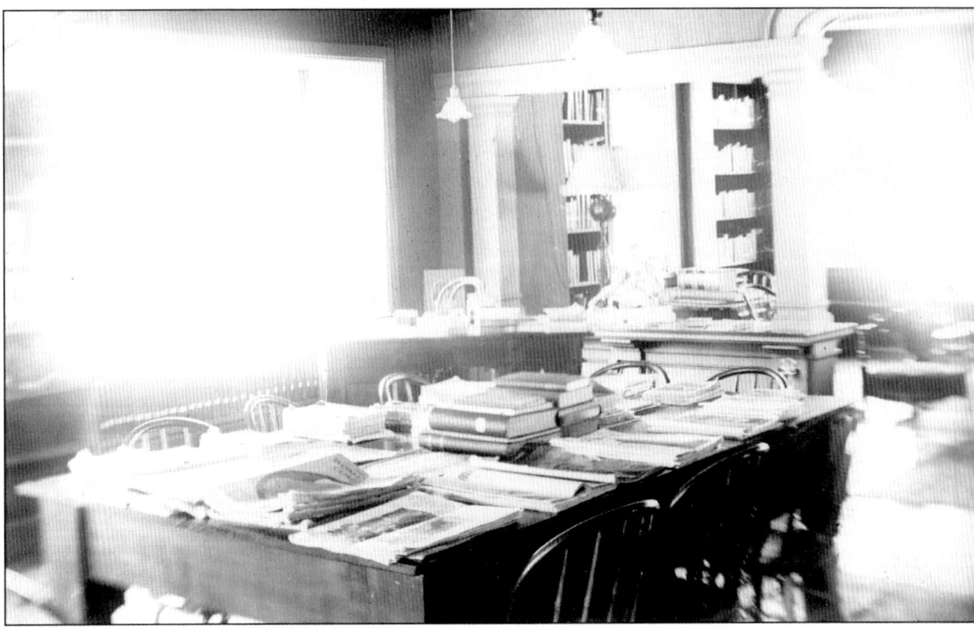

LIBRARY INTERIOR. Pride of place resulted in the photographic documentation of the library interior around 1905. The building was the recipient of a grant in 1998, and the exterior and interior were completely restored by the library board and ECHO. They used original photographs of the interior to guide in the restoration, including arranging into the proper spaces much of the original furniture that was intact.

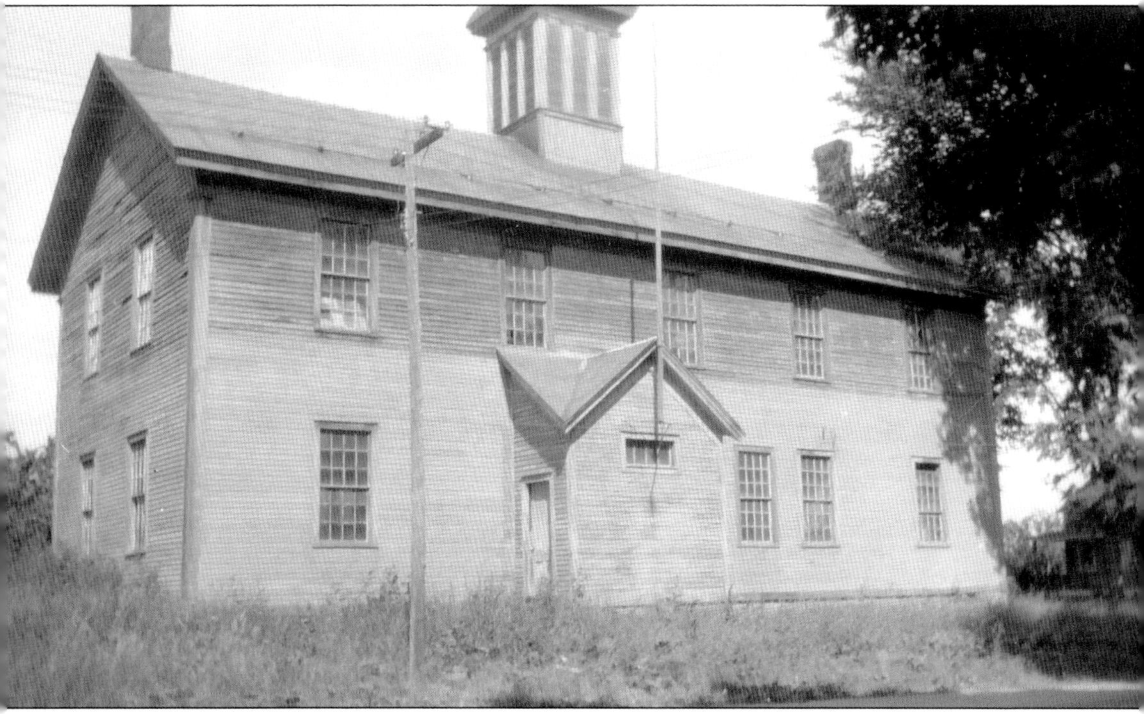

ESSEX UNION FREE SCHOOL. After the Civil War, Essex expected again to resume a period of prosperity. After all, this is what happened after the War of 1812, so the residents believed the same would happen this time. The immense Greek Revival design of the Essex Union Free School was constructed just down the road from the small brick school it replaced. As the county history records, "The 1867 Essex Union School was built at a cost not exceeding $5000; there are three teachers in constant employment, the average attendance at the school is about one hundred and thirty eight in 1885." The fact that the building seemed out of scale with its small frame neighbor residences represented the optimistic belief in education as a key to prosperity and future success following the Civil War. The Essex Union Free School allowed for a free high school education for both men and women. It was used until 1908. All of the architectural details remain intact, except for the pair of brick chimneys originally for heating stoves on each end of the building. The county history also states that portions of the original Gen. Ransom Noble residence were reused in this structure, perhaps testifying to an early effort at being green by Essex citizens. The cupola features a metal Moorish arch roof with a generic fish weather vane, just recently restored in 2008. In 2009 as the new Essex Heritage Center, the former schoolhouse will once again feature an educational and heritage recreational series of community programs.

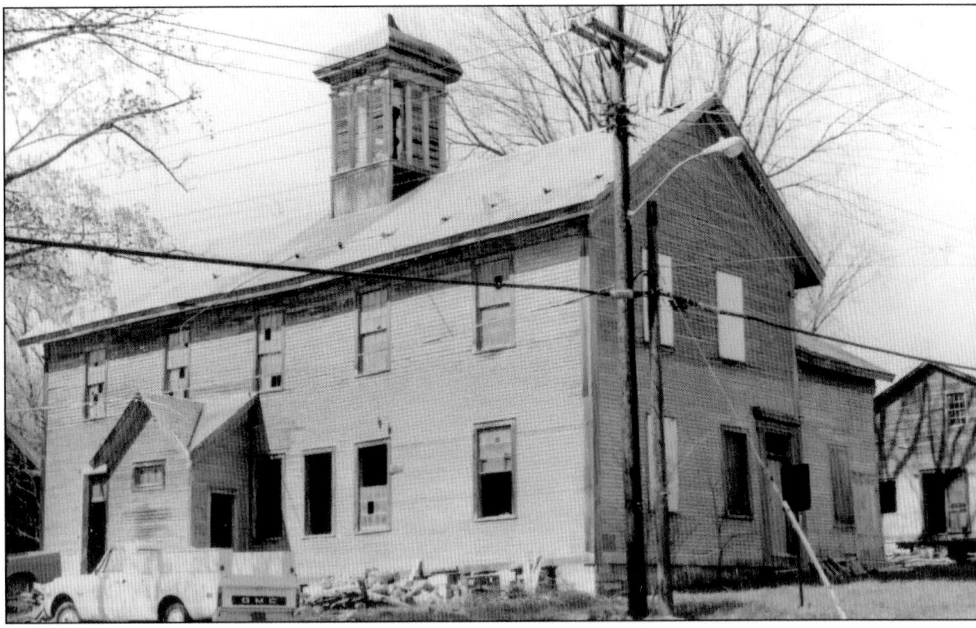

Union School Revived. In time, the Essex Union Free School fell out of favor, and by the mid-20th century, large garage doors were cut in its side. Dr. Bates Lowry, director of the Museum of Modern Art, summered in Essex and tried to develop interest in the built environment. The modern aspect of Essex was its architecture, which could be interpreted as folky in an American rural way, much as with the popularity of Nantucket.

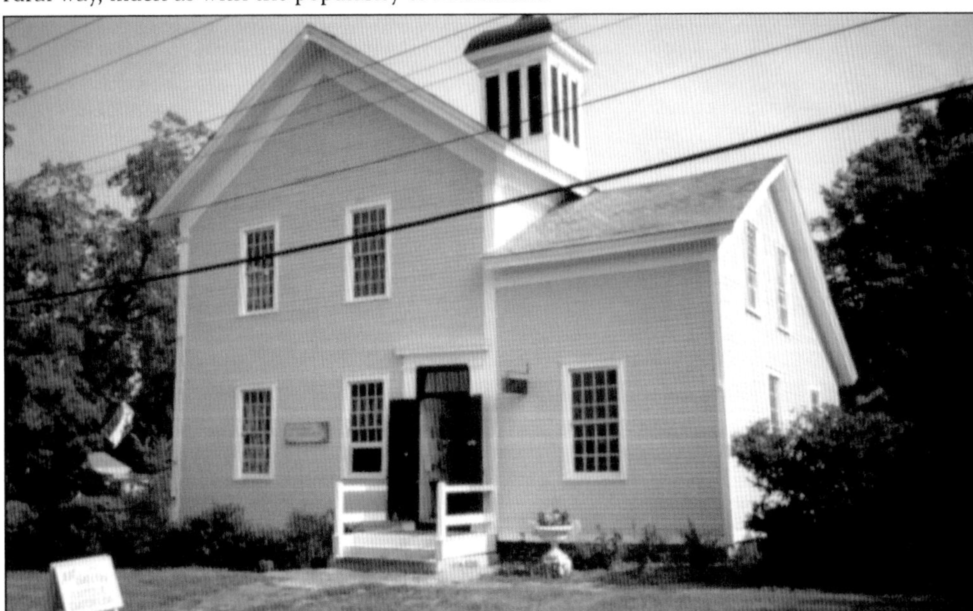

Essex Heritage Center from 1867 Schoolhouse. The Essex Union Free School then hosted the local Adirondack Art Association for several years. During a 1991 restoration, an inner board was removed, and this was written in pencil on the back: "On this date, January in 1867, the lake froze over." Finally, with another major restoration by ECHO, it became a museum and visitor center known as the Essex Heritage Center in 2009.

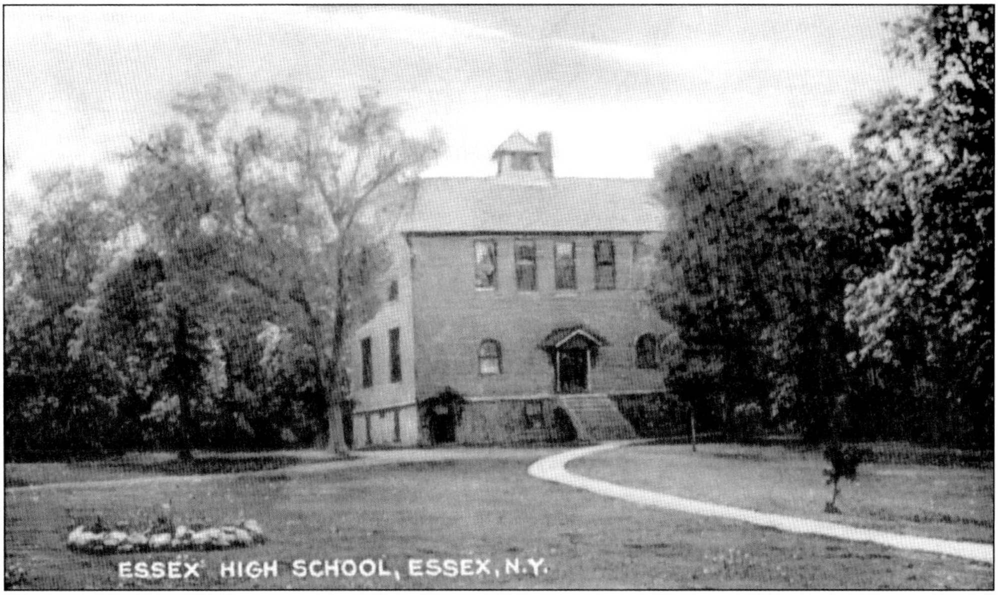

ESSEX HIGH SCHOOL. Again, time and changing education theory demanded a new school building, so in 1908, a massive stone-and-brick structure was constructed. Like most Essex buildings, the foundation was cut from the local limestone ledge. Massive stone foundations and solid brick construction characterized the construction of the new Essex High School in 1908. Principles of teaching, heating, and hygiene had again evolved, demanding another more modern school.

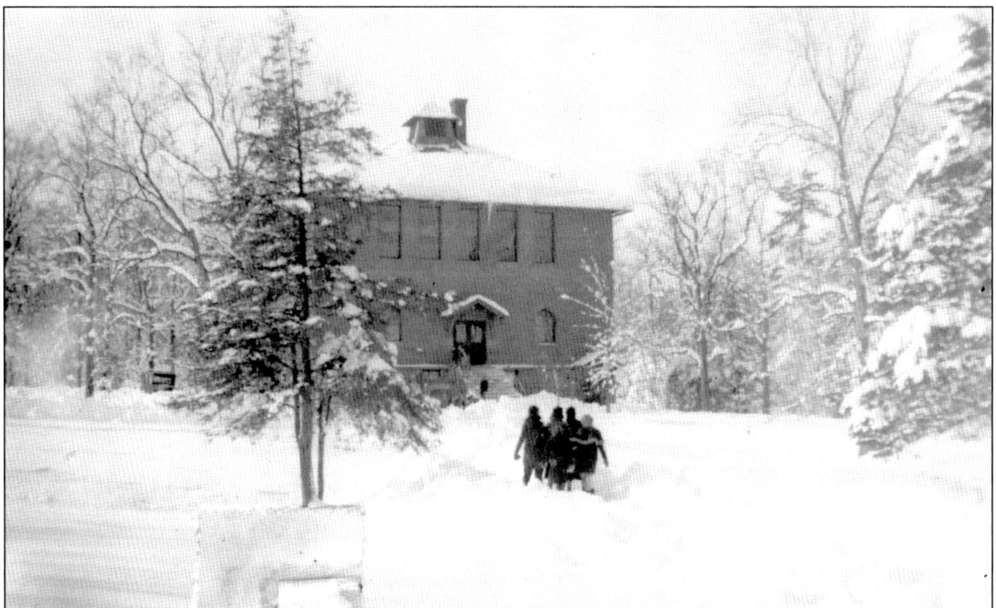

HIGH SCHOOL IN WINTER. The Essex Union Free School was replaced by the 1908 Essex High School in a style that appeared very strange at the time—a large foursquare, brick Romanesque building. This construction was well hidden slightly out of the village on the west end of town. Despite its name, it served both elementary and high school students. It was abandoned in 1952 when local schools consolidated.

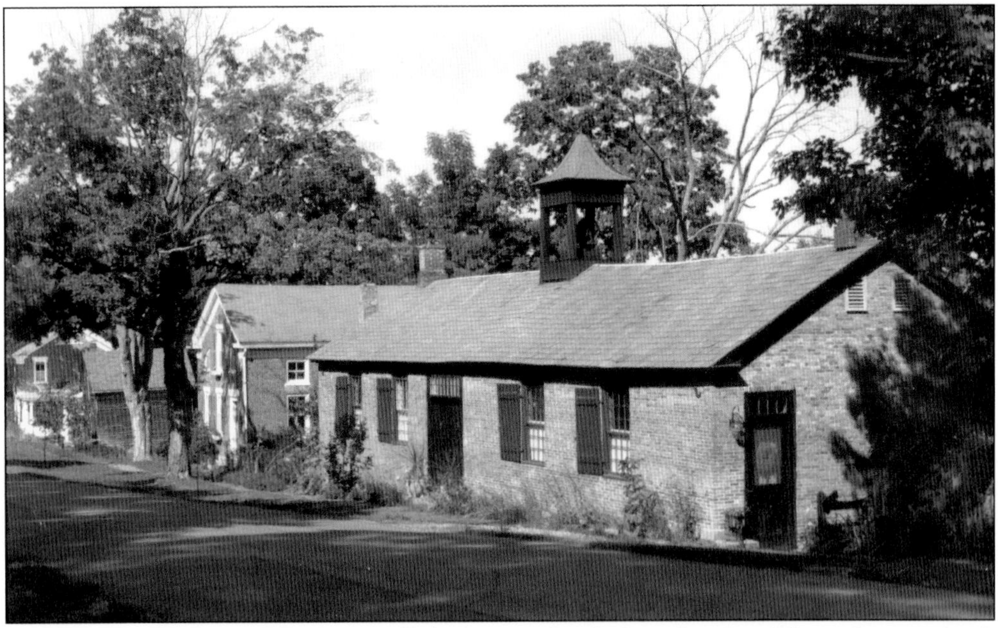

EARLIEST SCHOOLHOUSE. Essex actually has more schools than churches. The earliest is a brick single-story structure from 1818 that was enlarged in 1836, as the local population boomed on the thriving ship/canal boat–building industry after the War of 1812. The building was adaptively reused and converted to a residence in the early 1970s, one of Essex's first successful historic preservation restoration projects.

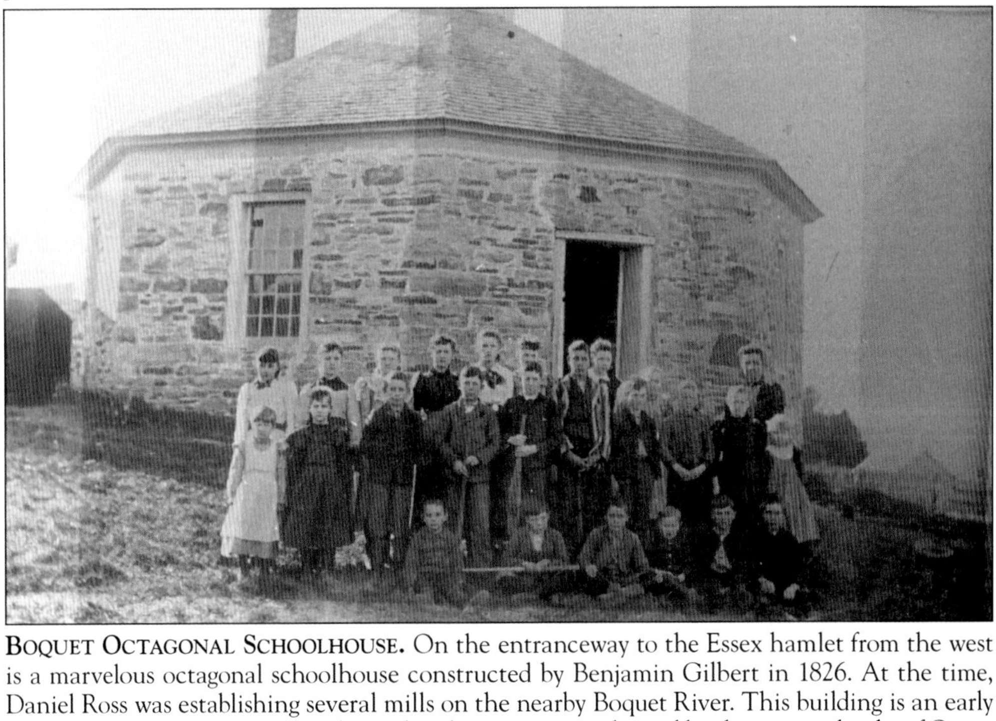

BOQUET OCTAGONAL SCHOOLHOUSE. On the entranceway to the Essex hamlet from the west is a marvelous octagonal schoolhouse constructed by Benjamin Gilbert in 1826. At the time, Daniel Ross was establishing several mills on the nearby Boquet River. This building is an early example of the octagonal fad of the mid-19th century, popularized by the pattern books of Orson Fowler, including *A Home for All* in 1849.

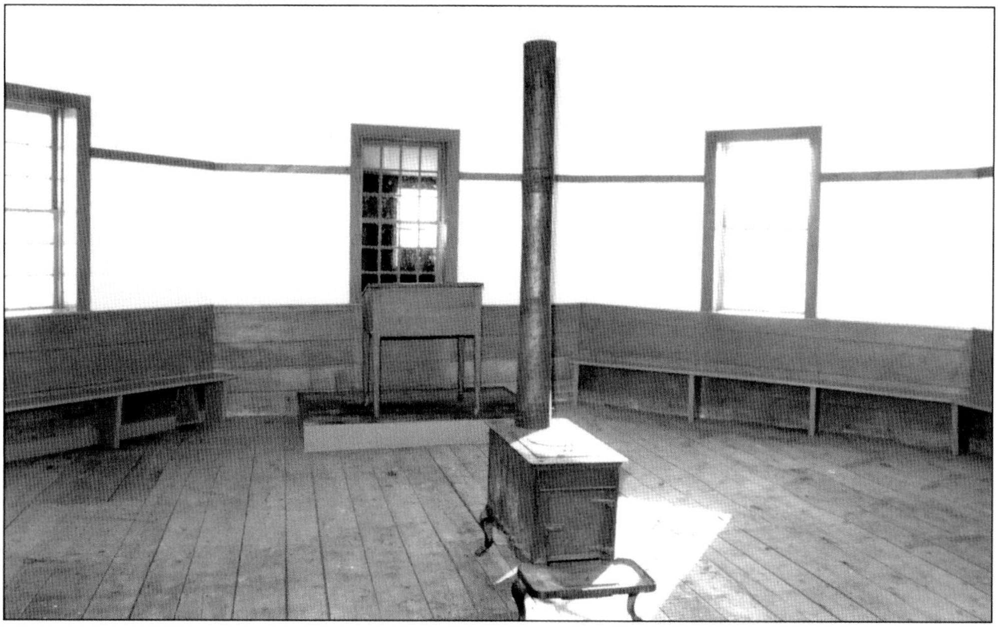

INTERIOR. The interior, seen here re-created in a 1980s restoration, featured wooden benches on the perimeter and a central woodstove. Later students used cast-iron and wood desks, and classes were held here until 1952. The schoolhouse has rubble Potsdam sandstone walls 12 feet thick. The building was restored by ECHO and the Town of Essex. It is listed on the National Register of Historic Places.

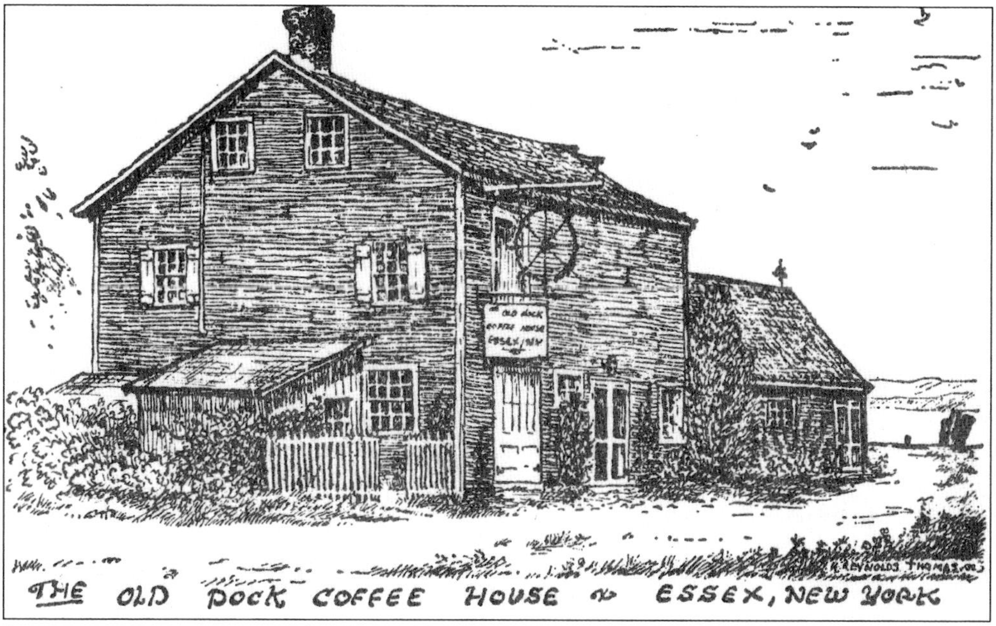

SKETCH OF OLD DOCK. Besides the Noble family, the Daniel Ross family settled in Essex before 1800 and stayed for generations. Just south of the Noble wharf, the Rosses built a dock and dock house. The Rosses competed with the Nobles for control of commerce at ferry crossings over the lake to Vermont. But the real wealth was in the lake commerce of shipping south through the Champlain Canal once that channel was completed in 1823.

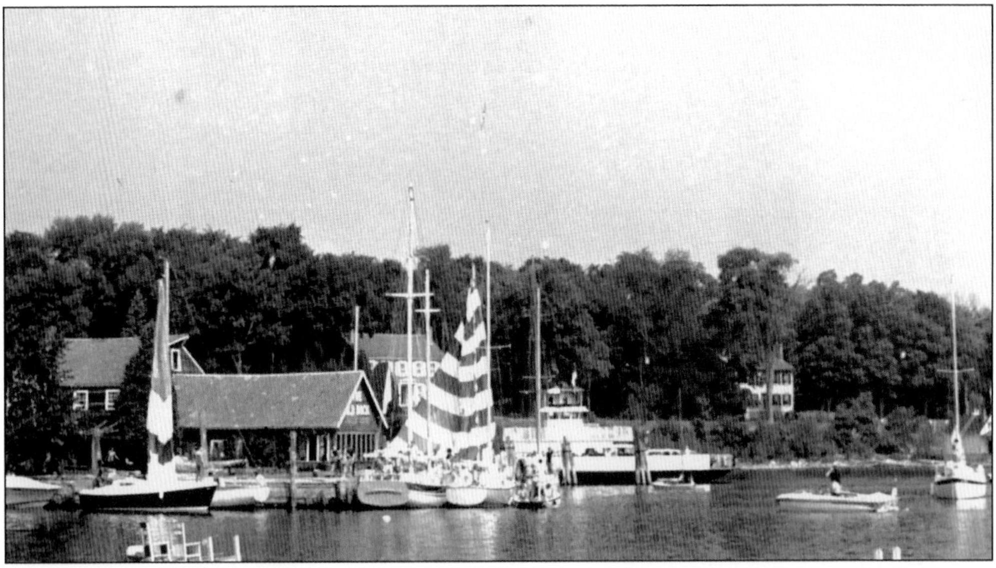

The Old Dock. By the 20th century, with lake shipping long in decline, the Old Dock was largely ignored until its rediscovery by tourism in the 1960s, when it became a coffeehouse. Restored and enlarged with a complete industrial kitchen in the 1980s, the now barn-red Old Dock has prospered as an eatery for over 20 years. The ferry moved over to the former Noble wharf, allowing the entire pier for restaurant use.

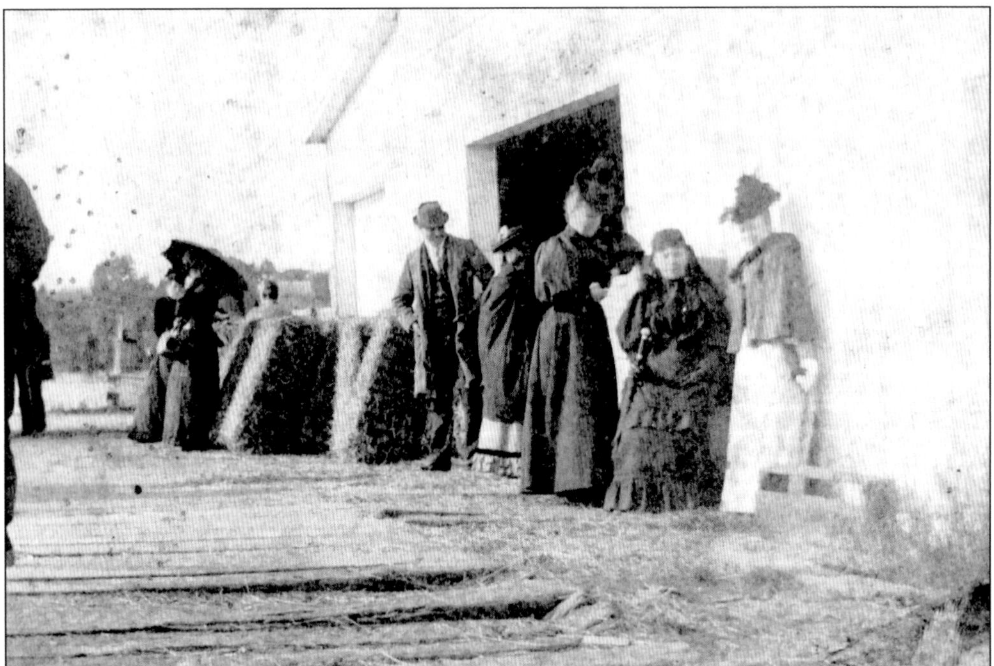

Steamboat Dock. The Old Dock was used mostly for commerce before the steamboats moved there. Here the dock on Beggs Point awaits passengers for the steamboat in an earlier era. (Courtesy of Tilly Close.)

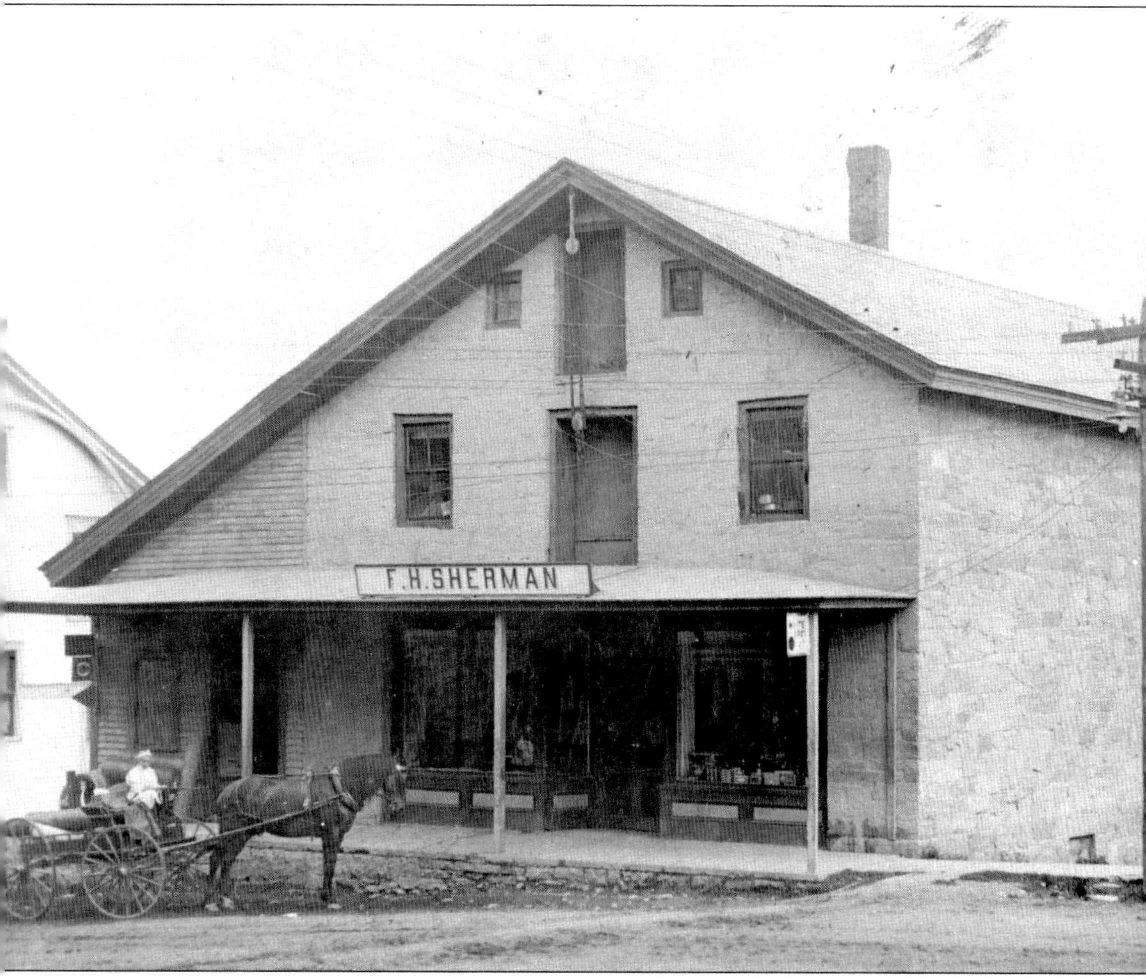

ROSS STORE. On the shore adjacent to the Ross wharf and the dock house, William D. Ross constructed a cut limestone store and law office. Note the little annex to the north, a clapboard enlargement to the original symmetrical Greek Revival design. F. H. Sherman ran a retail business here for many years. Only the Essex Presbyterian Church and Greystone were quarried outside the hamlet from the Frisbie quarry on Willsboro Point. The wires and telephone poles are visible at this period. The Champlain Valley, then not at all remote, received electricity relatively early in the century due to the availability of hydroelectric power. The Boquet River power-generating plant was in operation by the late 1890s. Nearby Elizabethtown had electricity in 1899. In the town of Essex, it is documented that the village was lit by electricity in 1905. A recent discovery was made at Rosslyn, the large Greek Revival house of William D. Ross, where documentation was found in the form of a note engraved on a slate near the old electrical entrance at the south basement window. It reads, "First electrical service in house Connected up June 13, 1908 by Guy H. Mason."

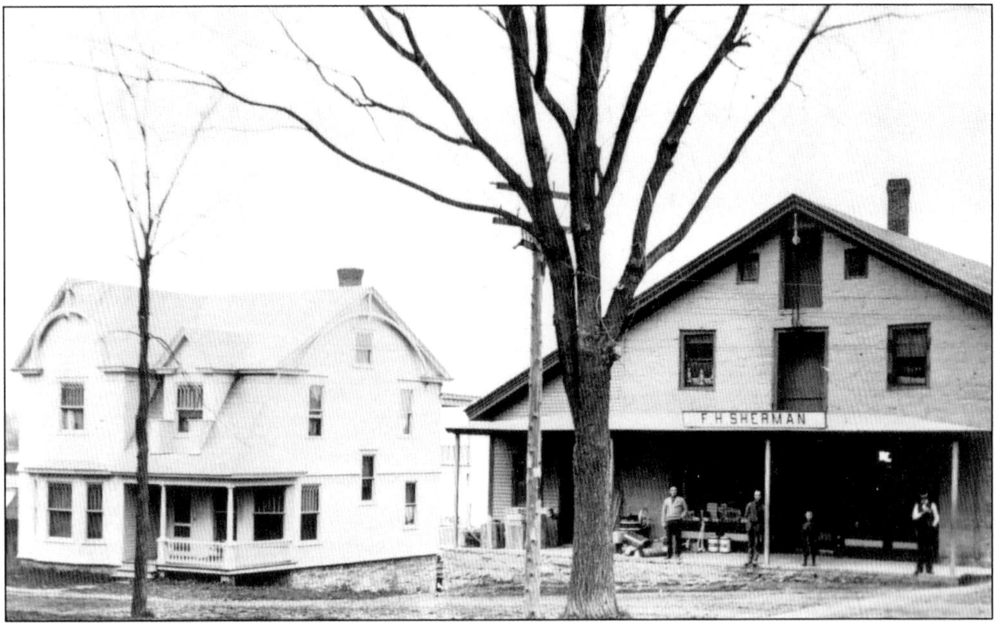

F. H. Sherman Store. In the 21st century, there is frequent debate about burying telephone wires. It is interesting to note that there have probably been poles with wires in Essex since at least the Civil War. Essex was an important town on the north–south New York-to-Montreal route and hosted the telegraph lines even before the railroad was completed. Telephone service came in 1910 to Essex, as this photograph shows the numerous lines and poles are all in place.

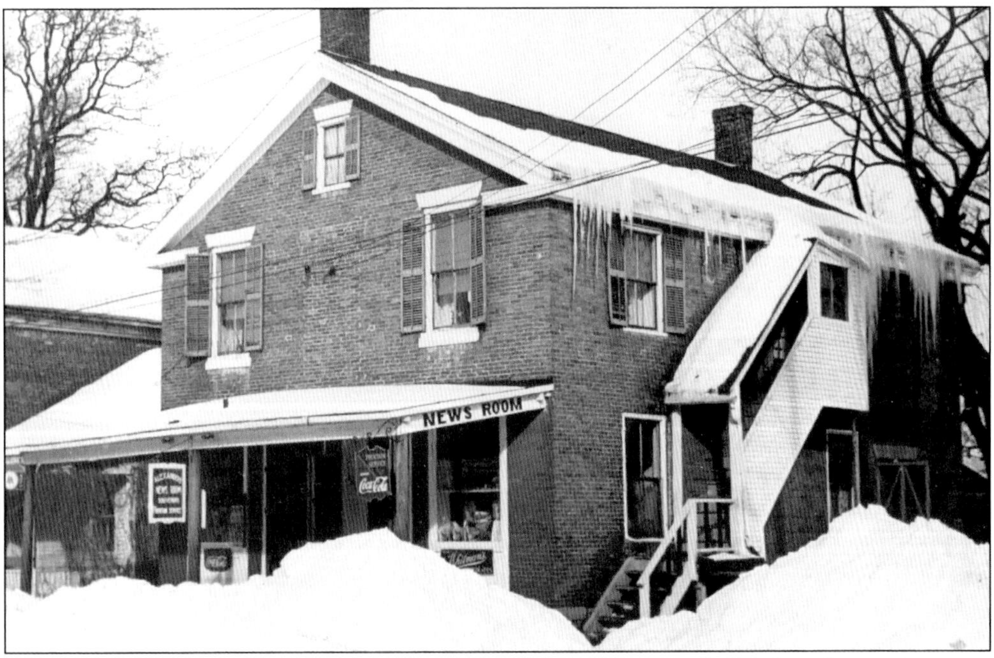

Alexander's News Room. A classic example of the gable end of a roofline facing the street is demonstrated on the front of this store. Without the later shed porch (no doubt a worthy addition due to the annual snowfall), the front elevation appeared, in a rural manner, as a Greek temple.

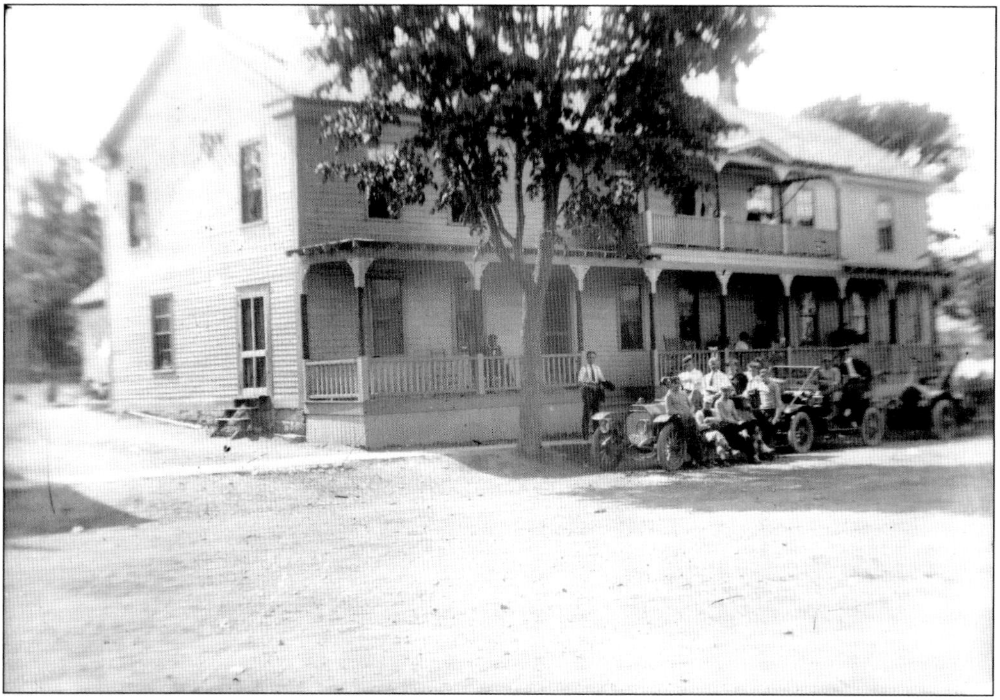

ADIRONDACK HOUSE. Daniel Ross built the southern half of this building in the Federal style in about 1790 to serve as a tavern and inn for the newly emerging cross-lake traffic from Vermont. Ross partnered in the ferry service sailing across the lake, and his was the other prominent family in Essex along with the Nobles.

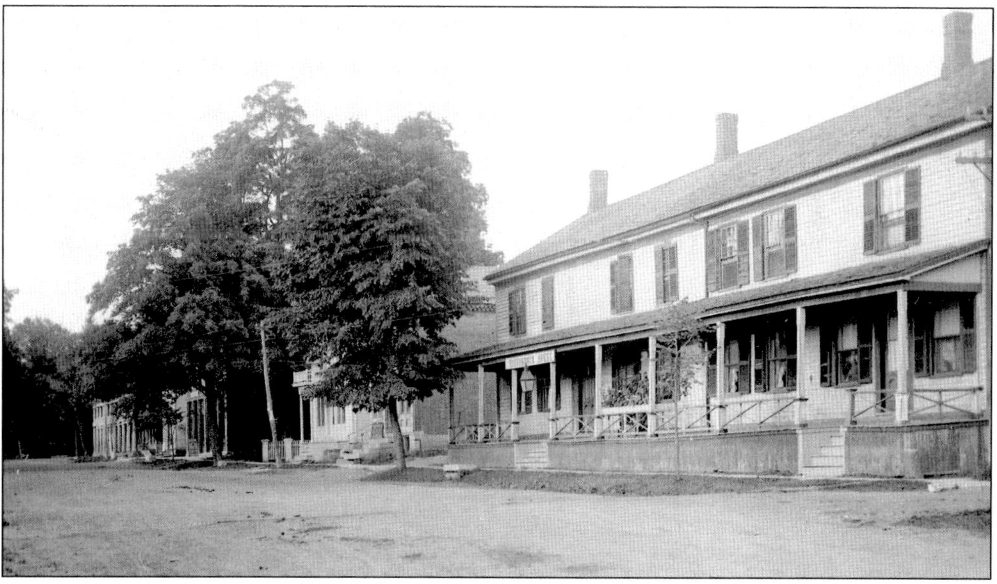

WRIGHT'S INN. Daniel Wright purchased the property by 1799, giving his name to the structure as Wright's Inn. The north section may have been completed in the early 1820s when traffic again boomed from the opening of the Champlain Canal that connected Lake Champlain to the Hudson River. A large Victorian part two-story porch eventually spanned both sections, giving them a uniform look.

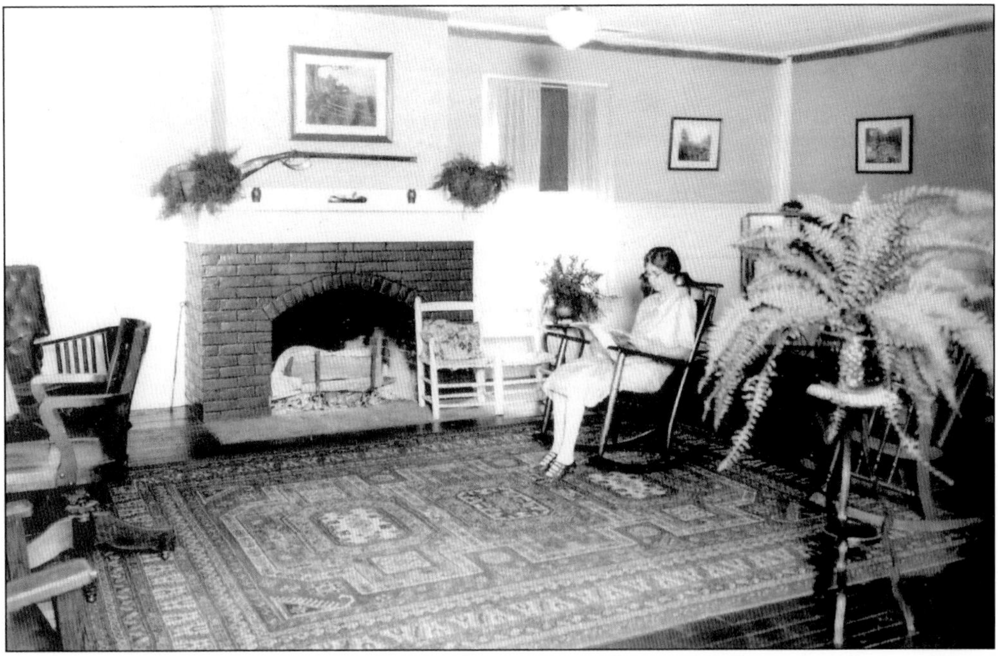

ADIRONDACK HOUSE INTERIOR. The Van Ornams owned several different buildings in Essex. At one point, they ran the inn then known as the Adirondack House. Daughter Geraldine Van Ornam is in the rocking chair. The Oriental rug and ferns transitioned from the Victorian to the Edwardian era.

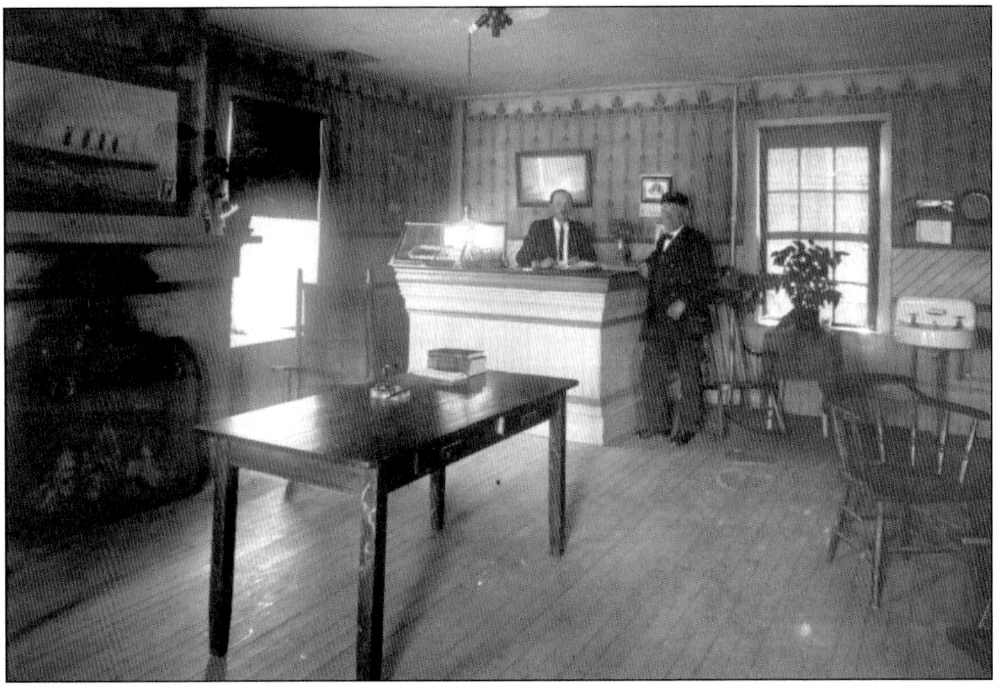

INNKEEPER. C. E. Van Ornam is in charge of the desk during an earlier era. A steamship, much like those of the White Star Line, is pictured over the mantel. No doubt the inn liked the associations with glamorous travel.

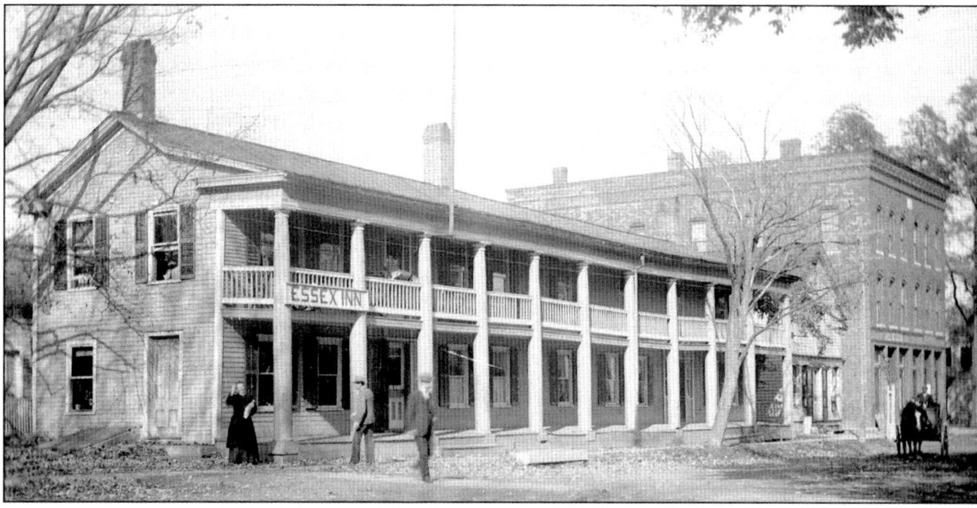

PENDANT. At the other end of the long block that forms the west side of Main Street is the Essex Inn. Close inspection of the entranceways reveals fine Federal detailing belying the inn's construction as a five-bay residence (southern portion) in about 1810. In a similar manner to the Wright's Inn and probably for the same reasons, the inn was enlarged in the 1820s. However, the prominent visual difference is the large Greek Revival porch added across the entire front about 1835.

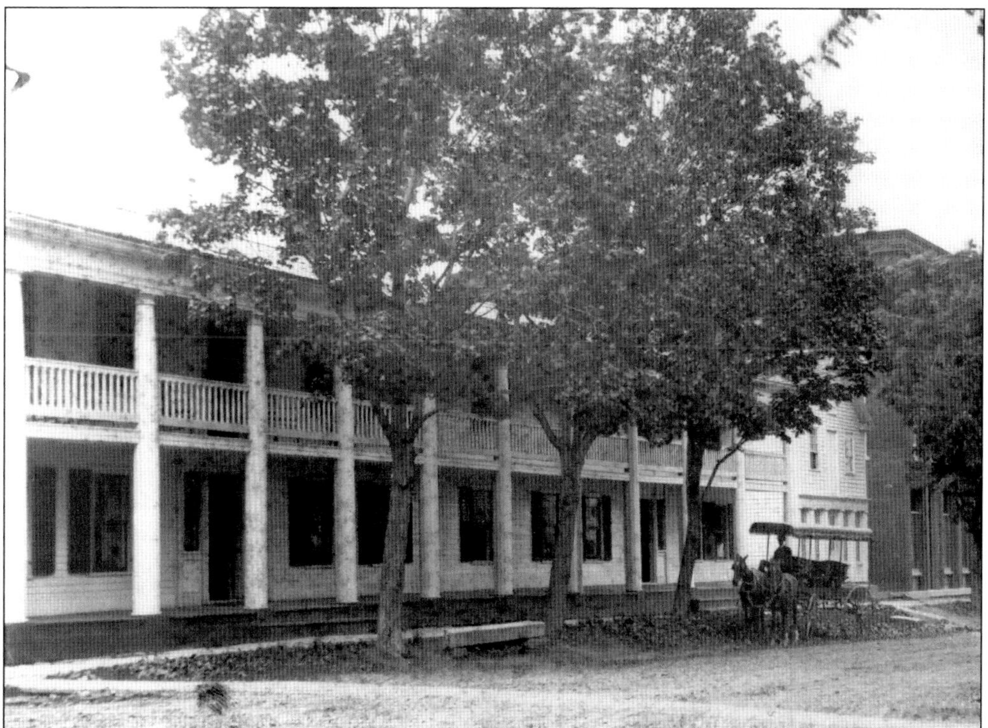

ESSEX INN. Here is the Essex Inn with a pair of horses and a fringe surrey carriage in front. The brick block is visible at the rear. No lower railing existed at the inn until modern safety codes forced the addition of a comparable low balustrade in the 20th century.

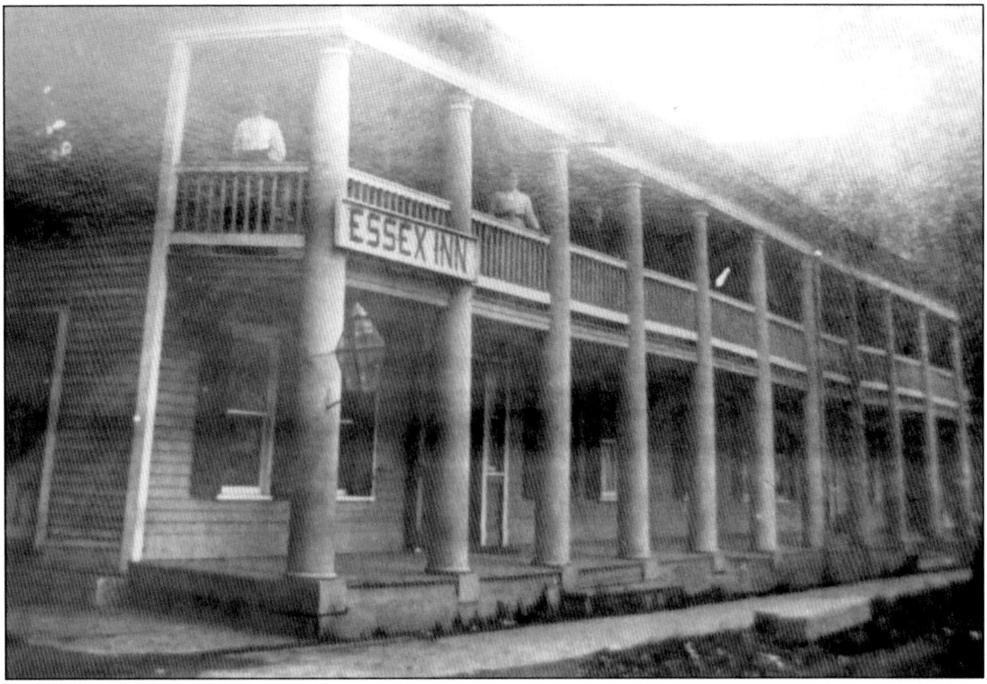

EARLY OIL LAMP LIGHTING. Oil lamps were the only form of lighting in Essex before electricity eventually arrived just after the dawn of the 20th century. The Essex Inn is the oldest inn still operating, despite a lapse of 50 years when it was used as a private residence.

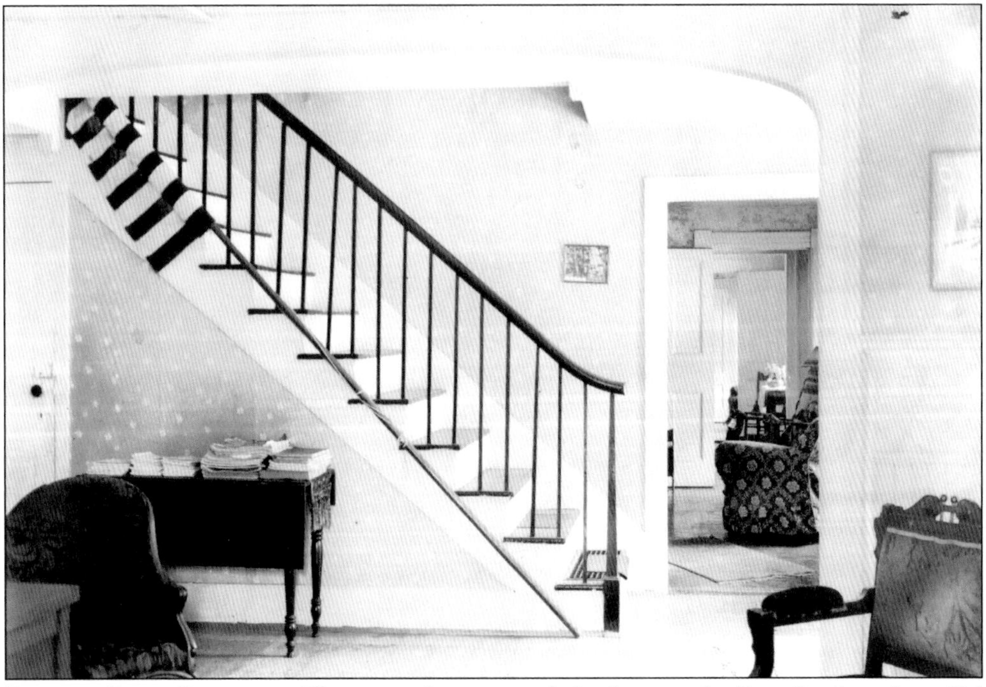

FEDERAL-STYLE STAIRCASE. The original structure of what became the Essex Inn has a beautiful staircase in the refined Federal taste. An elegant arched entranceway leads to the south parlor. Notice the flagpole with a flag stored alongside the staircase.

Six

Village Life and Country Life

The buildings of historic Essex are a tangible presence of the mid-19th-century era of prosperity in America. The Greek Revival architecture reminds one of the people who tried to live the classical ideal and develop a republic worthy of a democracy. Essex has been preserved for two centuries in its rural setting complete with its heroic tale of economic success and the embodiment of the first true national American style.

Just at the moment of westward expansion in America initiated by the opening of the Erie Canal in 1825, the Greek Revival style of architecture swept throughout Upstate New York into Ohio and Indiana. Americans dappled their hills with the porticoes of temples, their white painted woodwork standing out in the countryside. The Jacksonian era of successful commerce and canal building made Americans feel accomplished and civilized. Place-names across the country literally echoed the classical past, with diversity emphasizing the national expansion. There were Greek Revival town names in most extant states. For example, the town name Athens is found in Georgia, New York, Florida, Missouri, Kentucky, Alabama, and Maine. Similarly, the name Troy is found in New York, Vermont, South Carolina, Illinois, New Hampshire, and Wisconsin. As is apparent, the geographical breadth of the classical revival spanned the South, the North, and the Midwest.

The Greek Revival was not merely a copy of the past but a spirit of the times, symbolizing the new independence of America by associating it with the heroic struggles of the contemporary Greek revolution. The style filtered into the middle classes by the dissemination of pattern books so that master builders could copy the works of architects like Asher Benjamin and Minard Lafever.

One of the remarkable assets of Essex is the adaptation of academic styles into a vernacular form known locally as Essex style, such as the distinctive sunburst motif in the pediments of houses. While a regional variation is evident, the motif itself is actually derived from the fluted spandrel of the Federal period. Its use in pedimented gables of the Greek Revival is an interesting regional development, celebrated today by residents of the town and used as the official logo of Historic Essex.

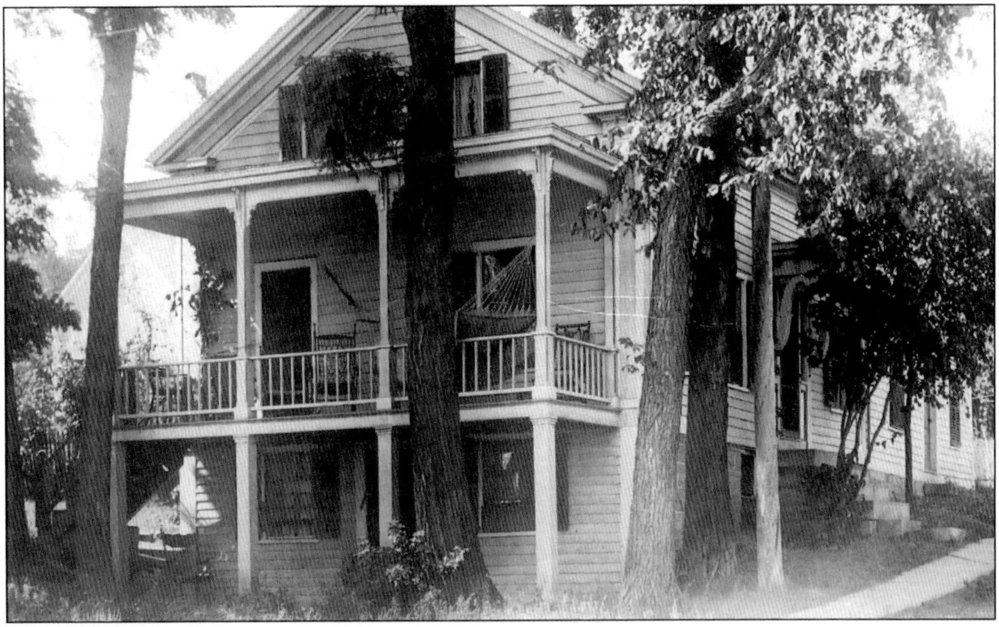

BULL RUN COTTAGE. Essex sits on a limestone ledge that gently slopes toward the lakeshore. This small 1840 Greek Revival cottage takes advantage of its siting to give an appearance of a three-story home with a two-story porch. The main entrance on the side street reveals that the house is essentially a story and a half. The hammock and rocking chairs are included as local summer furnishings.

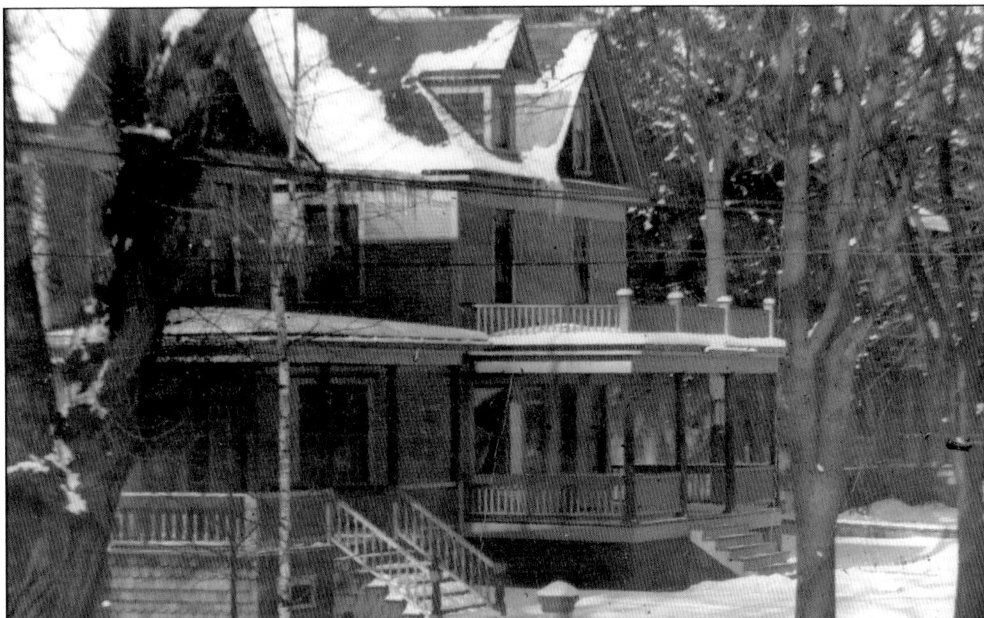

AMERICAN FOURSQUARE. An exciting residential boom, at least for Essex, was the construction of two neighboring houses just after 1900. These residences were designed in what has become known as American Foursquare style. The one in the center has been sensitively restored into the first environmentally green residence in town.

EDWARDS STORE. The ideal commercial building in Essex is one where the owner lives on the second floor and the business is operated in the first-floor space. Most commercial buildings in town were constructed to function in this manner, and a few still do so. The roofline of the gable here on the Edwards old brick store of about 1836 is ornamented in brick and termed a corbeled cornice. Henry Edwards was a tailor.

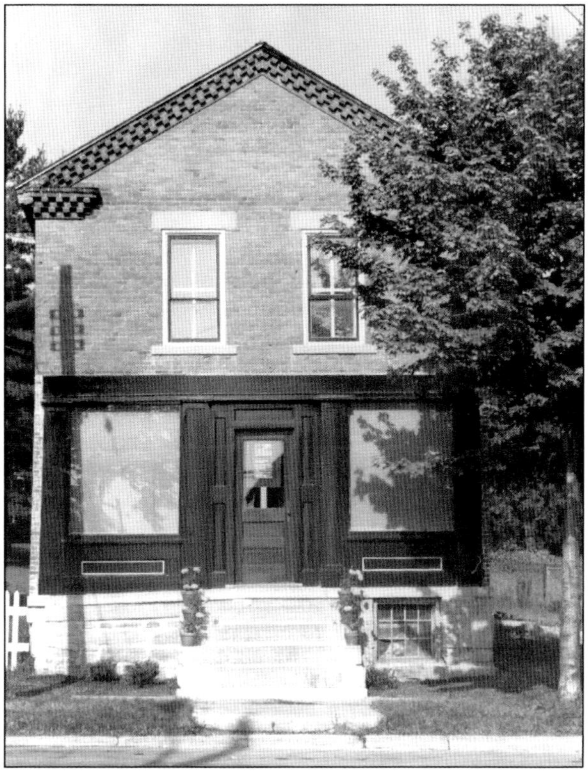

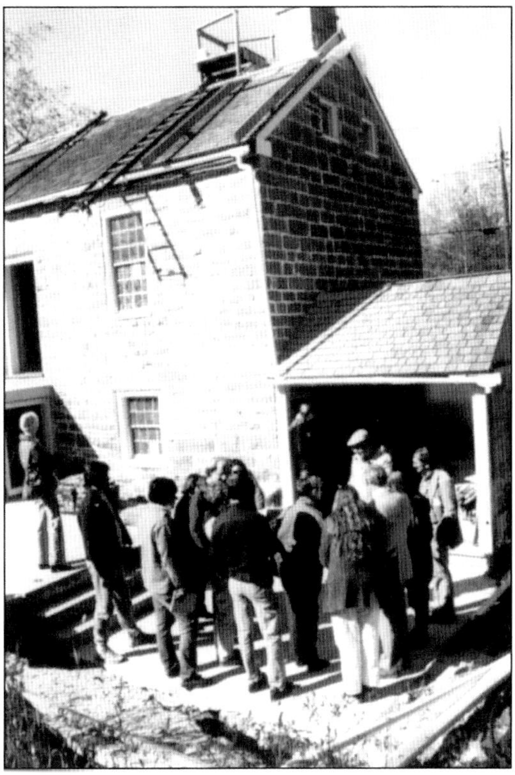

NOBLE TENANT HOUSE. The Noble family tenant house was built by P. P. Billings in 1828 and maintained by the Noble family for well over 100 years. The gray limestone was quarried immediately behind the house as was the stone for so many of Essex's building needs in the period. Under the guidance of restoration architect John I. Mesick, a detailed professional restoration has been ongoing for many years.

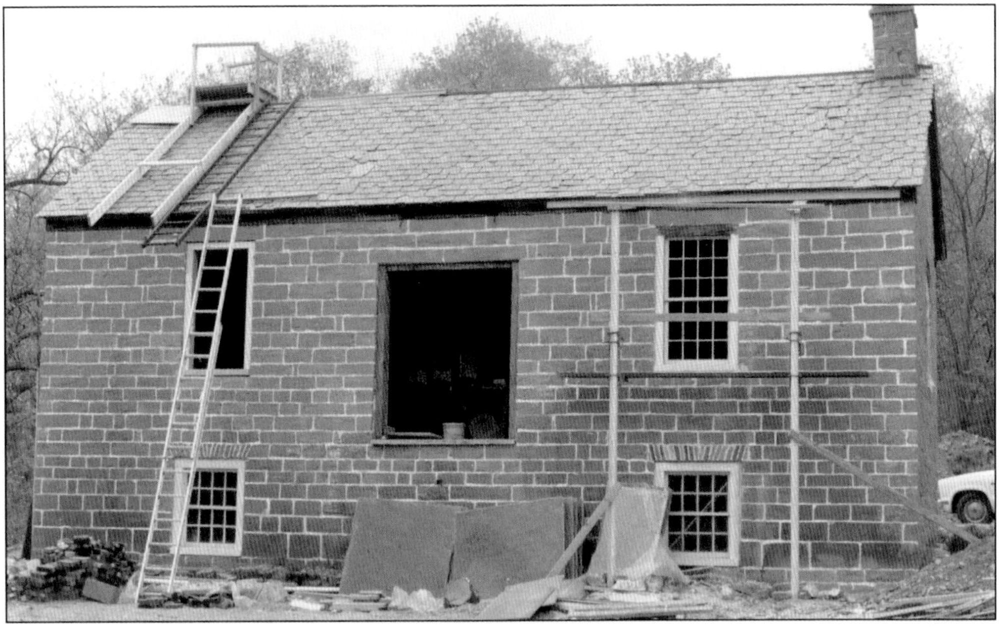

Meticulous Restoration. Local builders and craftsmen designed the porch and helped restore many of the missing architectural elements to the Billings/Noble cottage. The stonework indicates a solidity and permanence its owners wished to project. An inordinate number of stone buildings are on Main Street, with six clustered around the Noble family's Greystone, while the others are associated with the Nobles (Gould house, Noble tenant cottage).

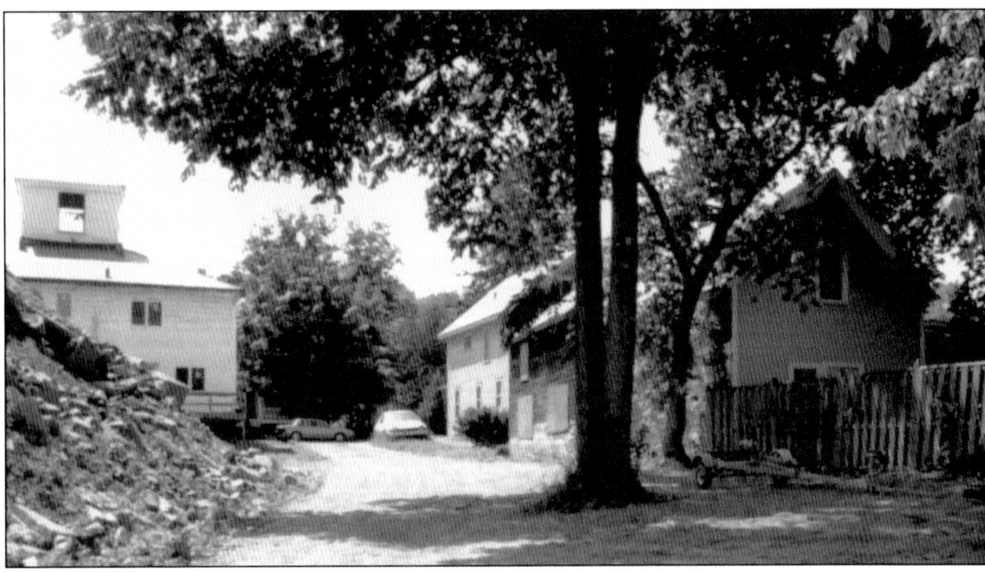

Essex Livery Stable. The barn on the right remains as a reminder of the horse transportation era when it functioned as a livery stable. The Cupola House on the left was restored in the 1990s and features fine gardens and elegant interiors. The front facade has a paneled entranceway with flat pilasters on either side.

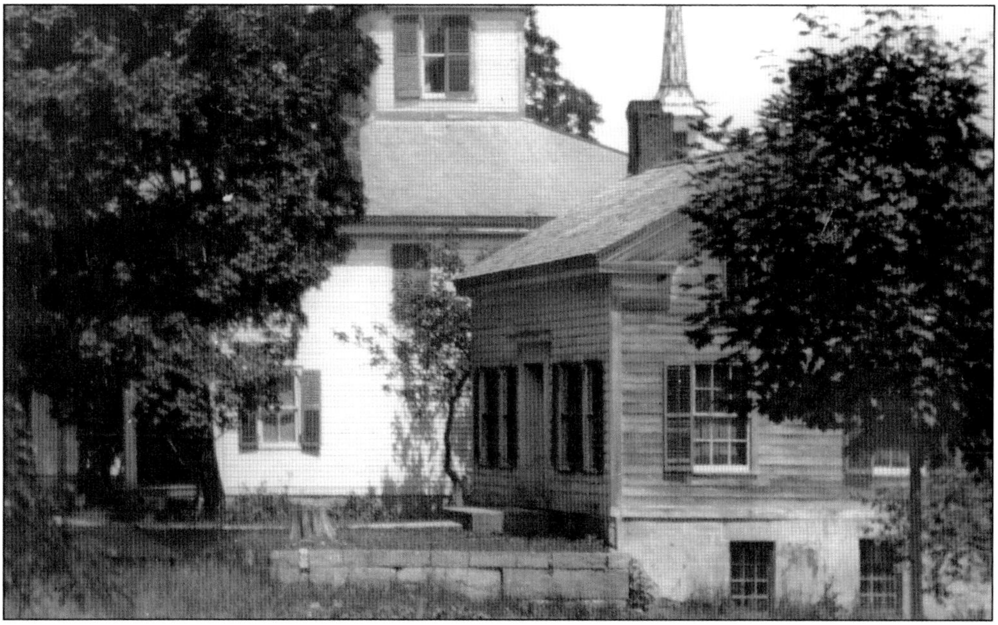

CUPOLA HOUSE AND 1813 HOUSE. Known as the 1813 house, its center hall entrance and five full bays facing the street give this small house presence. Like several Essex homes, the sloping terrain affords a full story below that is aboveground, with an external entrance to gardens. Behind it, the now-called Cupola House is a fine example of the vernacular Italianate style. It features a broad hipped roof surmounted by a large lantern or cupola.

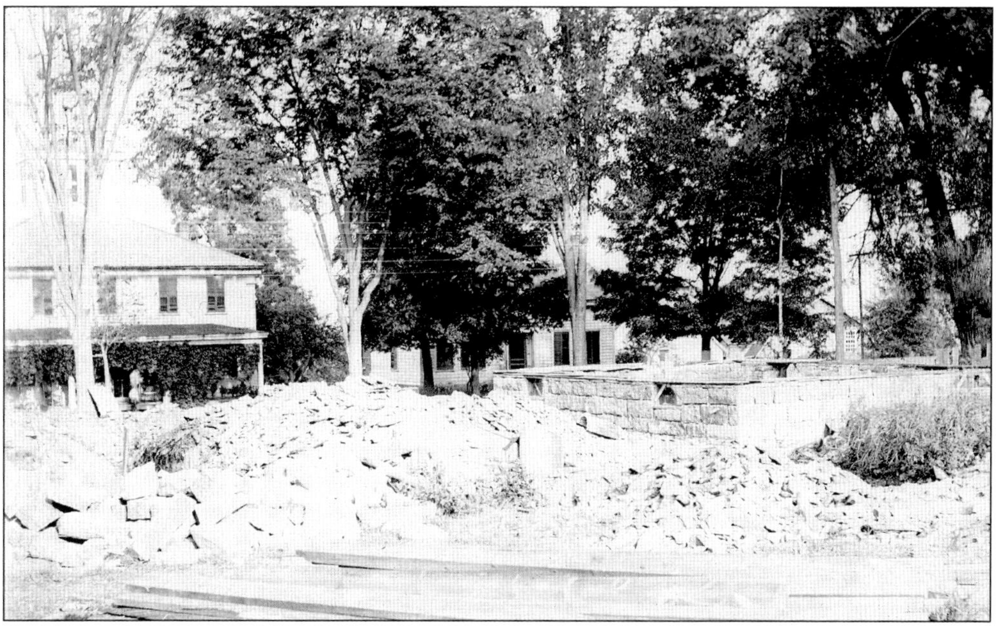

BUILDING BOOM OF 1900. Once it was thought that there was a dramatic building boom in Essex around 1900. In town, there are 13 American Foursquare buildings, including this pair. An ashlar foundation formed the basis of a house very different from the Greek Revival style nearly a century later. They usually had broad front porches and a third floor devoted to servant quarters.

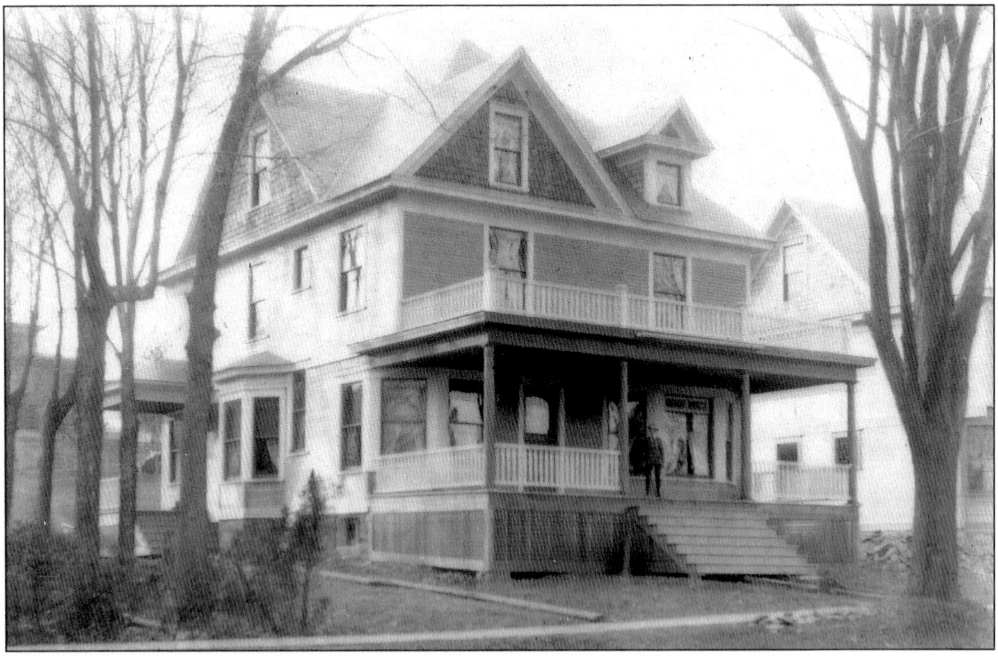

COMPLETED FOURSQUARE. The house from the previous photograph is shown completed here. For the first time, large plate-glass windows allowed for the near elimination of small panes and the absence of exterior blinds or shutters. Gables and dormers allowed the third floor to be used as servant quarters.

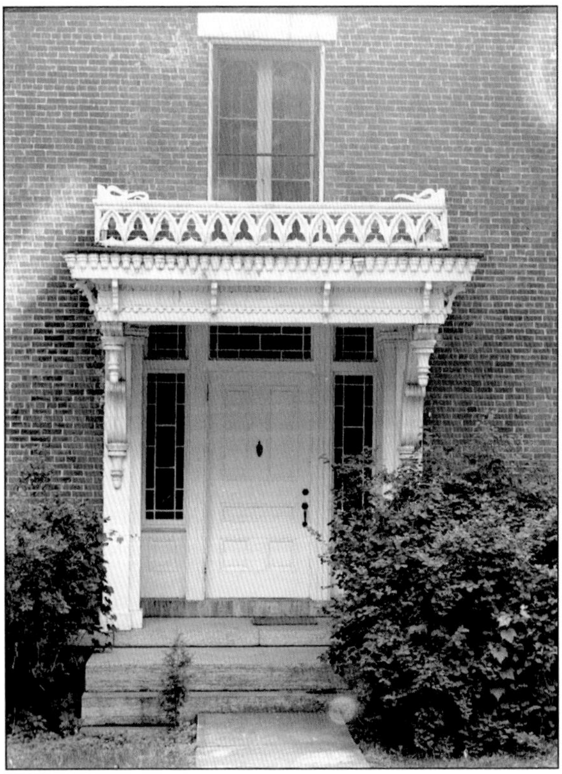

ITALIANATE DESIGN. Henry Gould, the brother of John Gould who built the wonderful stone classical house just across Main Street, constructed his own fine mansion of brick in the newer Italianate design about 1840. A Gothic Revival parapet with trefoils enlivens the entranceway.

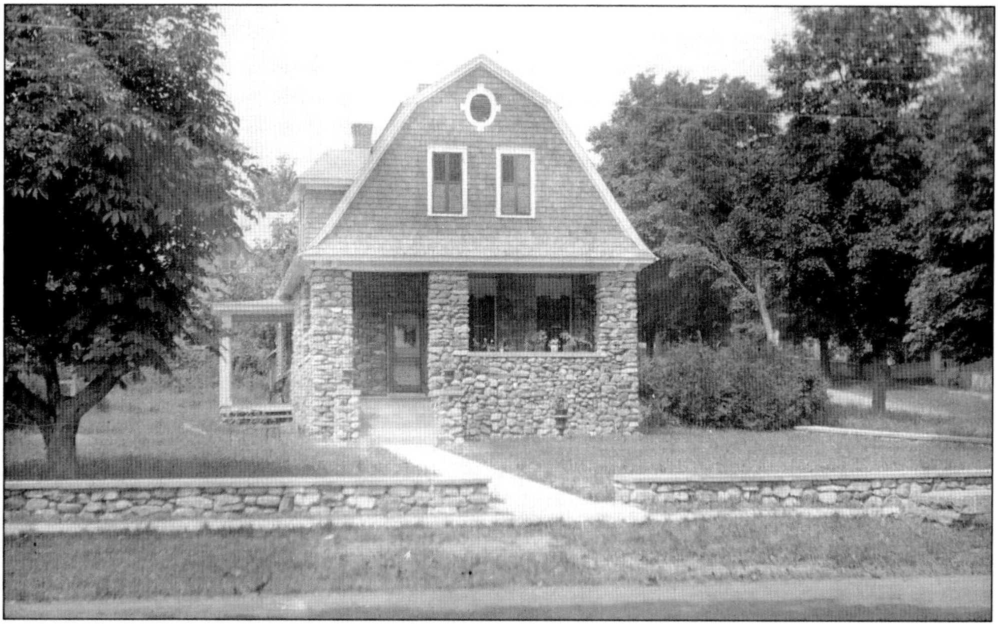

FIELDSTONE HOUSE, GAMBREL ROOF HOUSES. Several gambrel roof homes are noticeable, but when counted, there are only three gambrel roof houses, one each on Main, Elm, and Beggs Point Streets. On Main Street, the earlier cut stone structure that was part of the Palmer-Havens gardens was removed and the stones used elsewhere. Then a 1909 house with a gambrel roof was built noticeably of fieldstone in the arts and crafts tradition.

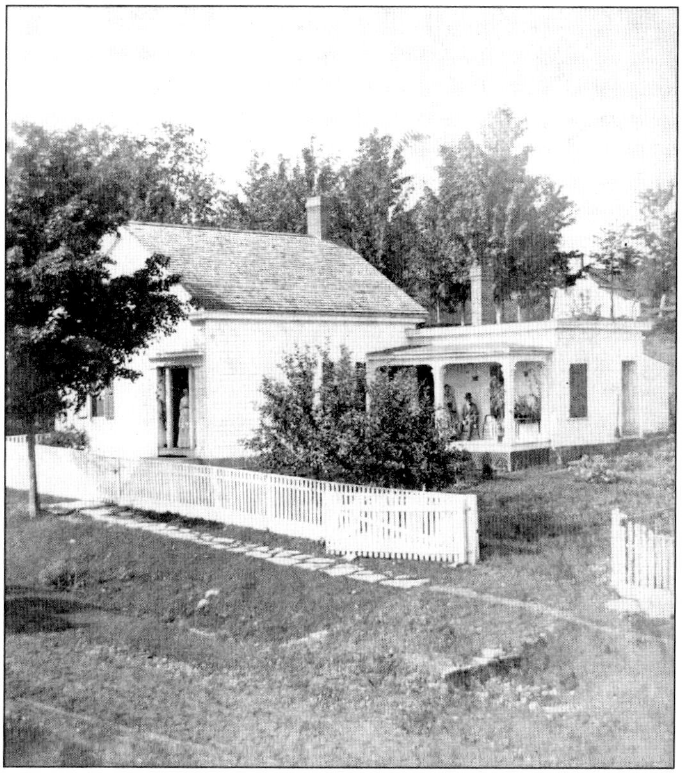

ELM STREET RESIDENCE. A wonderful surviving stereopticon card shows an Elm Street residence with its early dark-trim Victorian paint scheme and its outbuildings. The limestone sidewalk and picket fence add to the period details.

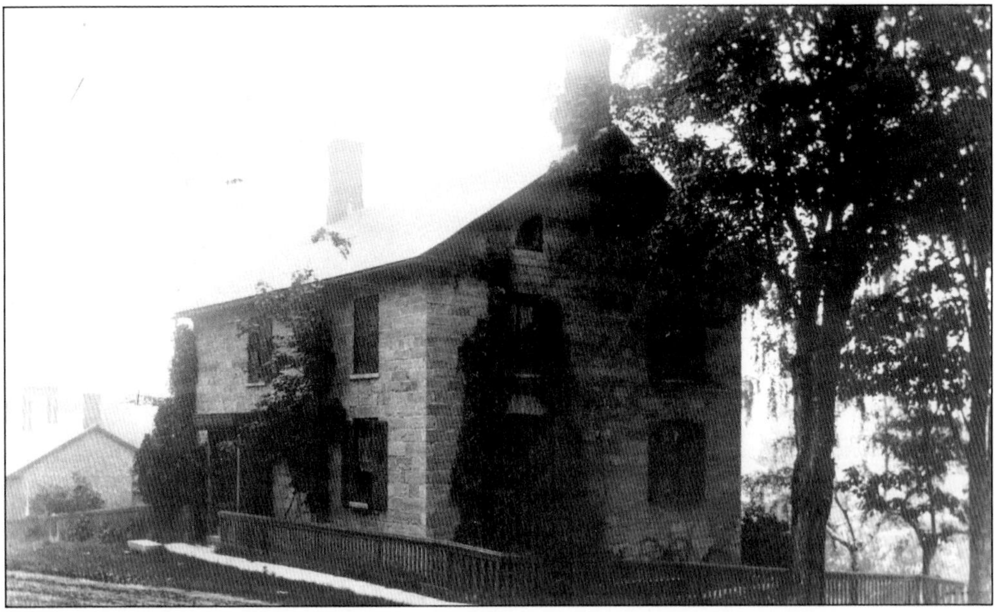

Shumway House, c. 1890. Despite the fact that a stone quarry has long existed in both Essex and nearby Willsboro, only 12 out of 142, or 8 percent, of the buildings are made of stone. All are made of the local limestone, popularly called Essex bluestone. Stone has always been more costly and more impressive and imposing than other materials. The Shumway house is one of the few that is not associated with the Nobles.

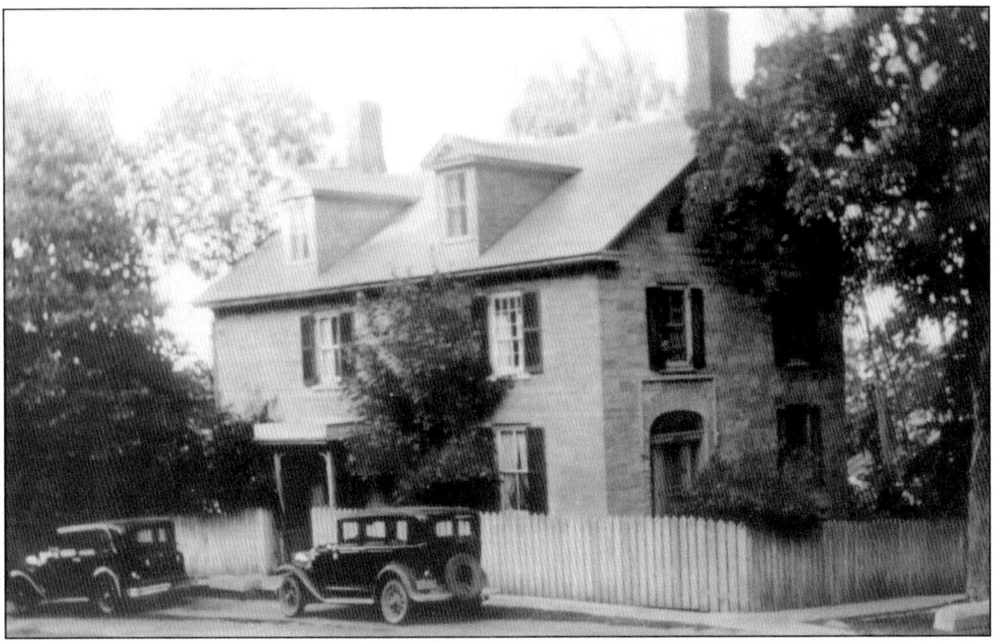

Shumway House, c. 1925. One visible alteration in the Shumway house is the addition of a pair of dormers to the roofline. Dormers can increase the usable space in the attic, making an area suitable for servants or, more in the present, guest rooms. In the 1920s postcard, the dormers are completed.

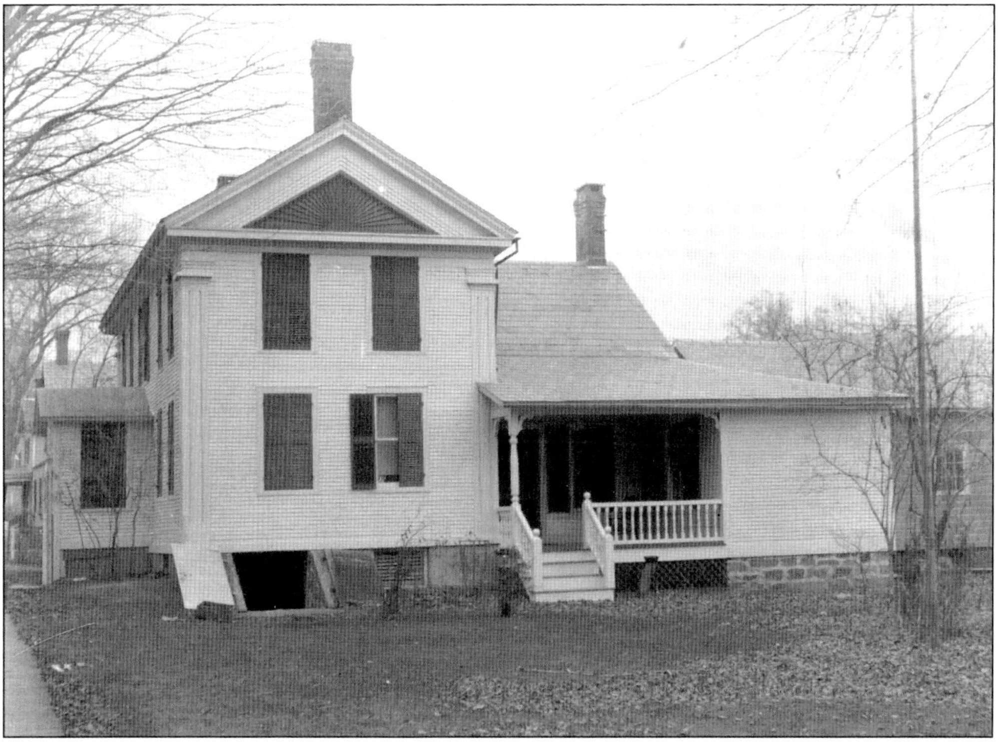

ESSEX SUNBURST MOTIF. The adopted symbol of Essex, the sunburst motif, can be seen in a splendid example on the gable of the roof here. The refined fluting matches the subtle pilaster on the corners of the house. The sunburst motif has been the logo of the Essex Fire Department, the art gallery, and various shops. Recently the new graphic design for Historic Essex incorporated the sunburst architectural motif.

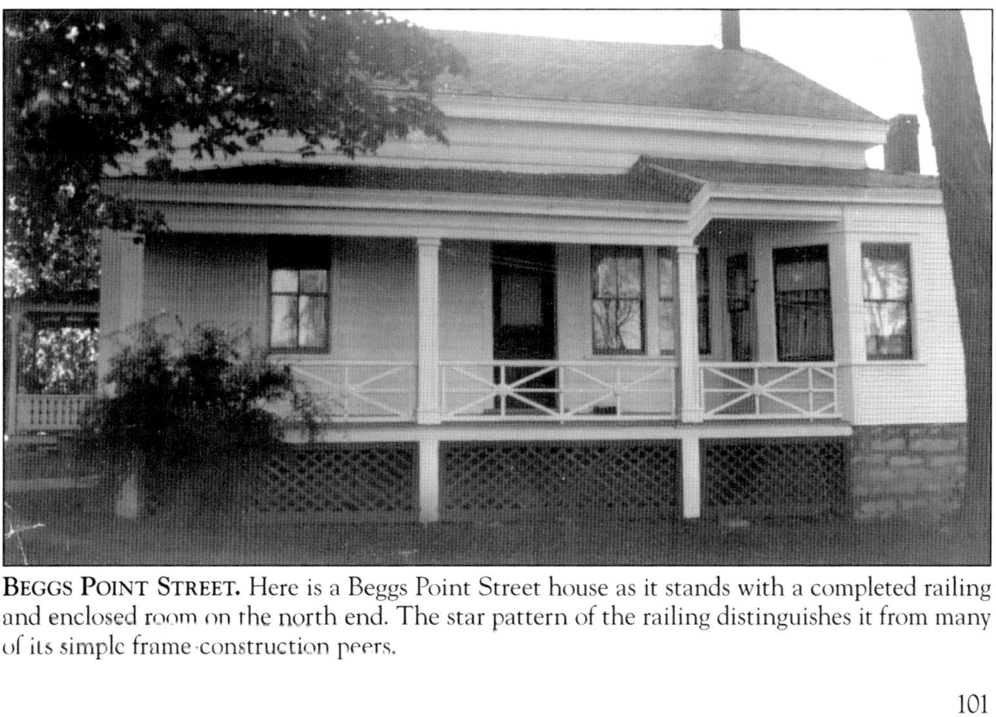

BEGGS POINT STREET. Here is a Beggs Point Street house as it stands with a completed railing and enclosed room on the north end. The star pattern of the railing distinguishes it from many of its simple frame-construction peers.

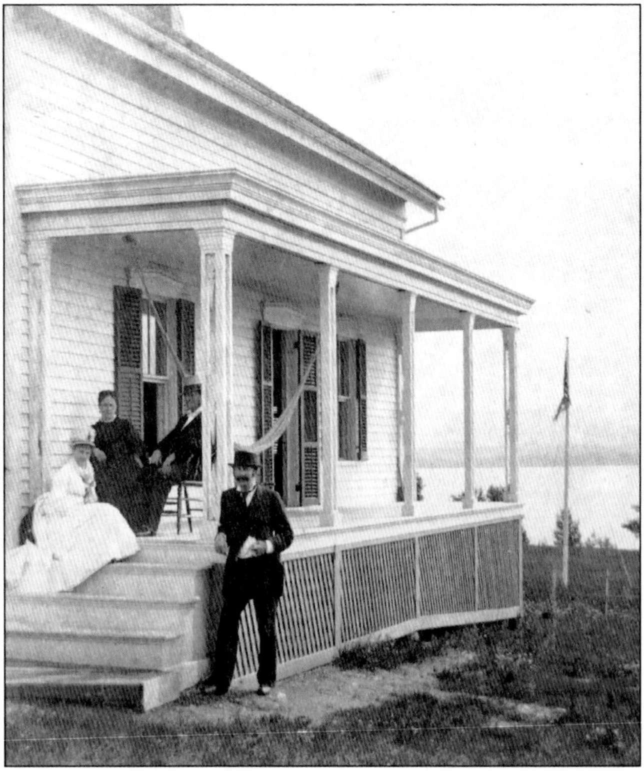

Earlier View. This is the same house as in the previous picture but in the 19th century, with an open porch and simple gable-end Greek Revival design. Less landscaping and no neighbor to the north allowed a lake view at the time.

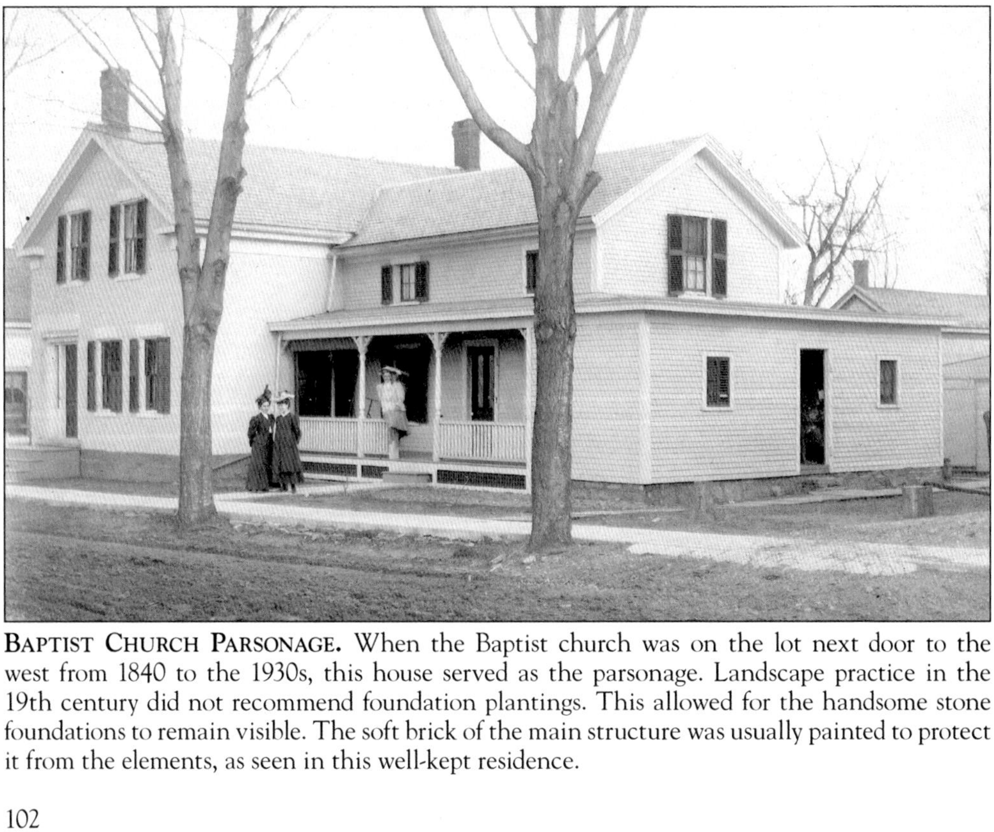

Baptist Church Parsonage. When the Baptist church was on the lot next door to the west from 1840 to the 1930s, this house served as the parsonage. Landscape practice in the 19th century did not recommend foundation plantings. This allowed for the handsome stone foundations to remain visible. The soft brick of the main structure was usually painted to protect it from the elements, as seen in this well-kept residence.

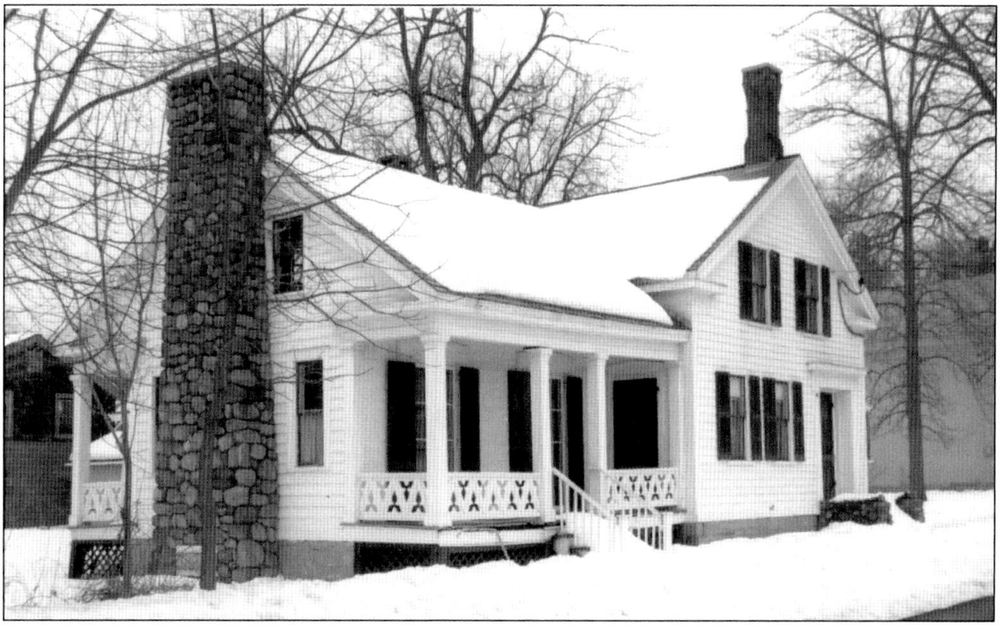

GOTHIC PORCH DETAIL. The finest feature of this Beggs Point house is the Gothic trefoil detail on the porch railing. The Gothic Revival came into prominence in the 1830s in England, where it was thought to be the only proper English style. In the mid-19th century, Gothic was one of the popular common tastes promoted by Alexander Jackson Davis and Andrew Jackson Downing in their widely circulated and influential style books.

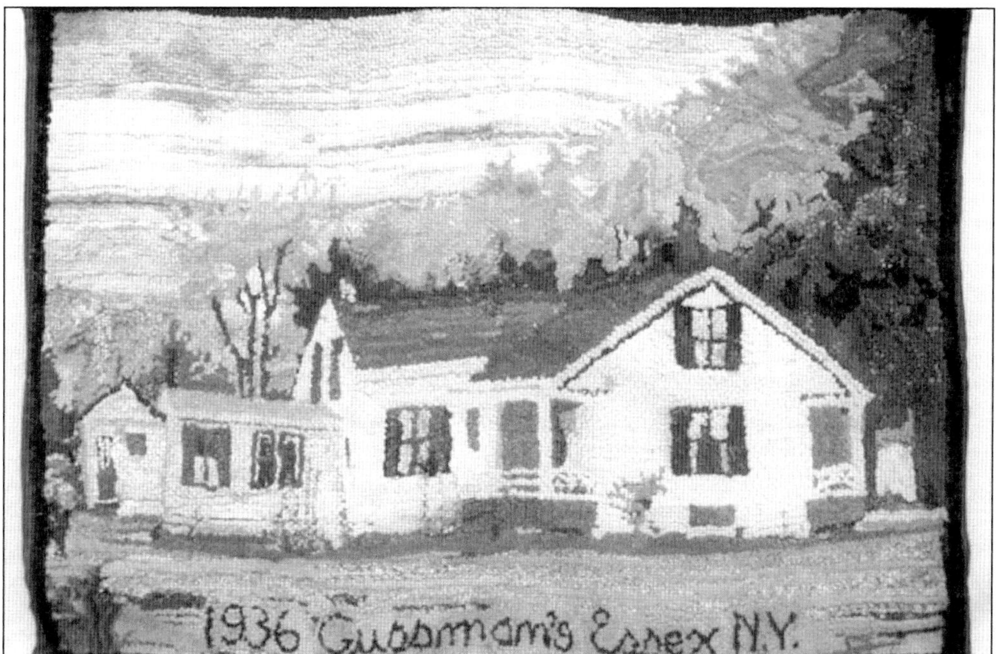

FOLK ART RUG. This is a splendid folk art hooked rug from the above house, made during the Depression years. The massive fieldstone chimney there today had apparently not been constructed yet. It must have been too difficult to hook the detail of the Gothic railing.

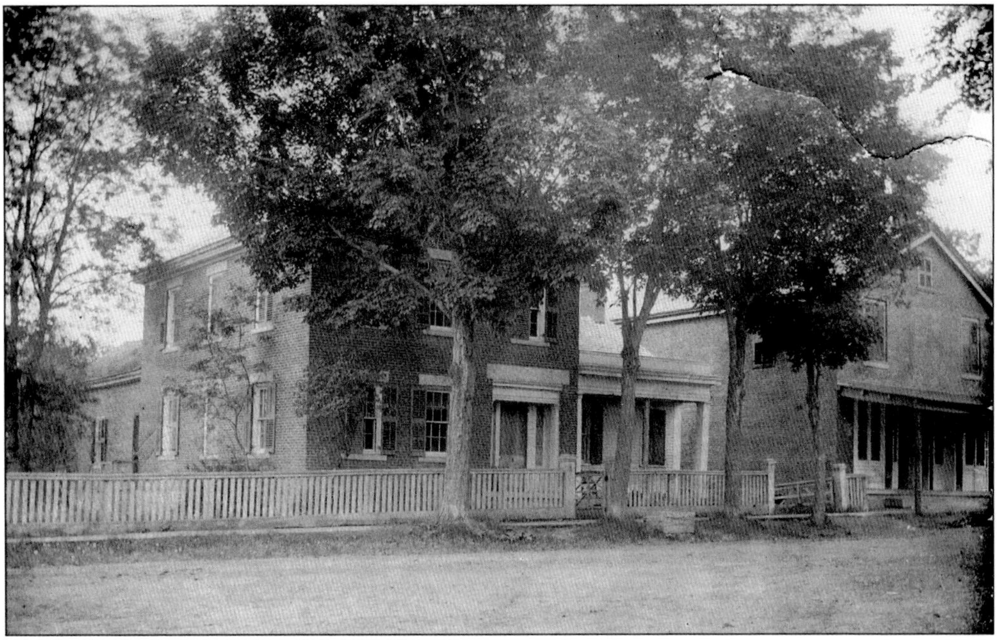

THE MANSE. Originally a private residence, this brick Greek Revival building was given to the Essex Presbyterian Church for use as a rectory. Ever since, it has been known as the Manse and has housed church appointees and staff. The original fence is lost.

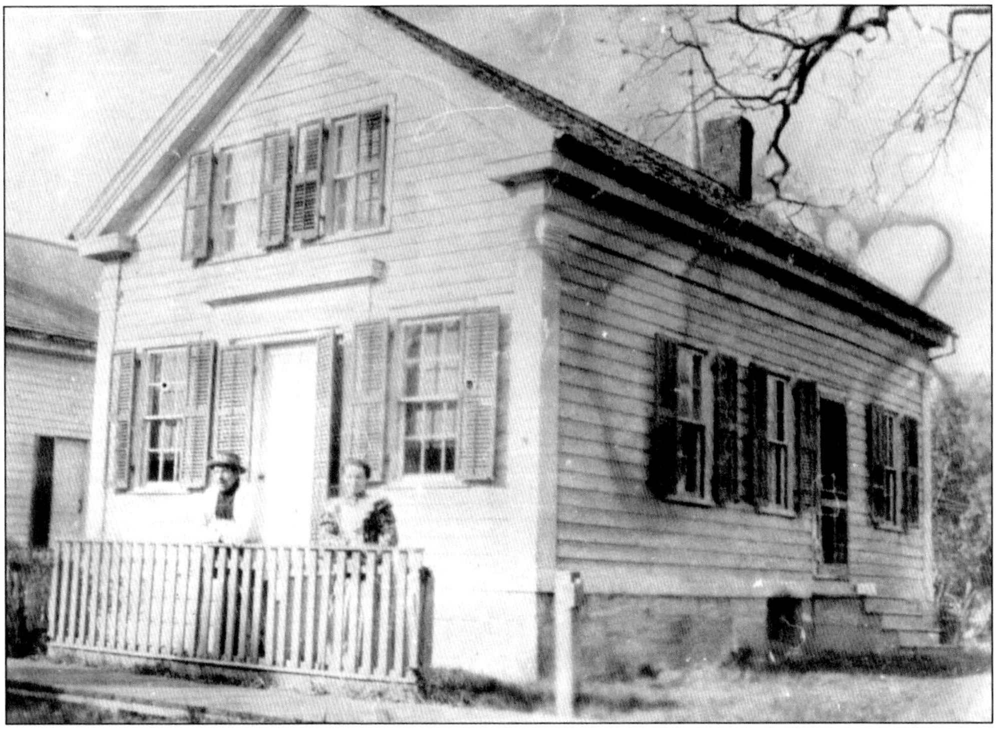

EARLY PALMER HOUSE. The earliest known photograph of the Palmer house, located on Orchard Street, shows it as a simple Greek Revival structure with the gable end facing Orchard Street. Somewhat unusual are the two windows so closely placed together in the gable.

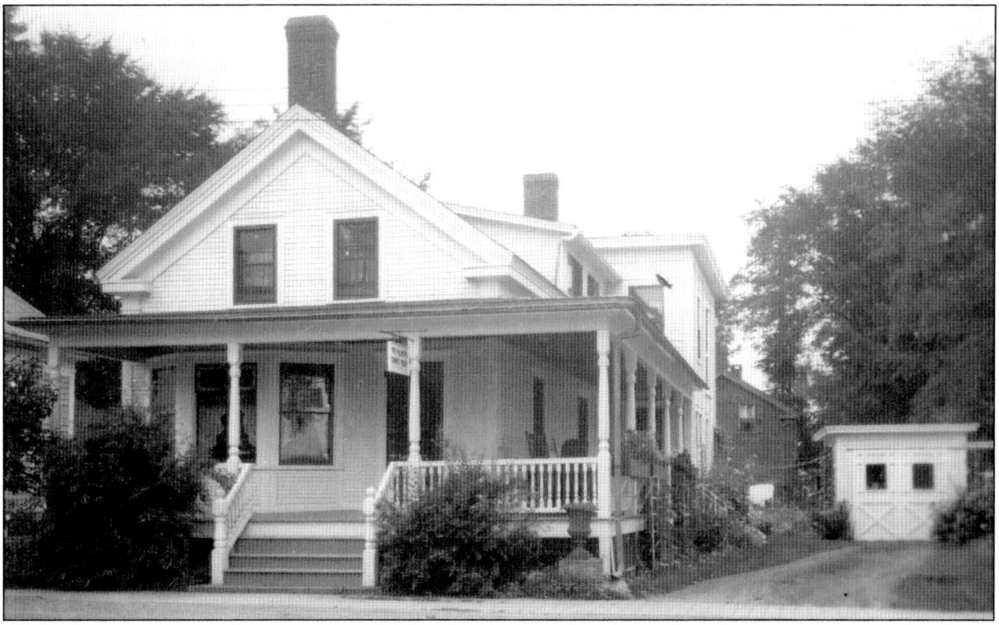

Palmer House Additions. In the early 20th century, the good fortunes of the Palmers enabled them to construct several additions. Amazingly, the records of all the construction projects survive and enable researchers to learn the names of all the contractors, suppliers, and builders in the projects. The front door has been moved to allow the construction of a bay window. The addition in the rear of the Palmer house allowed for more room for family and summer guests.

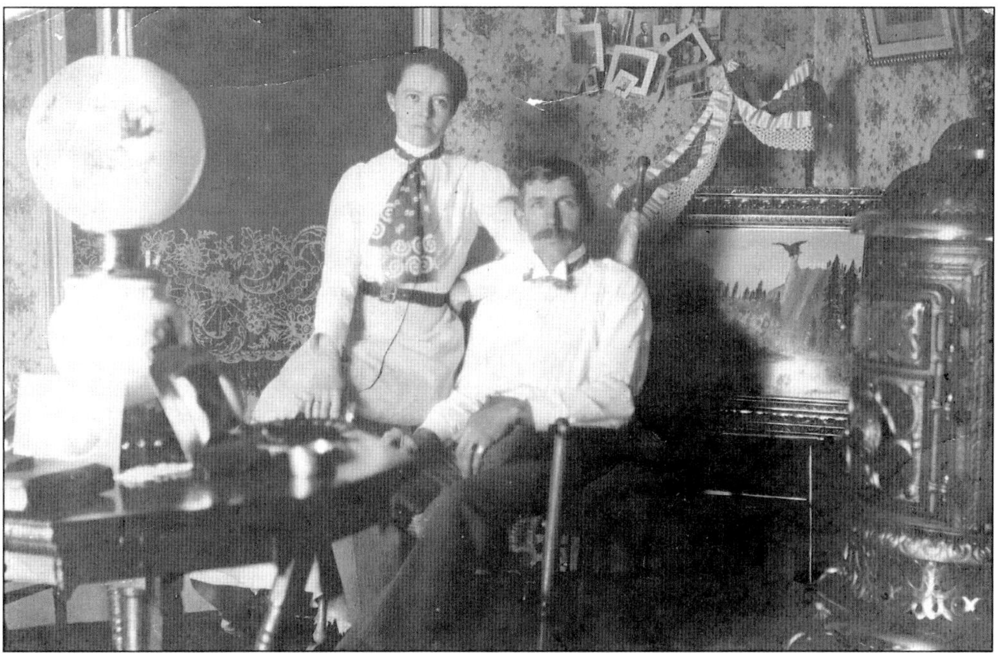

Victorian Interior. A rare photograph of the interior of the Palmer house shows Essex family life. While many families in society had the interiors of their elegant homes professionally photographed, it was only with the advent of George Eastman's Kodak company in the 1890s that photographic documentation became available to the middle class.

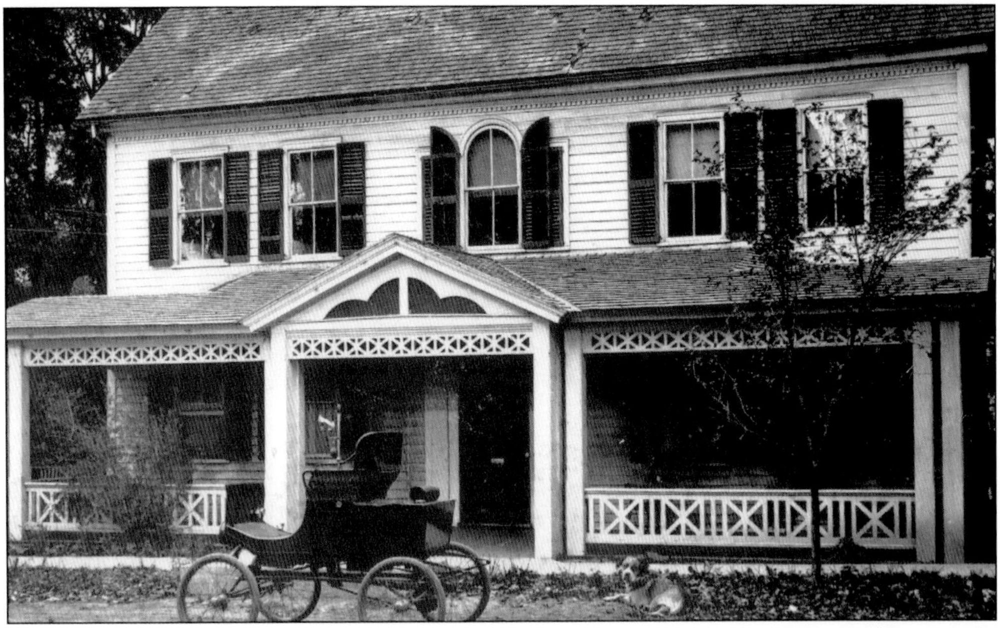

Hascall House. With Kodak cameras, the earlier stages of a house's existence could be visually recorded. The widespread use of these cameras by the 1890s allowed an archival record that was beyond the mere physical evidence of past construction. By 1900, the Hascall house of about 1800 had an added one-story porch that ran the full width of the house. The ornament indicates it may have been added by 1870.

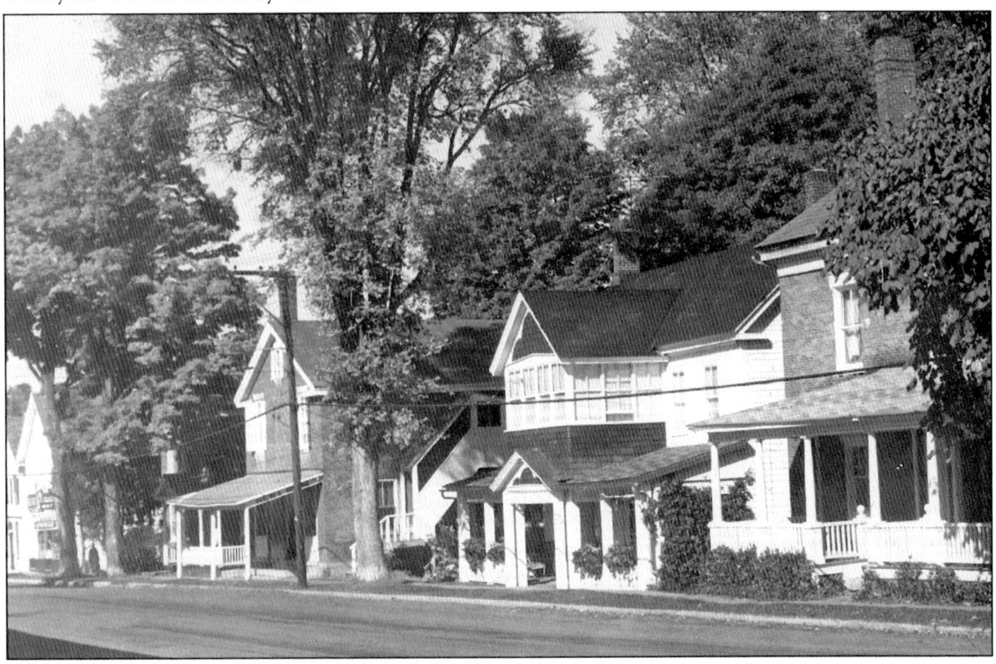

Cure Porch on Hascall House. Beside the addition of a front full-length porch, a sleeping porch added onto the second story greatly altered the appearance of the Hascall house. Such porches were often called cure porches after their associated use in the treatment of tuberculosis, especially in communities of the Adirondacks, such as Saranac Lake.

Seven

Merchant Row Mansions

A rare surviving feature found in Essex is the fact that the social hierarchy is intact from great mansions to detached worker housing. This was a typical pattern in 19th-century towns until it was disrupted permanently in the 20th century with the arrival of the automobile. The Merchant Row mansions in Essex all overlook the inner harbor once filled with canal boats, tugboats, and barges. They are immediately adjacent to the wharves and warehouses, and the mansions, village shops, churches, schools, and residences are all intermingled. The laborer and worker housing lines the adjacent area on the south side of town or on Station Road to the west. Thus, owners and workers alike could walk to their places of business.

Another point in the architectural integrity of Essex is that not only are most exteriors intact, but also many buildings have intact original interiors, some with original decorative motifs. Essex is fortunate in that four principal residences have an exceptional amount of original interior fabric.

The Daniel Ross house of about 1785 forms the northernmost boundary of the prominent lakeside Merchant Row in Essex. This linear park of four large residences presents a unique vista along the shoreline to those arriving from Vermont by ferryboat. It is a comment on the wealth and tradition of the builders that all four houses appear to be roughly contemporaneous, despite a span of nearly 70 years and differing building materials. Dating from 1785 to 1856, all are Georgian in style, with a center entrance doorway flanked by two windows on each side. Each has a gable roof with the long side facing the street and is two stories in height set among lawns and greenery, with the front elevation facing Lake Champlain. The oldest is constructed of wood and covered with clapboards. The second and third oldest are brick, and the newest and most costly is built of cut stone. Each residence has an extensive servant wing to the rear. All have barns, stables, or a carriage house on the grounds, although typically now many are converted to automobile garages.

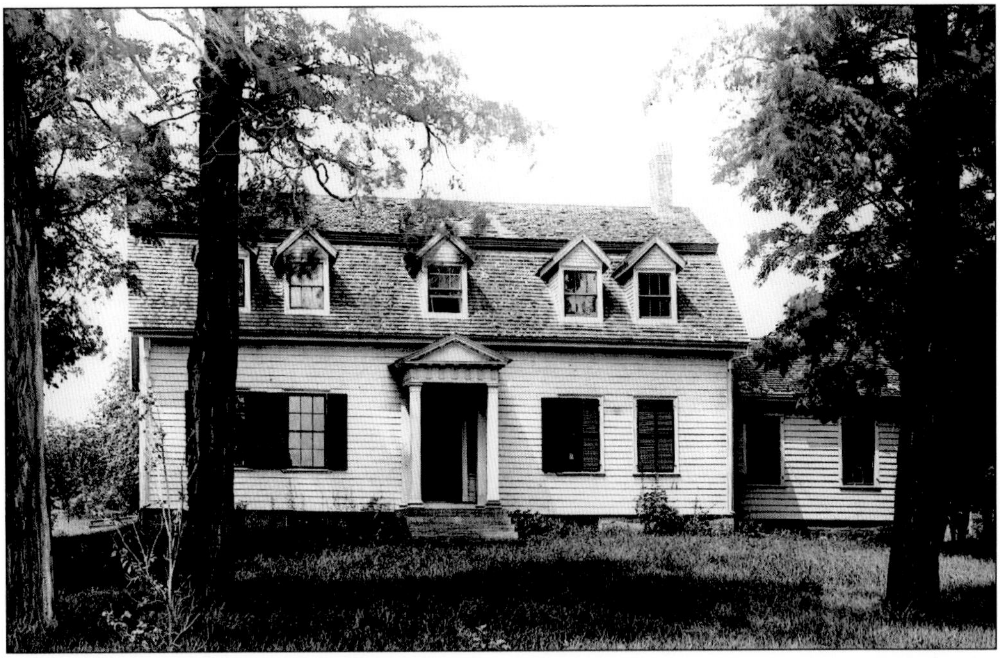

DOWER HOUSE. Essex founder William Gilliland constructed the residence about 1785 after he returned to the region in the aftermath of the American Revolution. His daughter Elizabeth married Daniel Ross. This white clapboard dwelling has a gambrel roof and dormers derived from an earlier Colonial style. In turn, this was derived from the English Georgian style with five bays, a central entrance, and windows arranged symmetrically, two to each side.

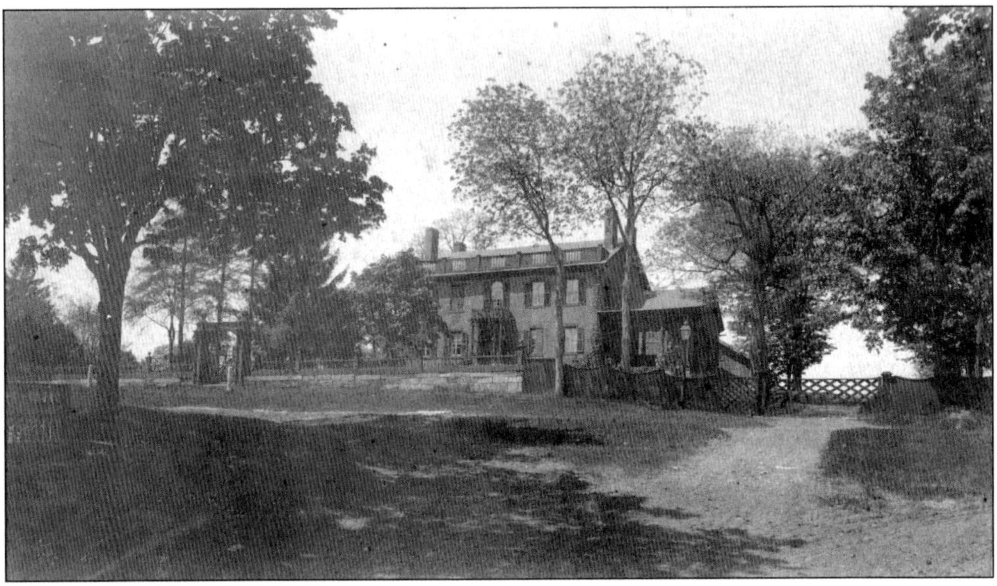

HICKORY HILL. The main house, named Hickory Hill, is documented by family history to have been constructed about 1822 and modeled after a house the family left behind in Salem, New York. The house was built in the classical Federal style, with an impressive arch and globe finials for an entrance gate. This view of about 1890 shows the gate still in place. The stone plinth is all that remains of the fence today. (Courtesy of Tilly Close.)

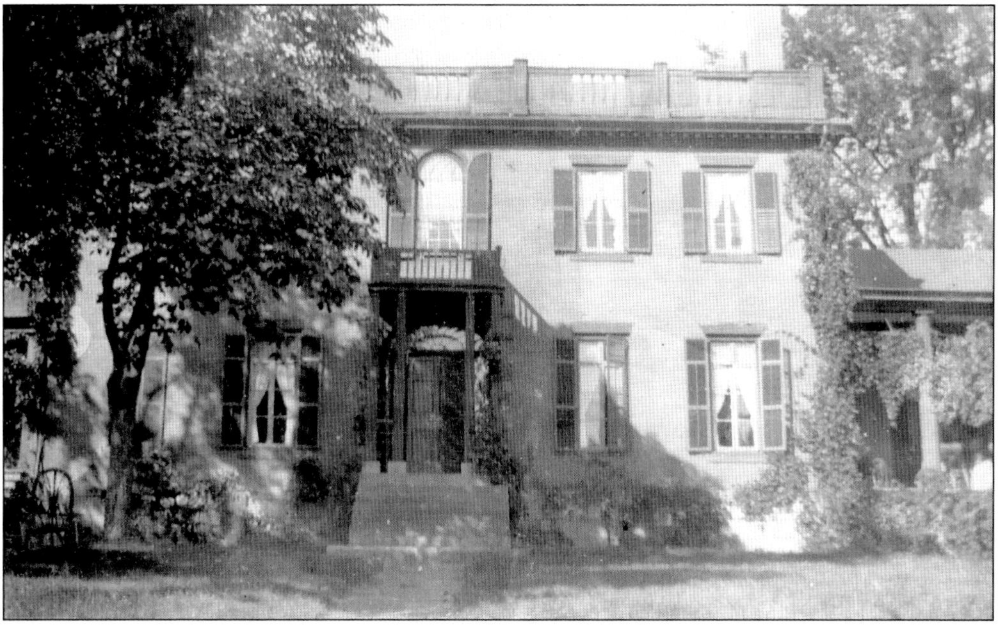

Law Office Addition. When an addition was added to Hickory Hill in 1845 as a family law office, the bold pattern-book style of the Greek Revival was added to this north wing of the Federal-style house. The front windows of the addition to the right are large floor-length sashes that open onto a front porch. In the frieze, there is a spectacular carved guilloche detail similar to that published in 1823 by Peter Nicholson. (Courtesy of Tilly Close.)

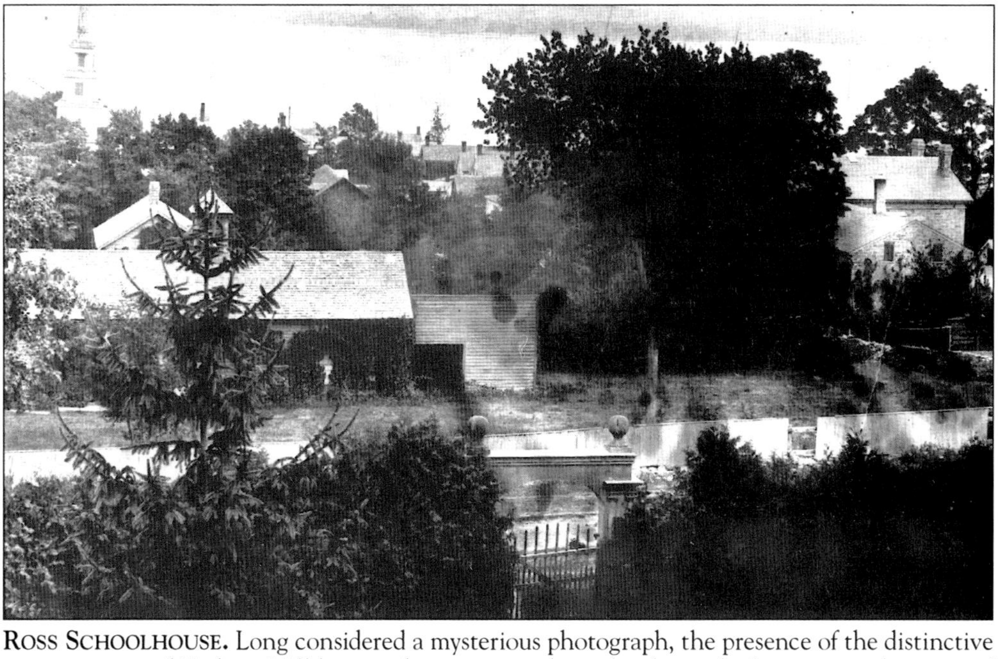

Ross Schoolhouse. Long considered a mysterious photograph, the presence of the distinctive entrance gate of Hickory Hill locates the picture as from that house looking out to the town of Essex beyond. The reason for the apparent confusion is that what looks like a schoolhouse in the foreground is exactly that, dating this photograph to before the Ross family schoolhouse was converted into St. John's Church in 1880.

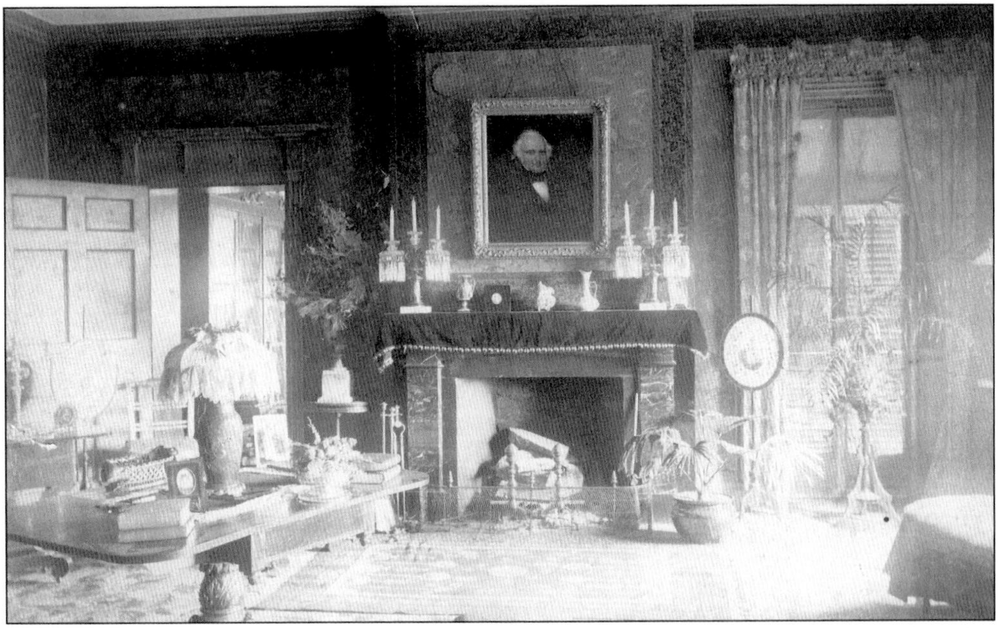

INTERIOR AT HICKORY HILL. As with many genteel families, the Ross family hired a photographer to document the interior of their manse. The 1892 view of the north parlor reveals the interior has remained unchanged since the Greek Revival marble mantel and plasterwork was added in the 1850s. A prominent oil portrait of Henry H. Ross is over the mantel. (Courtesy of Tilly Close.)

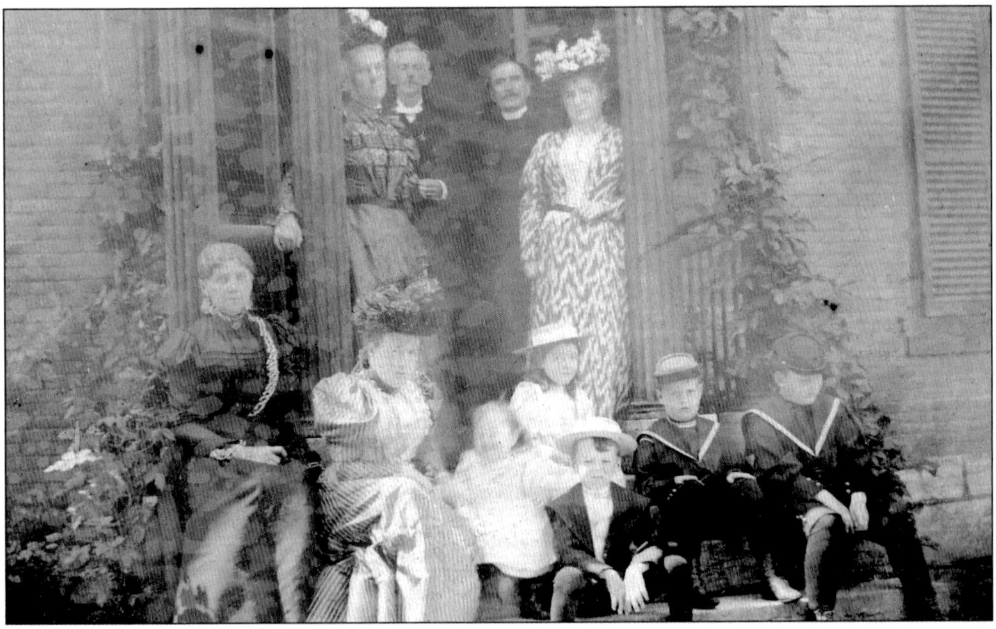

ROSS FAMILY. The Ross family descendants are seated in the office addition in 1892. As early as the 1920s, the decorative arts of this house were preserved by the family, and Geraldine Van Ornam described how she was hired by Mary Towsend in 1926 to be the curator of Hickory Hill and open it to the public. She did this for one season, organizing all the decorative arts by year according to use and period. (Courtesy of Tilly Close.)

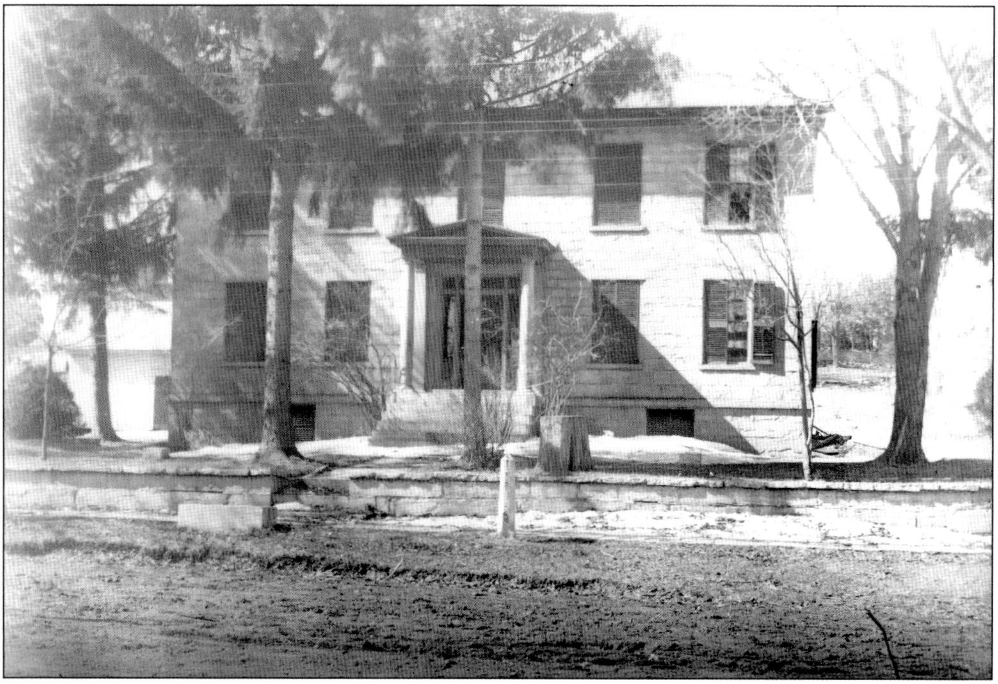

John Gould House. The remarkable John Gould house was built of limestone blocks in 1833. The central entrance and cut gray limestone construction make it appear as a precursor to the later Greystone of 1853. The Goulds and Nobles later intermarried.

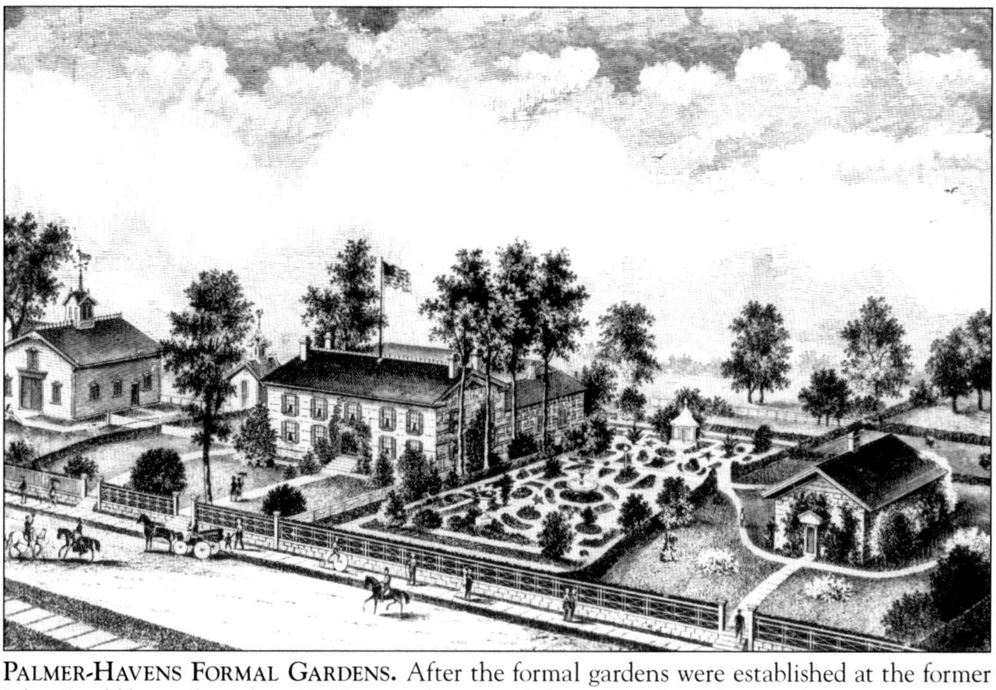

Palmer-Havens Formal Gardens. After the formal gardens were established at the former John Gould house by Palmer E. Havens, the grounds became a showplace, and an engraving and photographs were published and widely circulated. The elegant fencing has been lost.

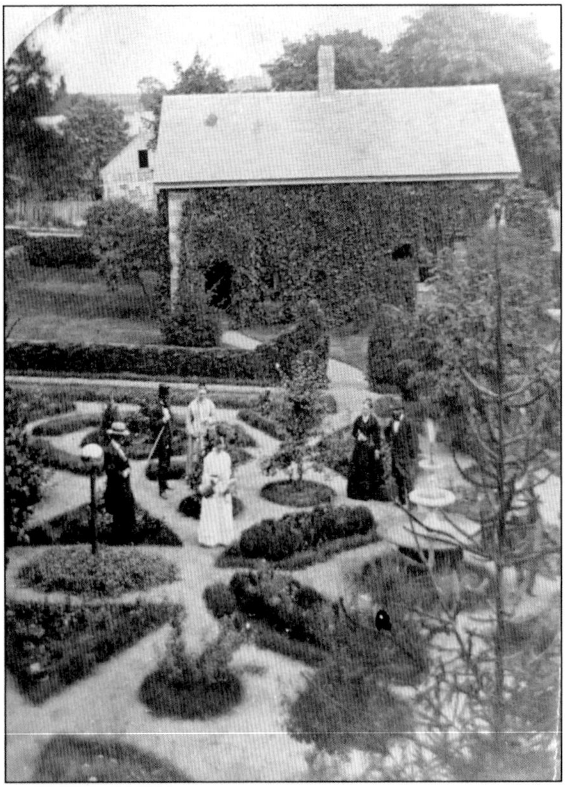

PALMER-HAVENS GARDENS STEREOPTICON. So attractive were the Palmer-Havens gardens that soon a stereopticon was created, seen here as one-half of the double image. The space still retains its original Victorian summerhouse and part of the cast-iron fountain.

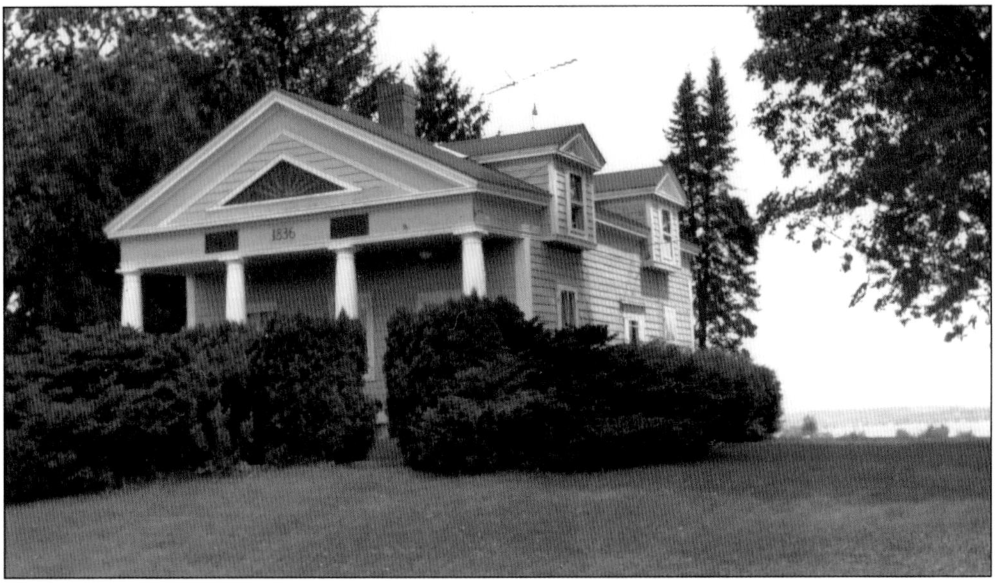

BLOCKHOUSE FARM. The only complete temple-form Greek Revival house in Essex is Blockhouse Farm of 1836. There is a full pediment turned to face the road that is supported by four freestanding Doric columns. This large pediment makes the house appear as a porticoed Greek temple. It contains what is sometimes thought to be an Essex original—a carved sunburst fanlight. Note the south-facing dormers added in the 20th century and Lake Champlain behind.

VICTORIAN ESSEX FAMILY. A Victorian Essex family poses formally for a portrait. At Blockhouse Farm, the large two-story carriage barn reportedly was constructed using timbers from the original blockhouse. Blockhouse Farm is now beautifully preserved, but it narrowly missed being reduced to lakeside residential development of modern vacation homes in the 1980s.

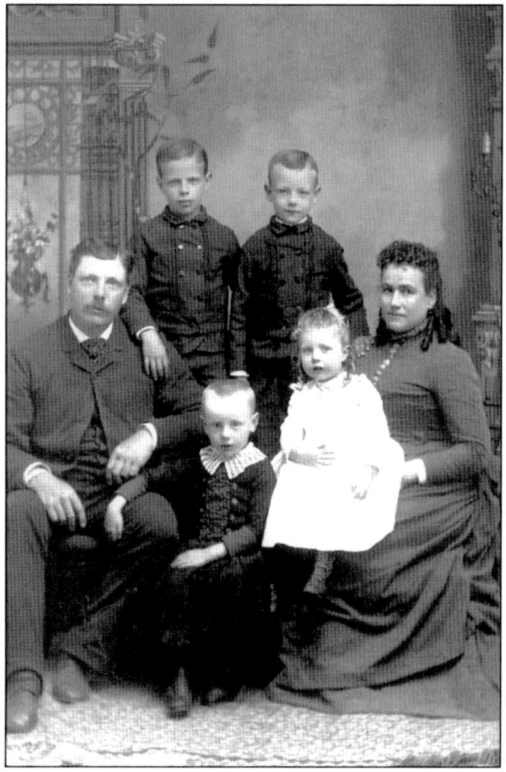

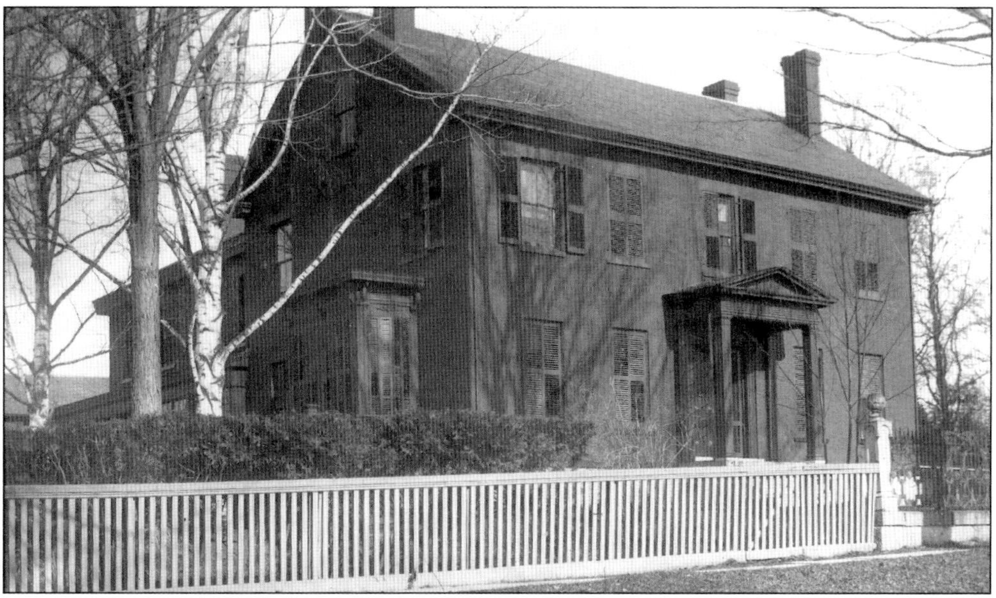

SUNNYSIDE, THE 1835 HARMON NOBLE HOUSE. Nested squares are the familiar Greek key design, a motif from ancient Greece often found in classical ruins in Athens. In Essex, the Harmon Noble house of 1835 displays an entrance porch carved with the Greek key on all three sides of the architrave. A highly similar variation of the Greek key appears inside at Greystone next door. The inclusion of the Greek key may be further indication of design harmony between the Noble brothers' houses.

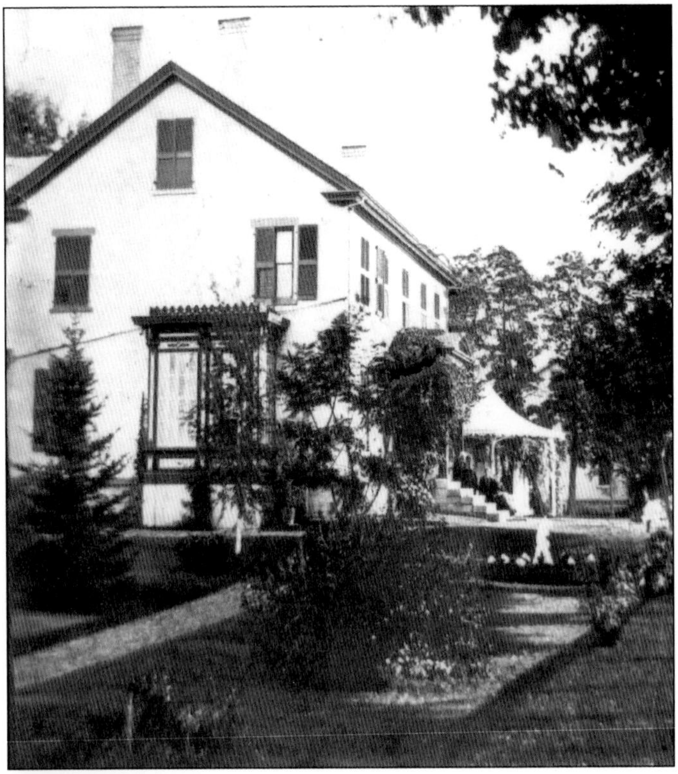

SUNNYSIDE. The redbrick house must not have always been red, as documented by this photograph from about 1880. Clearly here the body color is lighter than red. The Harmon Noble house was purchased by Maud Noble of Greystone in 1896. "Henry H. Noble sold red house in 1896 to Maud but still lived there." Maud returned the redbrick house to Harmon Noble heirs after she died in 1932.

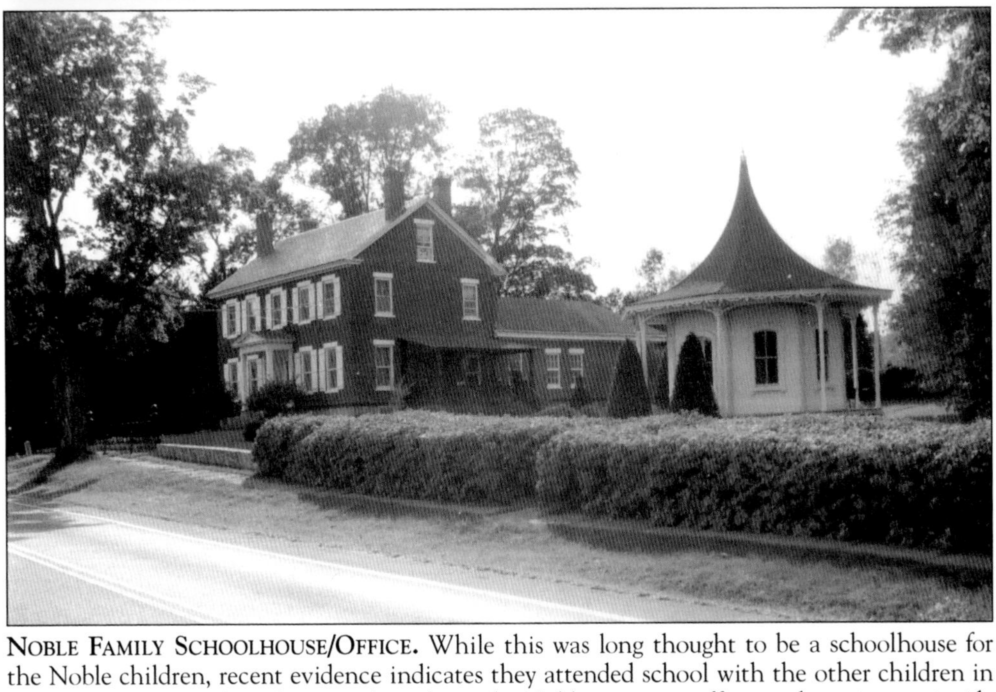

NOBLE FAMILY SCHOOLHOUSE/OFFICE. While this was long thought to be a schoolhouse for the Noble children, recent evidence indicates they attended school with the other children in town. This octagonal pavilion may have been the Noble company office, as the existence inside of a large partner's desk suggests. Octagonal structures proliferated in the Italianate period, here combined with Gothic Revival details.

NOBLE CLEMONS HOUSE. The owner of the Essex Inn decided in about 1850 to construct a residence in the latest architectural style, Italianate. The house was square with a central entrance and five bays with bracketed eaves. The south side had a large enclosed porch. The cupola on the roof contained the top of a central spiral staircase and featured seats for viewing the distant lake.

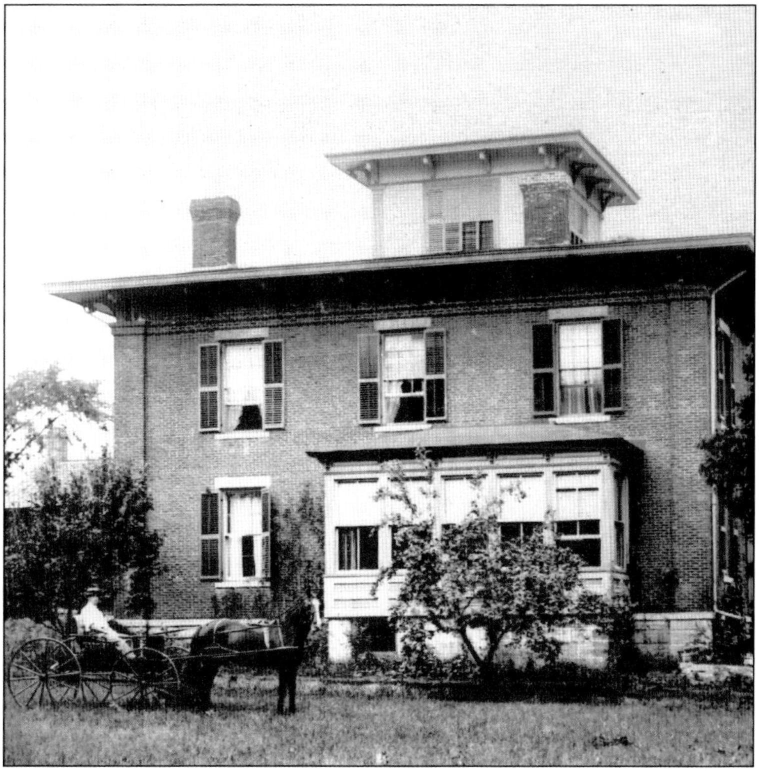

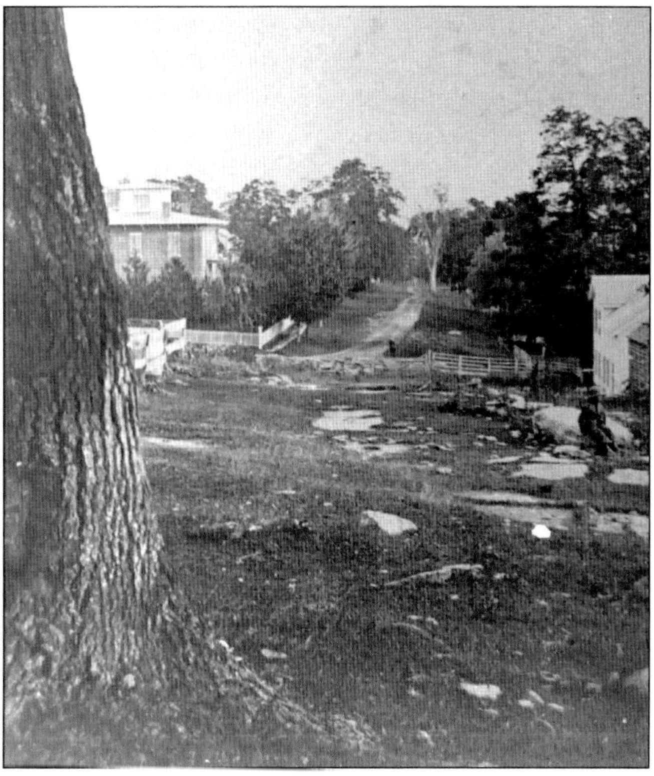

ELM STREET. A stereopticon card of about 1880 looks north on Elm Street. The Noble Clemons house of about 1850 was built in the fully developed Italianate style with a large cupola and broad overhanging roof with bracketed eaves. A formal cast-iron and wood fence surrounds it. The rutted roadway and bucolic setting enhance the rural village feeling.

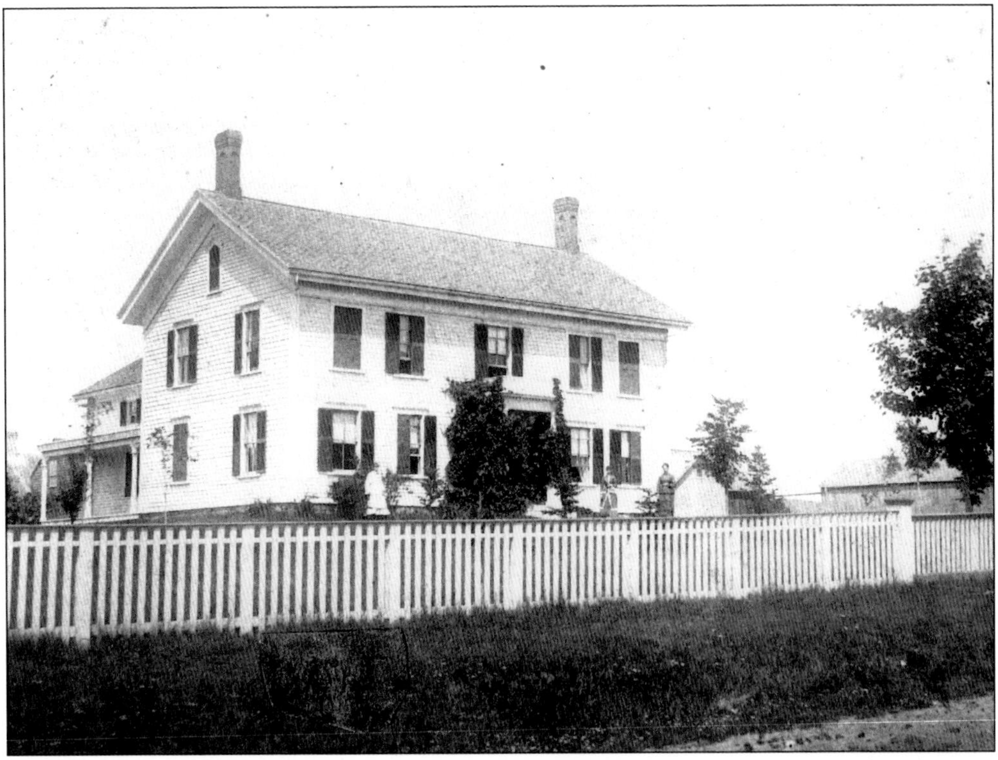

CRYSTAL SPRING FARM. Built in a simple but elegant Federal style, this residence later became known as Crystal Spring Farm. The house was the beloved home of early Essex historian Albert Hayward.

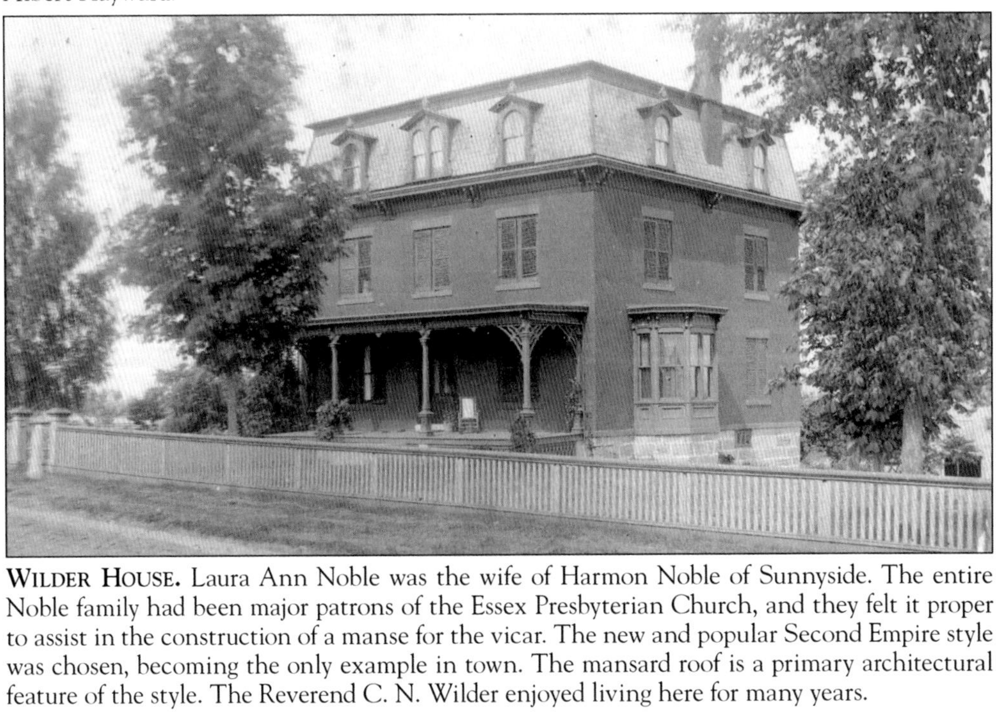

WILDER HOUSE. Laura Ann Noble was the wife of Harmon Noble of Sunnyside. The entire Noble family had been major patrons of the Essex Presbyterian Church, and they felt it proper to assist in the construction of a manse for the vicar. The new and popular Second Empire style was chosen, becoming the only example in town. The mansard roof is a primary architectural feature of the style. The Reverend C. N. Wilder enjoyed living here for many years.

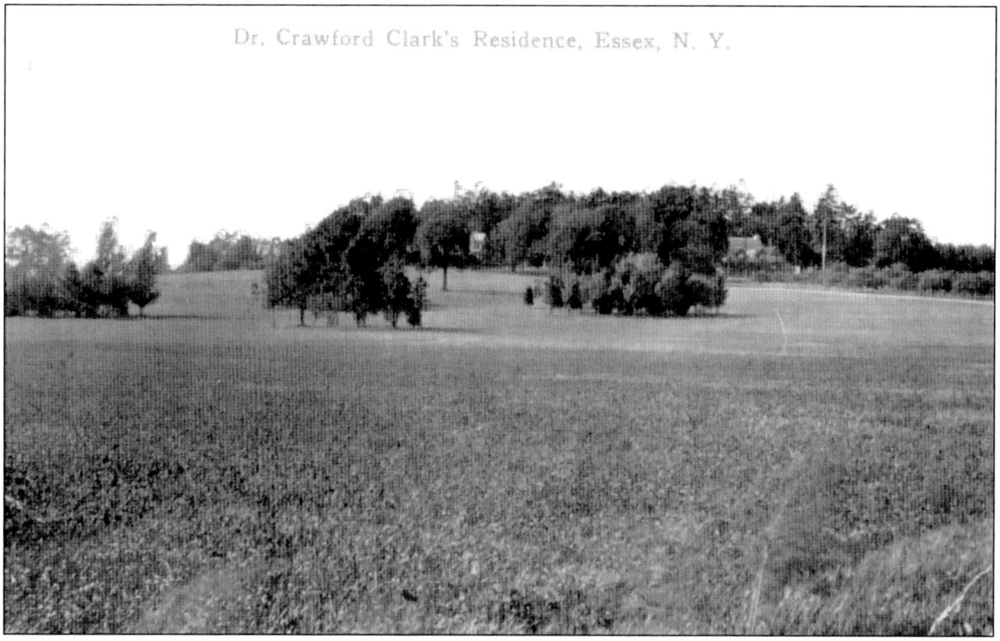

KEYSER RESIDENCE. On the northern boundary between Essex and Willsboro, a large shingle house was constructed for the Keyser family on 600 acres of land. Later it was called the Fulton Estate until 1934, when it was purchased by the Scholastic Brothers of the Oblates. It has returned to being a private residence.

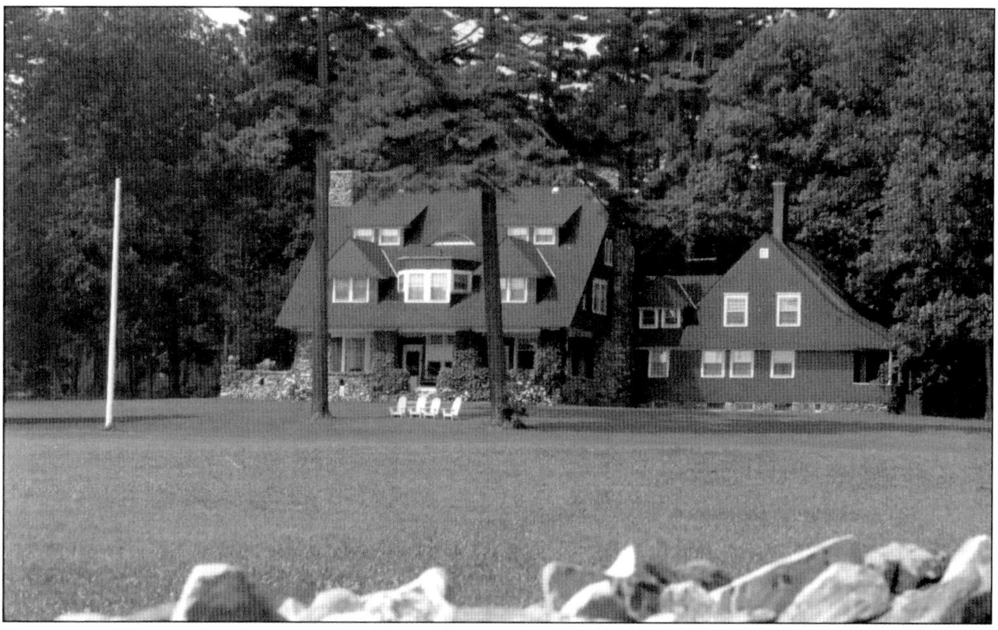

BRAIDLEA FARM. At the north border of Essex near Willsboro, the Dr. Crawford Clark estate straddles the border and extends into the town of Willsboro. Many resort towns that developed toward the end of the 19th century favored construction in the popular shingle style. The compound of three residences at Braidlea has broad, low porches and irregular shapes covered in natural cedar shingles.

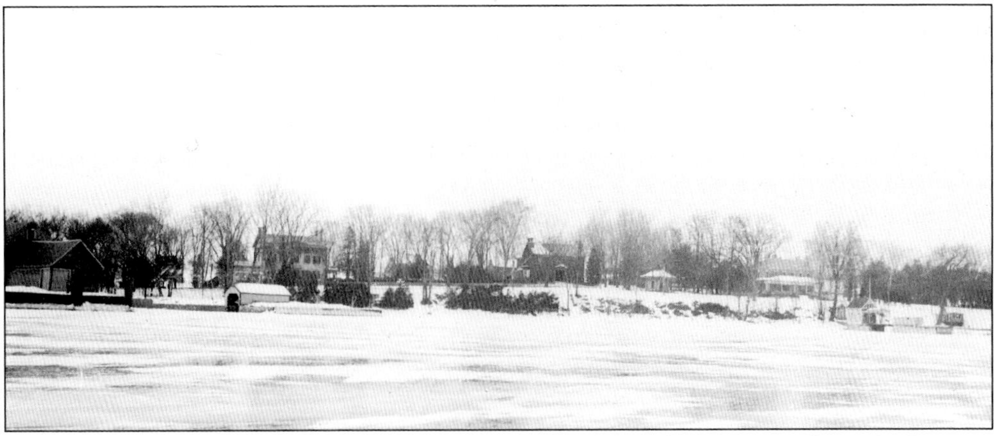

NORTH SHORE FENCES. An important feature of village life is the numerous fences built not to keep anyone out but rather to keep domestic life within its owner's property. The entire north coast of Essex had fencing running along it from the Dower house to the Essex Presbyterian Church. Mostly made of wood in a simple classical style, the fence line became elegant cast iron in front of Sunnyside and Greystone.

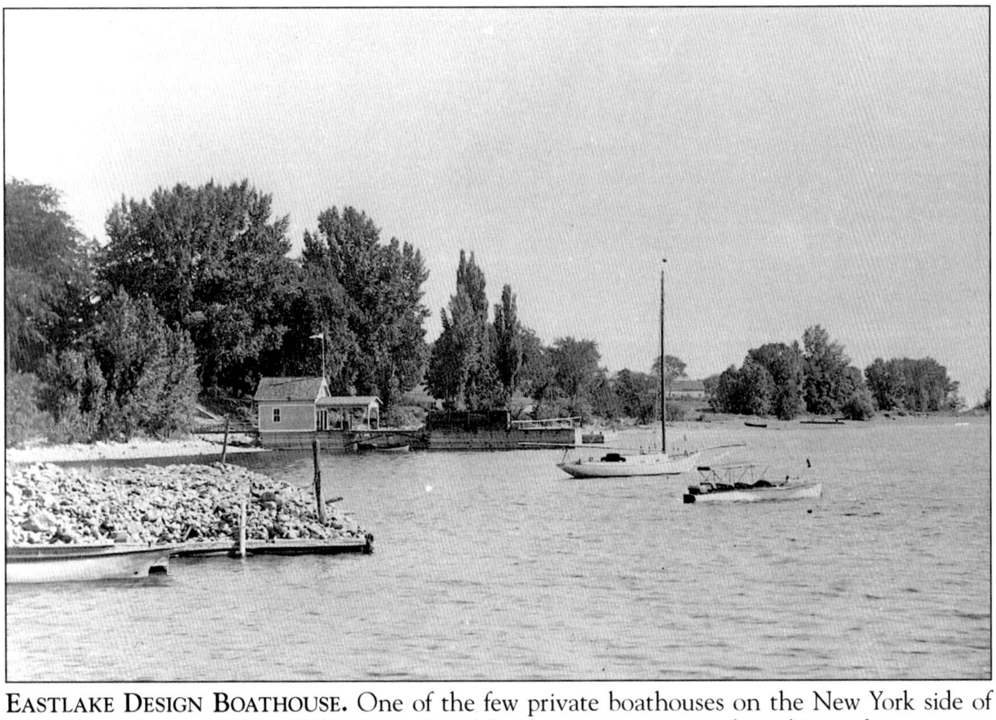

EASTLAKE DESIGN BOATHOUSE. One of the few private boathouses on the New York side of Lake Champlain, this late-19th-century Eastlake-design structure is the subject of many town views. Note the rubble remains of the Noble wharf before it was rebuilt.

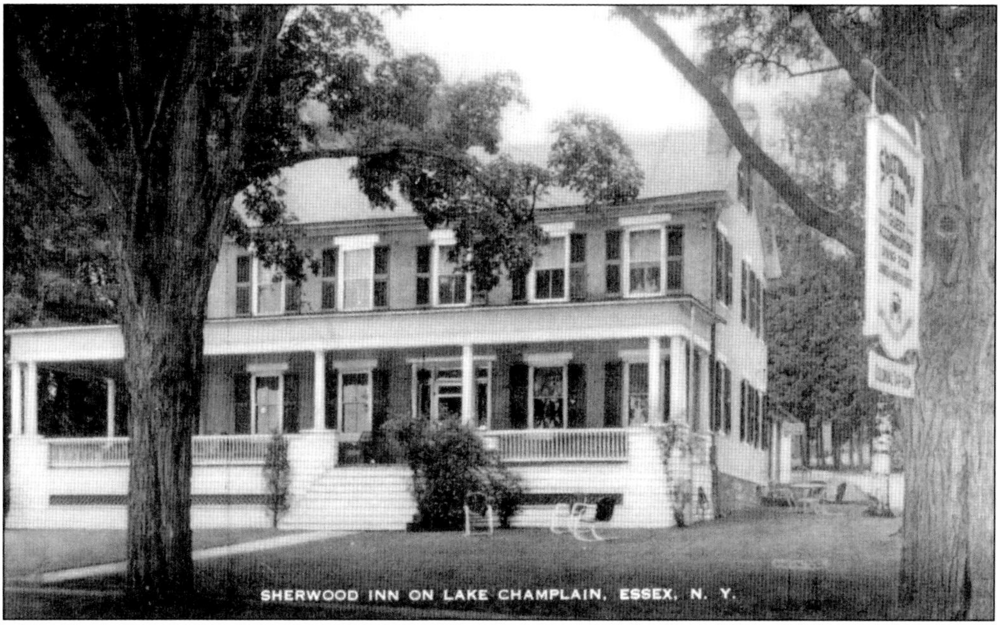

SHERWOOD INN POSTCARD. When William D. Ross married Mary Ann Gould in 1826, the house consisted of an addition of two bays to the south of an already existing three-bay residence. It originally had a Doric, fluted column entrance portico, since restored in the early manifestation of the Greek Revival. The completed five-bay facade is important in the evolution of a traditional Greek Revival style in Essex.

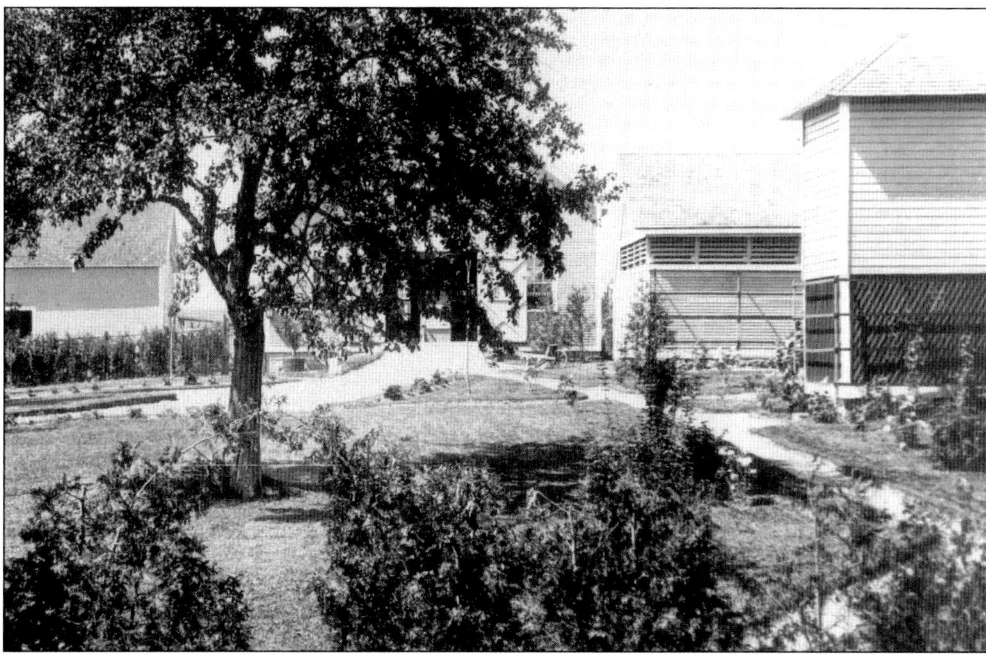

ROSSLYN OUTBUILDINGS. In the romantic movement of the Victorian era, the house was called Rosslyn after the Ross family name. The large house was adaptable for conversion to the Sherwood Inn in the mid-20th century. Several barns, a granary, an icehouse, a privy, and a carriage barn were located near the main house.

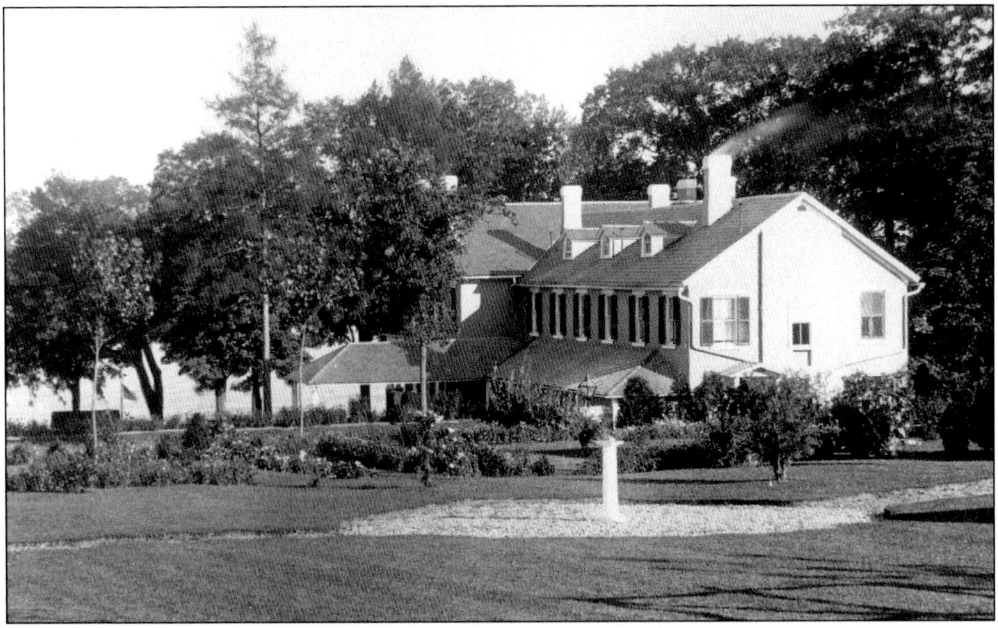

ROSSLYN REAR WING. The significant rear wing held extended family and servant quarters. The designed residential landscape in Essex echoed design sources of the period, such as Bernard M'Mahon's *The American Gardener's Calendar* that recommended a wide variety of necessary foods grown at home. The section on flower or pleasure gardens reflects the pioneering landscape guides of American landscape architect Andrew Jackson Downing.

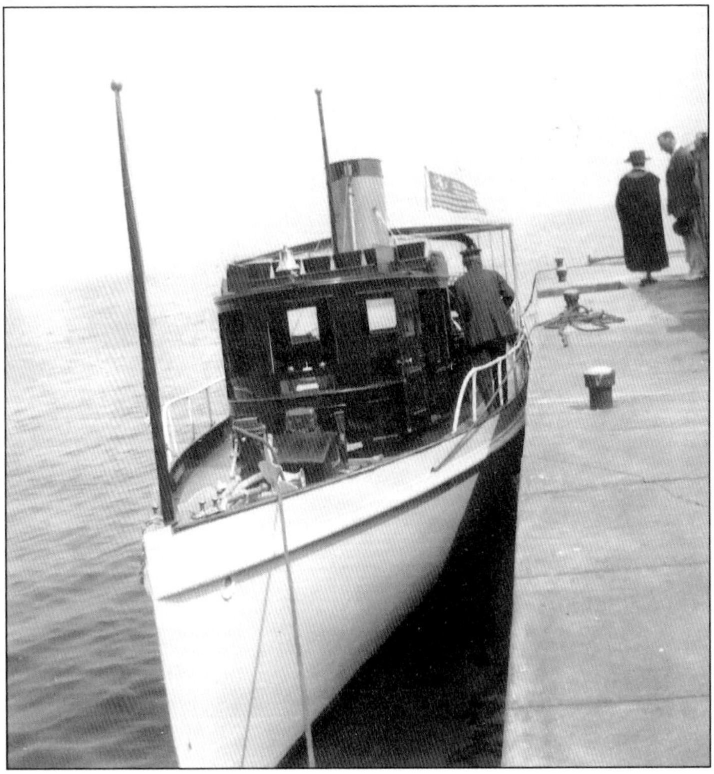

YACHT *KESTREL*. The *Kestrel* was a magnificent vessel constructed with mahogany woodwork. Here it is at dock at the William D. Ross house. The boathouse is one of the few on the lake. (Courtesy of Tilly Close.)

GREYSTONE. Greystone was constructed of cut limestone blocks between 1853 and 1856 by Belden Noble, the youngest son of Essex patriarch Ransom Noble. This monumental high-style Greek Revival house is remarkable in that it maintains a conservative five-bay facade on the front. While this is not the popular image of the temple-form portico Greek Revival, it is the most common, being the easiest modification of the Colonial style with the addition of Grecian details.

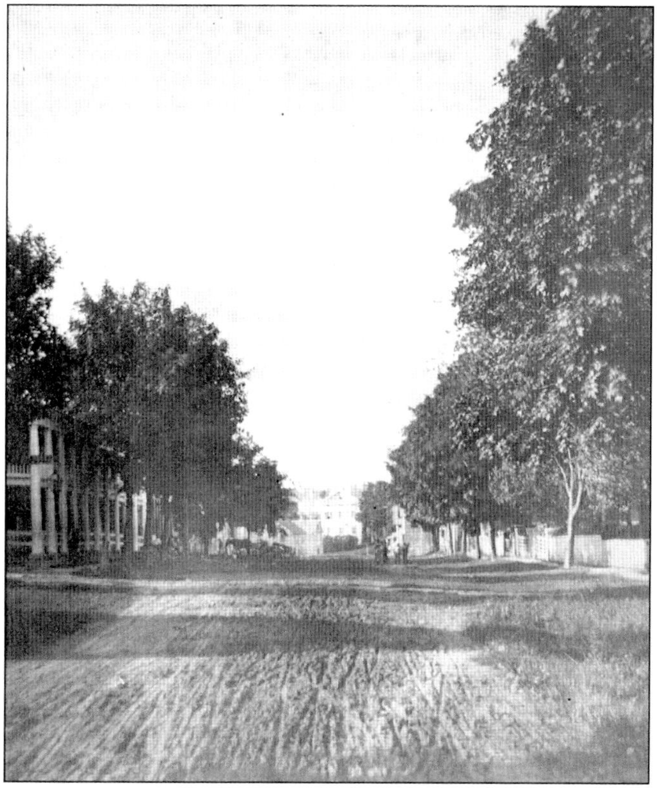

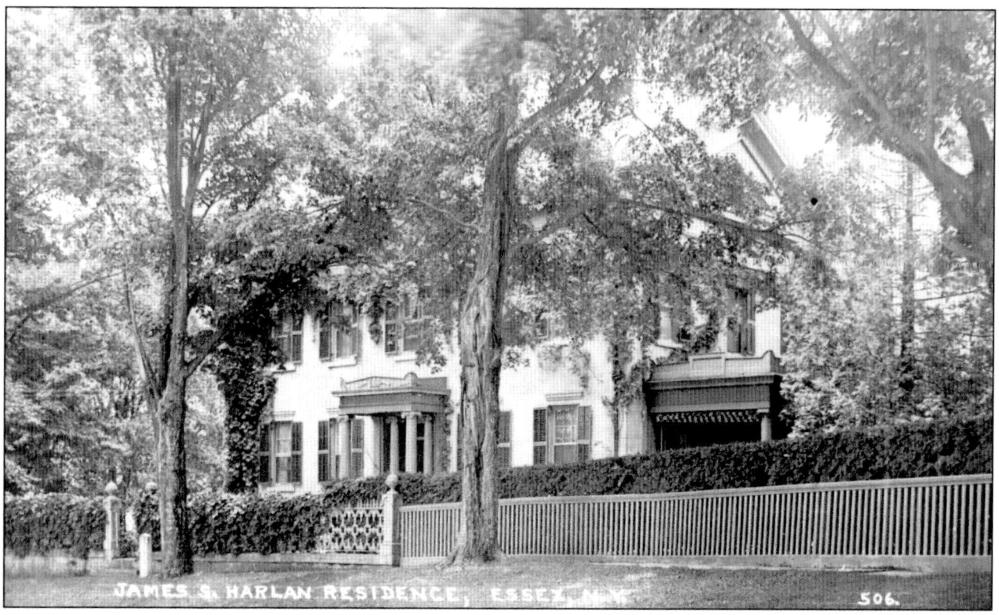

JUSTICE JAMES S. HARLAN RESIDENCE. As suggested by the other mansions nearby, it is believed that the Noble family wished to maintain at Greystone the integrity of the uniform look of five-bay houses along the lakeshore. The Nobles could see right down the main street from their south windows. James S. Harlan married the daughter of the house, Maud Noble, in 1897.

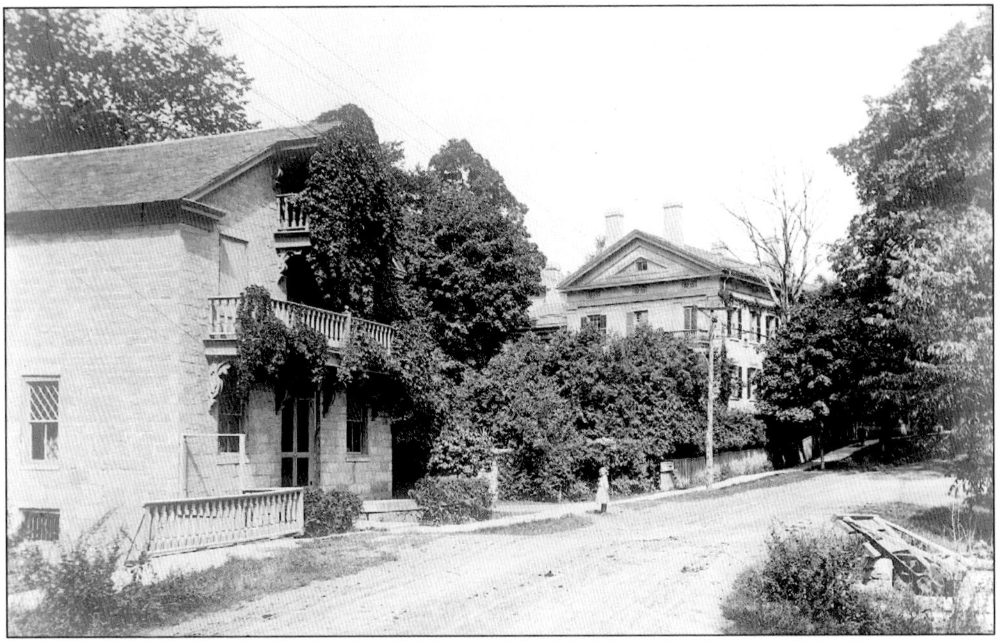

Tannery Store. When Ransom Noble settled in Essex in 1800, he established a tannery at the brook that crosses under this road. He then built a store at the edge of the road to sell his wares. Later it became a general store, and finally it was converted to a library. Adeline Noble left the library to the town in memory of her husband, thus it is named the Belden Noble Memorial Library.

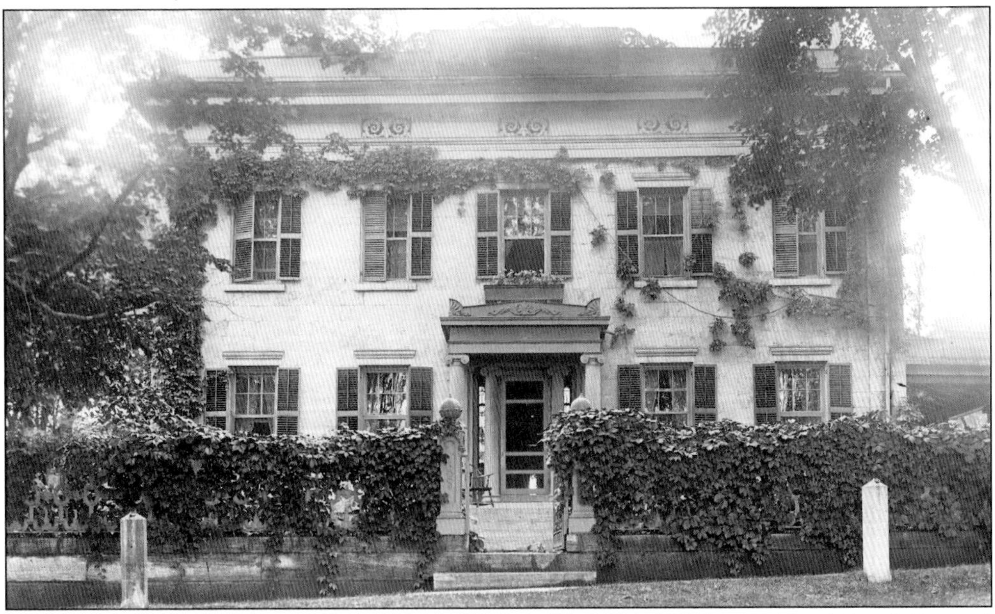

Great Greek Revival Architecture. Greystone has many fully developed Greek Revival ornaments. Its fundamental massing includes a repressed third floor hidden behind a row of frieze windows with cast-iron grills. The gable ends, while not turned toward the road, are still massive complete pediments of the classic temple form. The entablature is correctly Grecian Ionic and is on all four sides of the main block of the house.

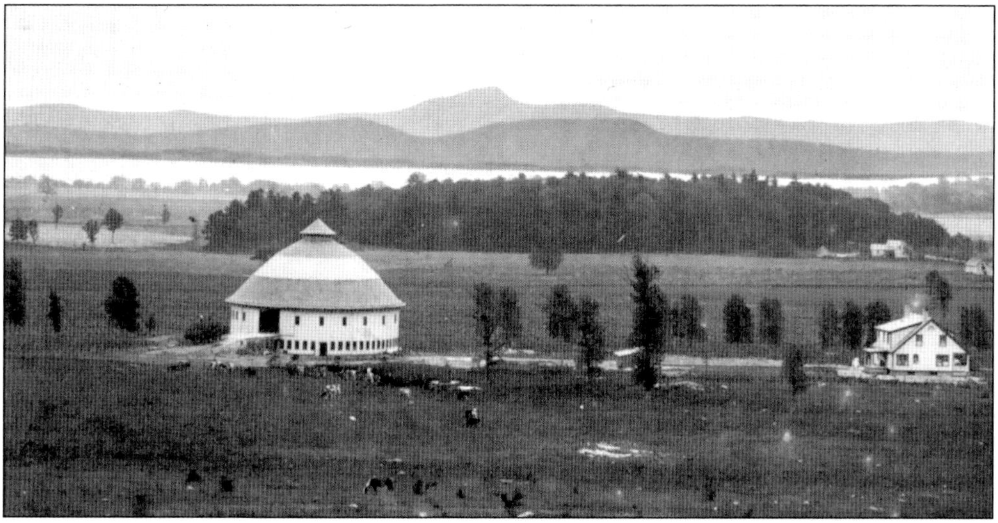

ESSEX FARMS. The Nobles owned more than 500 acres on the north side of town. Part of the acreage was devoted to raising farm products for the family. By 1900, however, the era of the gentleman farmer had arrived, and Justice James S. Harlan was eager to farm. He now owned the magnificent round barn for his exotic beef herds. Note the Green Mountains of Vermont in the distance across Lake Champlain, centered on Camel's Hump, which is always visible from Essex.

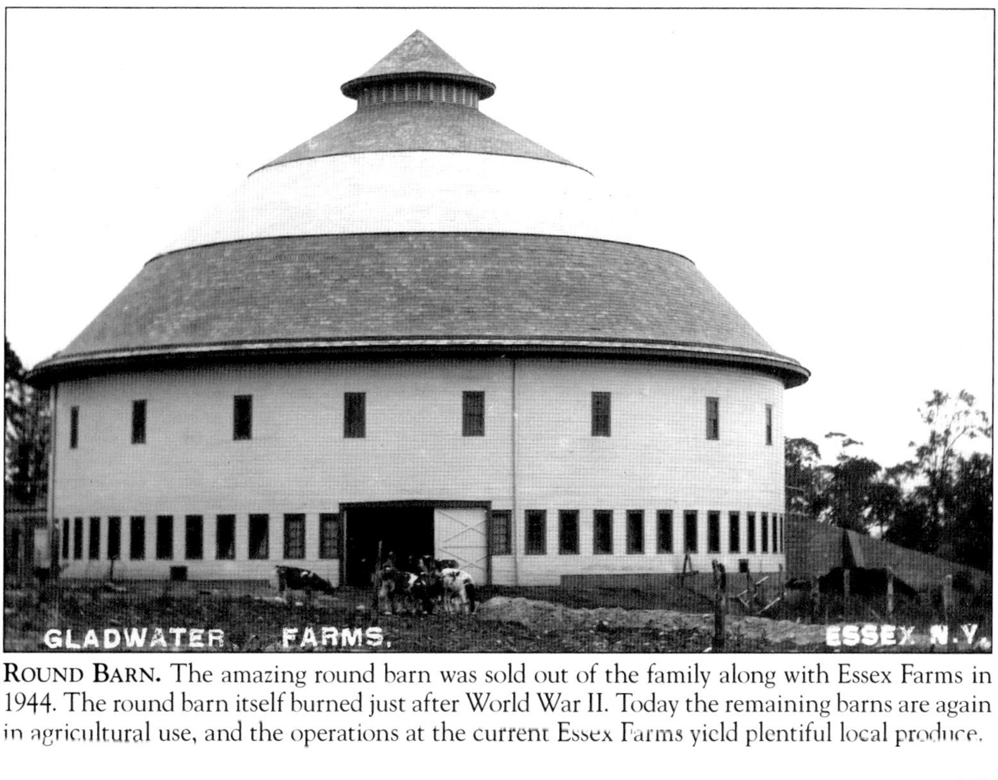

ROUND BARN. The amazing round barn was sold out of the family along with Essex Farms in 1944. The round barn itself burned just after World War II. Today the remaining barns are again in agricultural use, and the operations at the current Essex Farms yield plentiful local produce.

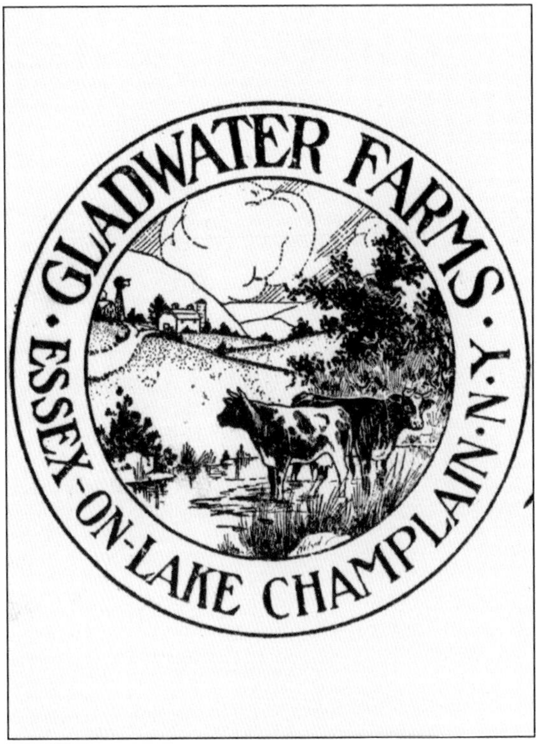

Gladwater Farms. James S. Harlan devised a seal for his Gladwater Farms. It was a cut-brass plate mounted on wood that could be used on stationary (in reduced form) or on bottles. Now renamed Essex Farms, the property has once again returned to serious farming under a new generation of determined local-production philosophy young farmers.

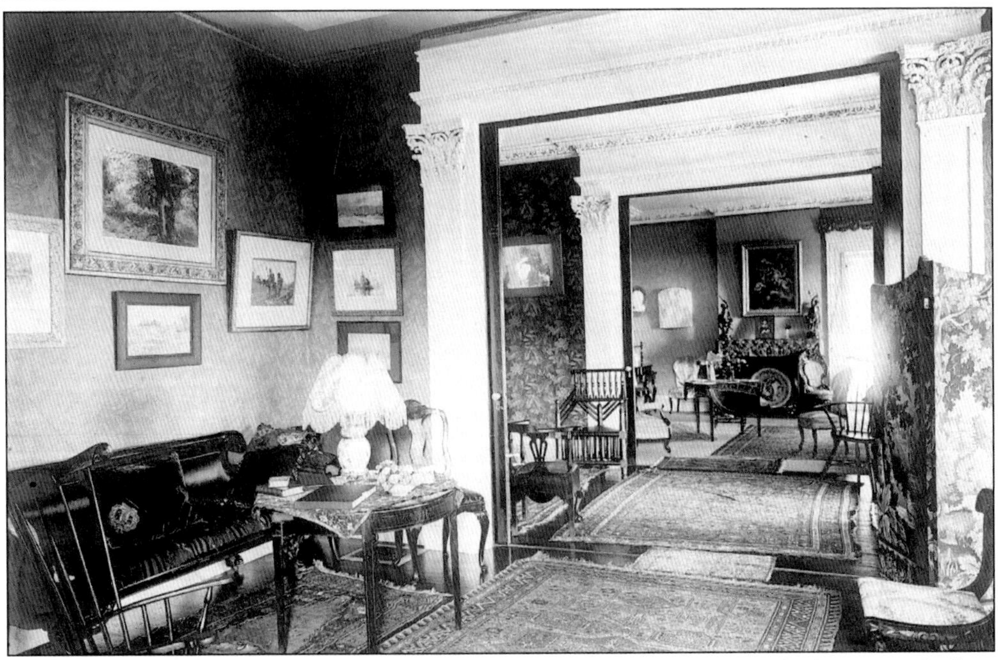

Parlors at Greystone. This view looks from the south parlor through the center hall to the north parlor of Greystone. The walls were always papered from 1856 until the 1950s. The large-scale pattern here may be from the original decoration. Furniture includes a mixture of Edwardian chairs and family pilgrim century chairs. Note the plaster pilasters, dark polished floors, and black marble fireplace surround.

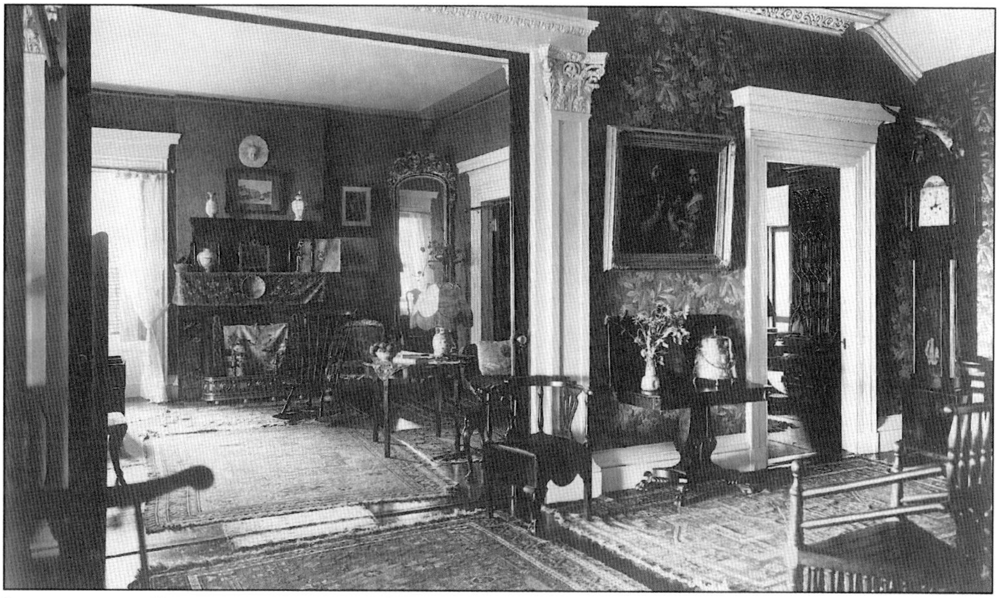

INTERIOR OF GREYSTONE. Here is the center hall of Greystone looking into the south parlor, showing some of the library and the great Gothic Revival bookcase. Greystone has a library and archives that house primary material on the Justice James S. Harlan era and the Ransom Noble family. Almost all of this material is being published and will add to the written record of Essex, which, when combined with the artifact record, presents a nearly complete documentation of a mid-19th-century American village.

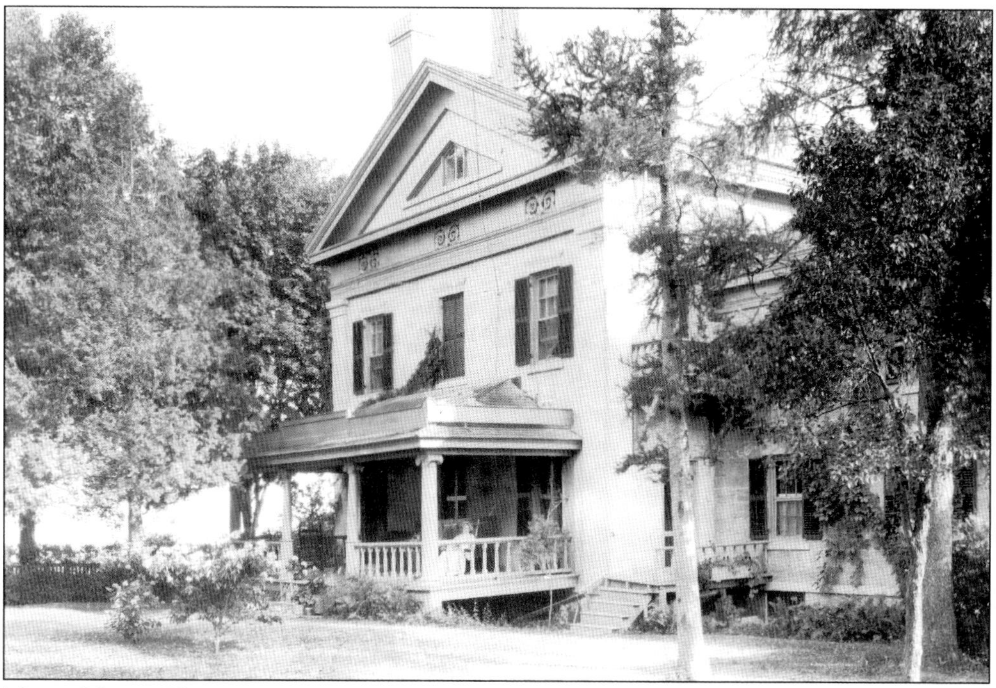

MAUD NOBLE HARLAN ON NORTH PORCH OF GREYSTONE. The porch was originally not enclosed; however, the sequence of biting bugs in the Adirondacks soon forced the issue of constructing screening. Note the casual landscaping with ferns and more informal plantings.

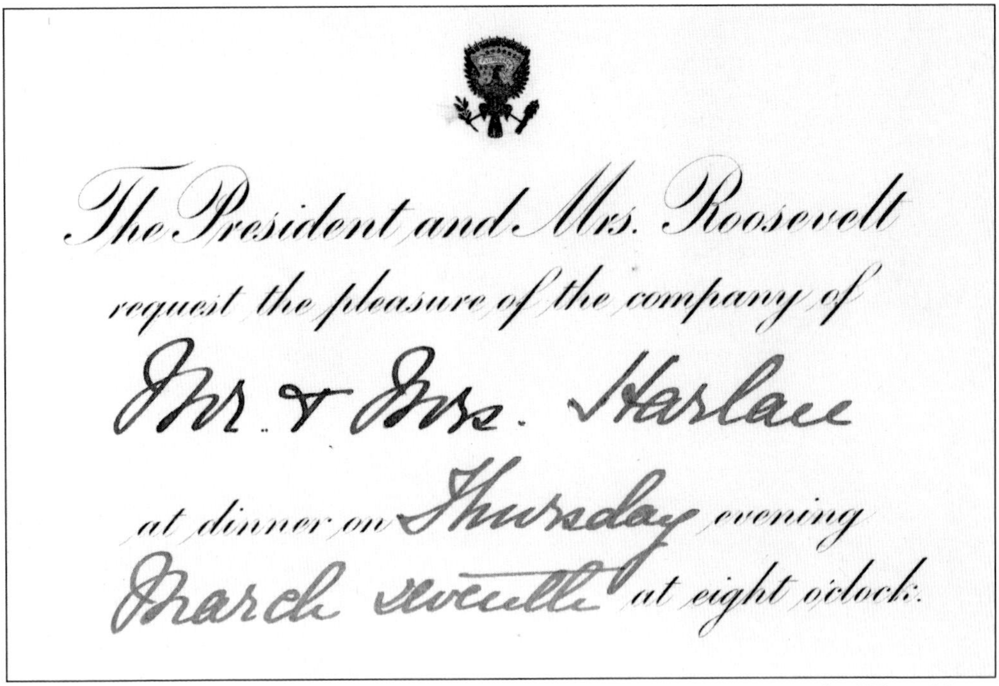

The President and Mrs. Roosevelt
request the pleasure of the company of
Mr. & Mrs. Harlan
at dinner on Thursday evening
March seventh at eight o'clock.

WHITE HOUSE INVITATIONS. The Greystone archives contain invitations to the White House under five U.S. presidents. In 1907, the Harlans attended dinner with Pres. Theodore Roosevelt, who had appointed James S. Harlan to the Interstate Commerce Commission.

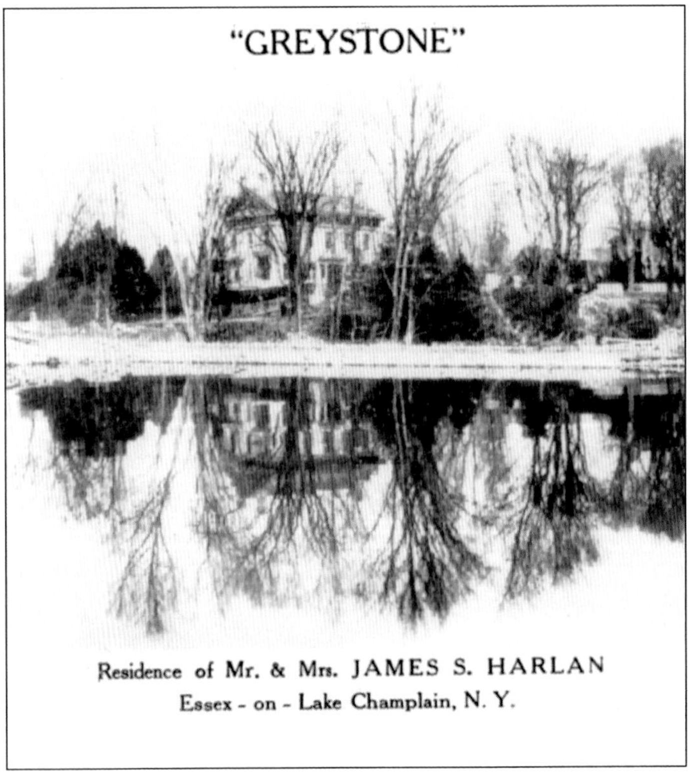

GREYSTONE CARD. Reflections of *c.* 1856 Greystone in Lake Champlain are seen on this card custom printed by James S. and Maud Noble Harlan. The new room on the south side had not yet been constructed. The canopy of American elms has become Essex history.

BIBLIOGRAPHY

Adirondack Park Agency. *A Citizen's Guide to Adirondack Park Agency Land Use Regulations*. Albany: New York State, 1982.

Belden Noble Memorial Library. *Essex, New York: An Early History*. Essex, NY: Belden Noble Memorial Library, 2003.

Cooper, Wendy A. *Classical Taste in America 1800–1840*. New York: Abbeville Press Publishers and the Baltimore Museum of Art, 1993.

DeSormo, Maitland C. *John Bird Burnham: Klondiker, Adirondacker, Eminent Conservationist*. Saranac Lake, NY: Adirondack Yesteryears, 1978.

Glenn, Morris F. *Lake Champlain Album*. Vol. 2. Alexandra, VA: Self-published, 1979.

Hill, Ralph Nading. *Two Centuries of Ferry Boating on Lake Champlain*. Burlington, VT: Lake Champlain Transportation Company, 1972.

Howard, Hugh. *The Preservationist's Progress: Architectural Adventures in Conserving Yesterday's Houses*. New York: Farrar, Straus, and Giraux, 1991.

Kennedy, Roger G. *Greek Revival America*. New York: Stewart, Tabori and Chang, 1989.

McNulty, George, and Margaret Scheinin. *Essex: The Architectural Heritage*. Essex, NY: Self-published, 1971.

Mesick, John, et al. *Essex: An Architectural Guide*. New York: Essex Community Heritage Organization, 1986.

Noble, Henry Harmon. *A Sketch of the History of the Town of Essex, New York*. Champlain, NY: Moorsfield Press, 1940.

Smith, R. P., pub. *Historical and Statistical Gazetteer of New York State*. Syracuse, NY: Self-published, 1860.

Trancik, Roger. *Hamlets of the Adirondacks Development Strategies*. Vols. I and II. Ithaca, NY: Self-published, 1985.

Upjohn, Everard, M. *Richard Upjohn: Architect and Churchman*. New York: DaCapo, 1968.

Watson, Winslow. *A General View and Agricultural Survey of the County of Essex*. Albany, NY: 1852.